THE INTERNATIONAL DICTIONARY OF

Event Management

D0018219

THE INTERNATIONAL DICTIONARY OF

Event
Management

SECOND EDITION

Dr. Joe Goldblatt, CSEP
Kathleen S. Nelson, CSEP
Editors

APPROVED BY

The International Special Events Society (ISES)

JOHN WILEY & SONS, INC.

New York · Chichester · Weinheim · Brisbane · Singapore · Toronto

This book is printed on acid-free paper. ∞

Copyright © 2001 by John Wiley & Sons. All rights reserved.

Published simultaneously in Canada.

This publication is designed to provide accurate and authoritative information in
regard to the subject matter covered. It is sold with the understanding that the publisher is not engaged in rendering professional services. If professional advice or
other expert assistance is required, the services of a competent professional person
should be sought.

Library of Congress Cataloging-in-Publication Data:

ISBN 0-471-39453-X

Printed in the United States of America.

10 9 8 7 6 5 4 3 2

Dedication

Klaus Inkamp
1944–1999

The second edition of *The International Dictionary of Event Management* is dedicated to the memory of a beloved member of the special events industry, Mr. Klaus Inkamp, CSEP. Mr. Inkamp served as chair of the International Special Events Society certification committee and devoted his professional life to helping others in the industry through education, professional development, and mentoring. He exemplified leadership by putting the goals of the industry ahead of his own personal wishes. A native of Germany and longtime executive at the Coca-Cola Company, Klaus Inkamp would be very proud to see that this second edition represents truly a global partnership to promote international understanding and growth for the special events industry.

Foreword

At last, we have a truly international reference base for the events industry. I say this advisedly, because I recognize how much our industry has developed beyond geographic borders to assume international status and legitimacy.

Having organized a major event across fourteen countries in four months, I can attest to the value of corralling our industry's jargon and phrases into a consolidated document. This is not simply to define our occupational territory, nor to monopolize our work, but to commence the long journey of formally accumulating our tribal knowledge. For too long we, as event practitioners, have gone about our work using similar expertise, practices, and techniques, yet our terminology has been distinctly different. This is despite the fact that many of our professional networks transcend international borders. While I concede that much of our expertise continues to be picked up with practice and through working experience, it is important that newcomers and seasoned professionals have a single reference point for our key phrases. A tangible legacy of our work is duly required. *The International Dictionary of Event Management* is an important first step for our industry.

Our success in staging major events in the past ten years has seen a plethora of people maneuvering on the edge of our field, quick to claim the title "event manager". Over time, the traditional event manager will continue to develop into a well-oiled professional with a new skills base which is applicable across many industries. There have been notable challenges our industry has faced in the past five years: None is more prevalent than our need to acquire more traditional management skills in the eyes of our clients. This has more to do with our success in developing into an established occupational grouping level with senior managers than a rationalization of what we do. Let's take, for example, when we are soliciting events. In addition to our traditional skills and experience, we are now expected to demonstrate our financial and project-management experience. This supports the view that event professionals are now being given full responsibility for projects from start to finish. Balancing the spreadsheet, tending to safety issues, and managing

employees are becoming all too familiar activities for the event professional. Single-event practitioners are required to develop these skills while
larger event-management companies are now supplementing their teams
with project and/or business planners. This reflects the shift from short
one-off events to multiple events linked as part of a wider corporate stra-
tegic framework.

I believe this expansion of our responsibilities as event managers
will continue to dominate the profession for the next five years. These
new responsibilities have much to do with the credibility we have es-
poused on the international stage and are certainly a step in the right
direction for our industry.

The second edition of *The International Dictionary of Event Management* is a giant step toward the global success we have earned. Use
this valuable book to "define" your future in this expanding global industry.

Di Henry, CSEP

Preface

On behalf of the International Special Events Society (ISES), I congratulate you on your decision to expand your resource library with *The International Dictionary of Event Management*. The authors of this valuable book, Carol McKibben, CSEP of the first edition; Dr. Joe Goldblatt, CSEP; and Kathleen Nelson, CSEP have diligently worked to create a meaningful resource guide that will transcend international boundaries as well as industry segmented nomenclature. Their efforts, to create this important dictionary is truly a noble task. It reinforces that the special events industry is a legitimate one. At the same time, the dictionary provides ISES with the opportunity to benefit from the profits of this book.

Whether you use this book to prepare to become a Certified Special Event Professional (CSEP), or reference it to familiarize yourself with an unfamiliar word, there is no doubt that this dictionary is the definitive resource of terms for the special events industry.

My congratulations to the authors, researchers, contributors, validators, editors and the publisher of this book for successfully completing a truly meaningful and valuable project in this dictionary, and to you its reader, for your interest and enthusiasm in expanding your professional horizons.

Robert W. Sivek, CSEP
International President
International Special Events Society

Acknowledgments

This book represents a true partnership between the academic community and the event management industry worldwide. The editors of this book were fortunate to enlist outstanding students from The George Washington University Event Management Program and the University of Nevada, Las Vegas William F. Harrah College of Hotel Administration to identify, verify, clarify, and classify the terms in this text. These students, the future leaders of the event management profession, were greatly assisted by many event management organizations that contributed their suggestions regarding the content and definitions for this book. Finally, industry professionals in five countries reviewed the entire manuscript to ensure widespread understanding.

The editors acknowledge the following sources that were reviewed in preparing the manuscript for this book and are grateful to the organizations who conducted the original research that contributed to the body of knowledge in this field:

American Association of Advertising Agencies.
Association of Destination Management Executives Glossary of Terms; Association of Destination Management Executives.
Black's Law Dictionary, abridged sixth edition; West Publishing Company; Henry Campbell Black, author.
Call to Order; Big Bay Publishing, Inc.; Herb Perry, CAE, author.
Catering Operations and Sales Glossary; Patti J. Shock, author. www.unlv.edu/tourism
Complete Guide to Professional Meeting and Event Coordination, The; George Washington University; Catherine H. Price, Ph.D., author.
Consumer Behavior; Dryden Press; James Engel, Roger Blackwell, and Paul Miniard, authors.
Convention Liaison Council Glossary; Convention Liaison Council.
Convention Liaison Council Manual, sixth edition; Convention Liaison Council.
Creating Special Events; Master Publications; Linda Surbeck, author.

Dictionary of Advertising: An Essential Resource for Professionals and Students; NTC Business Books; Laurence Urdang, editor.

Dictionary of Event Management, The; first edition; John Wiley & Sons, Inc.; Dr. Joe Goldblatt, CSEP, and Carol McKibben, CSEP, authors.

Dollars and Events: How to Succeed in the Special Events Business; John Wiley & Sons, Inc.; Dr. Joe Goldblatt, CSEP, and Frank Supovitz, authors.

Event Management and Event Tourism; Cognizant Publishing; Donald Getz, author.

Exhibit Industry Glossary of Terms; Trade Show Exhibitors Association.

Financial Management Glossary of Terms; International Association of Amusement Parks and Attractions; Alexandria, Virginia.

Folding Table Napkins; Brighton Publications; Sharon Dlugosch, author.

Glossary of Terms; International Association for Exposition Management.

How to Run Scientific and Technical Meetings; John Wiley & Sons, Inc.; Sara R. Torrence, CMP, author.

ISES Gold; International Special Events Society; Dr. Joe Goldblatt, CSEP, Linda Subeck, Betsy Wiersma, editors.

Marketing: Relationships, Quality, Value; Worth Publishers; William G. Nickels and Marian Burk Wood, authors.

Meeting Industry Terminology; International Association of Professional Congress Organizers.

Meeting Management; EPM Publications; Randy Talbot, author.

Meetings, Conventions, and Expositions: An Introduction to the Industry; John Wiley & Sons, Inc.; Rhonda J. Montgomery and Sandra K. Strick, authors.

Meeting Spectrum, The; Rockwood Enterprises; Rudy R. Wright, author.

On-Premise Catering; John Wiley & Sons, Inc.; Patti J. Shock and John M. Stefanelli, authors.

Planning Accessible Meetings: A Guide to ADA Compliance; American Society of Association Executives; Bill Scott, author.

Professional Meeting Management; Professional Convention Management Association; Edward G. Polivka, editor.

Professional Meeting Management: A European Handbook; Vanden Broele Grafische Groep; Tony Carey, CMM, editor.

Special Event Risk Management Manual, The; Alexander Berlonghi, author.

Special Events: The Art and Science of Celebration; John Wiley & Sons, Inc.; Dr. Joe Goldblatt, CSEP, author.

Special Events: The Best Practices in Modern Event Management, second edition; John Wiley & Sons, Inc.; Dr. Joe Goldblatt, CSEP, author.

Stay Out of Court; Prentice Hall; Rita Risser, author.

Table Setting Guide; Brighton Publications; Sharon Dlugosch, author.

The editors gratefully acknowledge the contributions of the individuals whose names appear below.

FIRST EDITION RESEARCH TEAM

The George Washington University Students

Karen Baker, Ayhan Bayer, Janna Bowman, Rob Caskey, Kimberly Collins, Arnold Ehrlich, Andrea Frank, Amy Galton, Michele Glemser, Tanya Headley, Dana Jarvis, Bill Knight, Laurie Lowe, Stephen Masten, Sara May, Cynthia McDowell, Erin McGee, Terrance Morris, Kari Nestande, Gabriel Ornelas, Kristan Quackenbush, Lisa Shafran, Kathy Siegfried, Traci Silke-Punke, Annie Stine, Arden Tellini, Tamera Thomason, Mary Toups, Darnyce Werth, Anita Wiler, Guion Williams, Nancy Yim, Suk Kyu Yoon, and Jennifer Ziehl.

SECOND EDITION RESEARCH TEAM

The George Washington University Students

Maren Biester, Danika Foster, Seung-Won Lee, Marisol Nolasco, Misty Piel, Corina Sumarna, and Jill Zeigenfus.

University of Nevada at Las Vegas Students

Irina Alenikova, Michelle Banks, Alice Bucklin, Gwek Nee Linni Chia, Yu-Shan Chiu, Christopher Drake, Wanda Fair-Murray, Mitch Gorelick, Dong-Joo Kim, Lisa LaPera, Shawna McNair, Wilisha Moore, Miyuki Mori, Nicole Rysedorph, Joshua Schwebel, Helen Syrpes, I-Hsuan Tseng, Chikako Tsuji, Anne Warren, and Ron Wu.

The following industry professionals generously shared their time and talent most to provide critical suggestions to ensure that the second edition reflects a true global perspective.

United States: Jaclyn Bernstein and Robert W. Hulsmeyer

South Africa: Leora Berger, Helen Brewer, Melanie Campbell, Sandra Collier, Susan Deerans, Liz Hart, Shelly Jones, Michael Kemp, Calton Kennedy, Janet Landey, CSEP, Nicky Kennedy, Rudy Kesting, Garth Kirkman, Lisa Loeb, Andrew Pennington, Miguel Pereira, and Paul Warner

Australia: Lena Malouf, CSEP

Great Britain: Tony Tims

Canada: Dana Zita, CSEP

The editors also wish to express appreciation to the following individuals and organizations whose friendship, inspiration, and encouragement supported the development of this book.

Suzanne Bristow, CSEP
Alice Conway, CSEP
Douglas Frechtling, Ph.D.
Max Goldblatt
Sam Goldblatt
Donald E. Hawkins, Ed.D.
Glen Kasofsky
Leah Lahasky
Nancy Lynner
Ruth C. Lynner
Carson Matheny
Elliot Matheny
Nancy Matheny, CSEP
Doris Morales
Chloe J. Nelson
Dan Nelson, CSEP
Jason A. Quinn
Don Saytar
Patti J. Shock
Millie Torres
Stephen Joel Trachtenberg
JoAnna Turtletaub
Reuben E. Walton

This book would not have been possible without the dedicated efforts of Corina Sumarna, who served as coordinating editor for this important work. Ms. Sumarna literally searched the world over to ensure that the broadest possible representations of event management terms were included in this text. Her attention to detail, creativity, and persistence are deeply appreciated by the editors.

The senior editor at John Wiley & Sons, Inc., JoAnna Turtletaub, has served as cheerleader, champion, and coach for this new edition, which also marks the first book in the historic new series of books entitled "The Wiley Event Management Series." Ms. Turtletaub is a major asset in the event management profession, and her dedication to the expansion of this profession is much appreciated by the editors of this volume.

Introduction

All human societies celebrate, and many also share a common language that binds them together in a tight cultural knot. The societies that share a common language communicate more effectively and through this communication sustain and expand their culture. Communication inevitably increases and expands the collective pride they have for their group.

Therefore, the second edition of *The International Dictionary of Event Management,* through your continued use, is potentially the cornerstone of our event management culture and should be used effectively to sustain our profession and increase the pride we have in our work.

The first edition of this book was created to support the competencies of the Certified Special Events Professional (CSEP) exam and provide a useful tool for professionals and students to study certification. Now, this second edition takes our common language to a new level.

This new book represents the collective input of event students and professionals from many parts of the world. The first book received input from North America (Canada and the United States) and Australia. However, this new book includes recommendations from event professionals and event management leaders in Australia, Great Britain, North America, and South Africa. Therefore, this revised edition has 100 percent more input than the previous edition.

As a result of this new input and the careful research by event management students of The George Washington University Event Management Program and the University of Nevada, Las Vegas William F. Harrah College of Hotel Administration, this revised edition has been greatly expanded from 1500 terms to over 3500 terms and definitions. *The book that you are holding is the most comprehensive compendium of terms and definitions ever assembled in one volume by this industry.*

To gain the most benefit from this book, you should first understand the new format. Although the previous book listed all terms in alphabetical order, this edition adds an important new reference dimension.

Part one of this book is an A-to-Z listing of the terms and their definitions, and part two lists each term within the individual categories of *administration, coordination, marketing,* and *risk management.* These four categories represent the body of knowledge identified for the International Special Events Society (ISES) Certified Special Events Professional (CSEP) program of study. Therefore, in part two you can find the terms that support your specific body of knowledge requirements for this CSEP exam.

In addition to more than doubling the number of terms and definitions and providing a universal classification system, this new edition also represents an attempt to specifically identify new terms in catering and other fields that were underrepresented in the first edition. The editors have also attempted to try to balance the four knowledge domains with an equal number of terms in each category. However, during the research for this book the editors soon discovered that the coordination category remains the most robust in the number of terms identified. Through diligent research this book now includes significantly more terms and definitions in the administration, marketing, and risk management categories, resulting in a more balanced resource for industry professionals.

Due to the newly expanded international terminology in this dictionary, we have included a table to assist you with converting U.S. standard measurements into the metric equivalent. This is but one example of how important it is for modern event managers to be able to operate in a global business environment.

METRIC CONVERSION TABLE

Measurement	United States	Metric Equivalent
Length	1 inch	2.54 centimeters
	1 foot	0.305 meters
	1 yard	0.914 meters
	1 mile	1.609 kilometers
Area	1 square inch	6.45 square centimeters
	1 square foot	0.093 square meters
	1 square yard	0.836 square meters
	1 square mile	2.59 square kilometers
	1 acre	0.405 hectares
Volume	1 cubic inch	16,387 cubic centimeters
	1 cubic foot	0.028 cubic meters
	1 cubic yard	0.765 cubic meters
Capacity	1 liquid ounce	0.029 liters
	1 liquid pint	0.473 liters
	1 dry pint	0.55 liters
	1 liquid quart	0.946 liters
	1 dry quart	1.101 liters
	1 gallon	3.785 liters
Weight	1 troy ounce	31.103 grams
	1 pound	0.454 kilograms
	1 ton (2000 lb.)	907.18 kilograms
Temperature	1 degree Fahrenheit	-17.22 degrees centigrade
	33.8 degrees Fahrenheit	1 degree centigrade

This book represents the work of many people working together to develop a common vocabulary and language for the event management industry. Anthropologists recognize culture, archaeology, biology, and linguistics (language) as the four fields that are fundamental to understanding the nature of human beings and the groups they form. Therefore, *The International Dictionary of Event Management, Second Edition,* is an important tool to build our common language and, with it and through it, to construct the future of the event management profession. Used well and often, this book will help you construct a career that through a common language guides you toward the common goal of establishing a respected and successful profession. We encourage you to use the words in this book wisely to build our profession so that that we and our heirs can take pride in the words *Special Events* for generations to come.

Dr. Joe Goldblatt, CSEP
Kathleen S. Nelson, CSEP

Disclaimer and Request for Assistance

The editors have carefully researched each term in this book; however, omissions and errors are inevitable with a project involving a profession that is in continuous development. Therefore, the editors and publisher are not responsible for omissions or errors included in this text and encourage readers to provide new terms, corrections, or other suggestions to the editors through e-mail at drevent@gwu.edu or by fax to (202) 994-0013. All suggestions and other contributions will be included in the third edition of *The International Dictionary of Event Management.* Thank you.

PART ONE

Terms and Definitions A to Z

A

AAAA—See American Association of Advertising Agencies.

AAF—See American Academy of Florists; see American Advertising Federation.

A and B roll editing—Editing that is done with two or more rolls of film or video, conforming and matching with alternate scenes which permits single or double exposures, multiple exposure, and hands-on reediting by the frame.

ABC—See Alcohol Beverage Commission.

above-the-line advertising—Sometimes called media advertising; relates to traditional commission-paying media: press, TV, radio, cinema, outdoor; media handled by full-service agencies.

abstract—1. A written summary of a presentation or paper, generally 200 to 500 words; see summary/brief or call for papers. 2. In laser presentations, graphic designs or patterns that are not representational of concrete objects; often waveform of lissajous patterns, which are abstract electronic patterns that appear organic in view. 3. A brief statement of content.

academic conference/seminar—See colloquium.

acceptance—1. Any agreement to purchase products or services under specified terms. 2. A time draft (or bill of exchange) that the "drawee" (the payer) has accepted and is unconditionally obligated to pay at maturity. The draft must be written on the face of the draft. 3. The drawee's act in receiving a draft and thus entering into the obligation to pay its value at maturity.

access panel—A removable panel, equipment, or section of an exhibit to permit access to lamps, projector mechanisms, etc.

accident report—1. A log that records chronological documentation and includes date, time, location, parties involved, and nature or description of previous incidents. 2. A log that is obtained from police to scope a venue location and assess the risk feasibility.

accompanying person—A person who attends an event with a participant or delegate; see significant other or spouse.

account code—A number system given to specific categories of income or expense; also known as **code of accounts.**

account executive—An individual who represents an organization and the client in servicing in a business arrangement.

accreditation—1. An official recognition or authorization by an independent accrediting organization. 2. The process required for receiving credentials for access to an event or a certain area of an event.

accreditation badge—An identifying tag used for official authorization.

accreditation form—A document for official authorization.

accreditation rules—An established principle or mode of action to be followed in order to obtain accreditation.

accreditation supervising committee—The committee who supervises the matters associated with receiving the official authorization to cover an event.

accrued expenses—The expenses that are incurred before the balance sheet date but that are not due until after the balance sheet date.

ACCED-I—See **Association of Collegiate Conference and Event Directors-International.**

acetate—1. A film positive or negative from which silk screens are produced. 2. A family of plastics for light transmission and surface protection. 3. A sheet used on overhead projectors.

acetone—1. A solvent and/or adhesive agent for bonding many plastic materials. 2. A solvent used as a remover.

acousto-optic modulation—A technique for chopping or colorizing laser images in which primary laser color (red, green, blue) passes through an acousto-optical (AO) crystal, electrically modulated to transmit color. These beams converge into a single beam that proceeds to the XY scanners and the projection surface.

acrylic—The family of clear, color, and translucent thermoplastic resins such as Plexiglas or Lucite.

acrylic emulsion—A water-based latex made of acrylic polymer and used for coatings and/or impregnations.

actionable—Conduct that can be the subject of a lawsuit or legal action. Not everything that is unfair is illegal, however.

action station—A type of station at receptions and buffet meals, at which food is prepared by chefs to order and served to guests; also known as **exhibition cooking** or **food station.**

active language—The language being used by the speaker.

act of God—An accident or event resulting from natural causes that is not preventable by reasonable foresight or care, for example, flood, hurricane, earthquake, and war; see **force majeure clause.**

Actors' Equity Association (AEA)—A professional union that represents performers, stage managers, and others who appear in live theater; also applicable in Canada and Great Britain with a few slight variations in rules.

ACTRA—See **Association of Cable Television and Radio Artists.**

actual cash value—Replacement cost of lost or damaged property less depreciation.

actuator—A solenoid-type device, usually two-position, used in laser light shows and activated by an electric closure. It is sometimes used for shutters, as well as beam-positioning.

AD—See **after date**; see **assistant director/associate director.**

ADA—See **Americans with Disabilities Act.**

ADAAG—See **Americans with Disabilities Act Accessibility Guidelines.**

additional insured—An individual or organization listed as covered by a primary insurance agreement.

additional seating—See **overset.**

add-on—See **tour option.**

ad hoc committee—A committee that is formed on a temporary basis to conduct a specific task(s); also known as **special committee.**

ad hoc group—See **preformed group.**

adjoining room—A room sharing a common wall with another room but without a connecting door.

adjournment of the meeting—The suspension of the meeting either indefinitely or until a later date.

adjustable standard—A vertical support that allows a shelf bracket to be affixed at any point in the support.

adjustment of debts—See **debt adjustment.**

adlux—A black-and-white photo transparency; also known as **negative.**

administration—The group that determines budget, staffing required (organization chart), and flow of communications, as well as develops the timetable and production schedule for an event.

admission—The ticket price charged by a facility for entrance. Admission can be full price, discounted, or complimentary.

admission card—See **congress card.**

ad valorem—According to value; see **duty.**

advanced life support (ALS)—A term used in South Africa for medical service; see **medical service.**

advance order—A product or service ordered before move-in date or commencement date.

advance registration—An enrollment to an event made prior to opening day.

advancing colors—The colors found on the left side of the standard color wheel, such as red, orange, and yellow.

adventure tour—A tour designed around an adventurous activity such as rafting, hiking, or ballooning.

advertised air tour—A published, planned travel program with assigned inclusive tour number usually at special airfare and requiring prepayment.

advertised price (in television or radio)—The published price of broadcast time in television or radio.

advertising—A message that media (newspaper, magazine, television, for example) is paid to distribute. The sponsor controls the message.

advertising agency—An organization that creates general consumer advertising and assists marketers in planning and implementing advertising campaigns.

advertising merchandise—See **advertising specialties.**

advertising specialties—Promotional items with an organization's name and/or advertising message; also known as **advertising merchandise.**

Advertising Standards Authority (ASA)—A national association of advertising agencies in South Africa.

advice note—See **clean bill of lading.**

adviser—An individual appointed to give specialist or expert information on a particular event; also known as **counselor.**

advisory capacity—A term indicating that a shipper's agent or representative is not empowered to make definite decisions or adjustment without the approval of the group or individual represented.

advisory committee—See **consultative committee.**

AEA—See **Actors' Equity Association.**

aerial advertising—Different types of advertising in the sky. Forms include skywriting with smoke; trailed banners; illuminated messages on wings of night-flying aircraft; advertisements projected onto clouds; two or three aircrafts linked together with banners; tethered balloons; and hot air balloons.

aerial beams—See **atmospheric.**

affiliation—The union of a society or political party with another without loss of identity.

affinity group—A group sharing common interests, usually people who are members of an organization; see **preformed group.**

affirmative action—The practice of recruiting, hiring, and promoting certain groups that otherwise would be underrepresented in the workforce; also known as **equal opportunities.**

affirmative action plan—The written document that implements affirmative action.

affixed merchandise—An exhibitor's or client's products fixed to a display.

affreightment (contract of)—An agreement between a steamship line (or similar carrier) and an importer or exporter in which cargo space is reserved on a vessel for a specified time and at a specified price. The importer or exporter is obligated to make payment whether or not the shipment goes ahead.

A-440—The designated international pitch to which pianos are tuned.

AFTA—See **Australian Federation of Travel Agents.**

after date (AD)—A phrase indicating that the date of maturity of a draft or other negotiable contract is fixed by the date on which it was drawn. The date of maturity does not, therefore, depend on acceptance by the drawee or payee.

after-departure charge—Charges (restaurant, telephone, or similar) that do not appear on the guest's account at checkout; also known as **late charge.**

afterimage—An illusory visual image remaining with a spectator after the actual image is no longer available; also known as **ghost image** in South Africa.

aftermarket—After a product or service has been sold, all those means of satisfying the customer, maintaining goodwill, encouraging recommendations, and achieving repeat or renewal sales, including sales of accessories.

after sight—A phrase indicating that payment of a draft or other negotiable instrument is due a specified number of days after presentation of the draft to the drawee or payee.

AFTRA—See **American Federation of Television and Radio Artists.**

Age Discrimination in Employment Act—Legislation that prohibits discrimination against people over 40.

agenda—A written schedule of an event, providing pertinent information, including time, sequence of topics and sessions, location, and presenters' names; also known as **running order** or **schedule.**

agent—1. An individual empowered to act on the behalf of entertainers, speakers, or other contracted people, for a fee, and who has no legal or financial responsibility other than for areas of professional liability resulting from those acts. 2. An individual who negotiates the buying and selling of goods or services without taking title to such products or services.

aggregate limit—The greatest amount of coverage possible that is stated on an insurance policy. Anything beyond this amount must be covered by an excess policy.

AGVA—See **American Guild of Variety Artists.**

AH&MA—See **American Hotel and Motel Association.**

AIA—See **Australian Incentive Association.**

AIFD—See **American Institute of Floral Designers.**

air-conditioning—The system that controls the temperature and humidity of the air in a room.

air-cooled laser—A high-intensity lamp creating laserlike beams and operating on a standard 115 VAC, cooled by air; used for indoor presentations. An air-cooled laser is primarily safe for an audience scan effect.

airfreight—Materials shipped via airplane.

air space—The space between air walls that separate event rooms.

Air Traffic Conference of America (ATC)—The division of the Air Transport Association (ATA) that establishes industry standards and methods of operation.

Air Transport Association of America (ATA)—An organization for members who are connected with airlines' operation.

air walls—A movable, sound-resistant barrier that partitions event areas; also known as **movable wall, partition, divider,** or **diving walls.**

air waybill—A bill of lading (B/L) that covers both domestic and international flights transporting goods to a specified destination.

aisle—A passageway between rows of tables, chairs, booths, or stands. The width is determined by local fire regulations; also known as **bridgeway** or **gangway.**

aisle carpet—A floor covering installed in passageways.

aisle sign—A notice of aisle numbers or letters, indicating locations of participant booths or stands.

à la broche—Cooked on a skewer.

à la carte—A menu with a separate price for each item as opposed to a fixed price for an entire meal.

à la grecque—Prepared Greek style with tomatoes, garlic, black olives, and parsley.

à la king—Cooked in white cream sauce with vegetables.

à la maître d'hôtel—Specialty of the house or a featured item on the menu.

à la mode—1. In the style of. 2. Ice cream on pie. 3. Mashed potatoes on beef.

à l'anglaise—English style.

à la Provençale—With garlic and olive oil.

à la russe—A method of food service in which each guest is served a plate completely set up; also known as **plated.**

à la vapeur—Steamed.

Alcohol Beverage Commission (ABC)—The United States state-level organization responsible for licensing and regulating the sale of alcohol.

alcohol risk management—Policies and procedures that are put into effect to assure the safety of the individuals when a function supplies any alcoholic beverages or condiments.

A-list—1. A list that consists of a catering department's steady, extra employees. They are the first ones called to work when temporary help is needed. 2. In Australia, known as pertaining to society's.

all-expense tour/all-inclusive tour—A tour covering all or most services (transportation, lodging, meals, portage, sightseeing, taxes, gratuities, etc.) for one price.

allocation of speaking time—The time given to a particular speaker to make his presentation.

allowances—Include expenses, rebates, refunds, and overcharges of revenue.

allowed time—See **dead time.**

all-risk coverage—Property insurance covering losses arising from any fortuitous cause except those that are specifically excluded.

all-space hold—A term that indicates all facility space that is reserved for one client.

alongside—A phrase referring to the side of a ship. Products to be delivered "alongside" are to be placed on the dock or within reach of the transport ship's tackle so that they can be loaded aboard the ship.

ALS—See **advanced life support.**

alteration—A production change made by the client after work has begun, and may be billed as extra charges.

AMA—See **American Marketing Association.**

amandine—Served with thinly sliced almonds sautéed in butter.

amateur—Anyone whose work in or for the theater is without financial gain.

ambient light—A level of illumination used to create a particular atmosphere using existing or additional lighting sources.

ambush marketing—A form of marketing in which a competitor attempts to grab media attention away from an official sponsor, which may cause consumer confusion and loss of negotiated coverage.

amenity—1. A complimentary item provided by facility management and found in a sleeping room, such as writing supplies, bathrobe, fruit basket, shower cap, shampoo, shoe-shine mitt, etc. 2. A complimentary service or product provided by a host or sponsor of an event for the purpose of advertising and goodwill; also known as **giveaway.**

American Academy of Florists (AAF)—A school based in Chicago, Illinois, that trains individuals in floral design.

American Advertising Federation (AAF)—A national association of advertising agencies based in Washington, D.C.

American Association of Advertising Agencies (AAAA)—A United States national association of advertising agencies headquartered in New York City.

American breakfast—A hotel term to designate a morning meal that consists of cereal, eggs, meat, bakery goods, fruits, juices, and beverages; also known as **full breakfast.**

American Federation of Television and Radio Artists (AFTRA)—A labor union that represents performers on audiotape, radio, television, and videotape.

American Guild of Variety Artists (AGVA)—A labor union that represents performers who appear in nightclubs, circuses, touring attractions, and other special events.

American Hotel and Motel Association (AH & MA)—An organization whose members work in hotels and motels and provide service and products for the hotel and motel industry.

American Institute of Floral Designers (AIFD)—An international organization that provides seminars and workshops to professional florists who display their designs in shows and events.

American Marketing Association (AMA)—A United States national organization for the promotion of improved marketing practices that publishes the *Journal of Marketing* and the *Journal of Marketing Research.*

American plan—Overnight accommodation that includes breakfast, lunch, and dinner; also known as **full American plan (FAP).**

American Society for Training and Development (ASTD)—A United States organization whose members are training specialists and those who provide services for the training industry, offering a myriad of educational opportunities and material for its members.

American Society of Association Executives (ASAE)—An organization providing information, resources, and education to its members, who are trade association executives and those who provide services and products for the association industry.

American Society of Composers, Authors, and Publishers (ASCAP)—An organization protecting the rights to its members by licensing and paying royalties for the public performances of their copyrighted works.

American Society of Travel Agents (ASTA)—An organization of travel agents throughout the world, whose members provide travel services and products; also provides information, resources, and education to its members.

American Standard Code for Information Interchange (ASCII)—The standard for the code numbers used by computers to represent all the uppercase and lowercase Latin letters, numbers, punctuation, etc.

Americans with Disabilities Act (ADA)—United States legislation passed in 1990 requiring public buildings (offices, hotels, restaurants, etc.) to make adjustments meeting minimum standards to make their facilities accessible to individuals with physical disabilities.

Americans with Disabilities Act Accessibility Guidelines (ADAAG)—The accessibility standards that are referenced in the Americans with Disabilities Act and that apply to public- and private-sector buildings and facilities that come under its jurisdiction.

amorphic lens—A special lens for projectors, used to eliminate distortion in abnormally wide throws.

amortize—To extinguish the value of an asset or a loan gradually and evenly over a period of time.

amp—1. Ampere; a standard unit measuring the strength of an electrical current. 2. Amplifier; also known as **power amplifier.**

amperage—The amount of electrical current transferred from one component to another. This specification is often important when considering the amplifier loudspeaker interface.

amphitheater—An oval or circular building with rising tiers of seats about an open space.

amplifier—An electronic device that drives loudspeakers in audio systems.

analog—A method of conveying data electronically in relation to a television, radio, or telephone signal by varying its frequency or amplitude.

anamorphic lens—A wide-angle lens designed to produce a wide-screen image.

anchor—An auger-type device used to secure the guy ropes of a tent to the ground, ranging in length from 30" to 48" with a helix of 4" to 8" in diameter. Anchors hold better than stakes do in bare earth and sand; also known as **stakes.**

angel—An individual who invests money in a theatrical, film, or event production.

angels on horseback—Baked bacon-wrapped oysters.

animation (slides)—A technique that creates an illusion of movement when used in rapid sequence; see **cel animation, computer animation,** and **slide animation.**

animation camera—A camera used for filming animation in which the camera drive meter allows the film to move forward one frame at a time.

animation stand—A precise, customized camera mount for animation usage, which is capable of accurate gradations of movement above the artwork, Peg-Board, or platen; also known as **crane.**

animation table—A flat table with a circular rotary inset to allow the cel to be turned to any angle for observations, matching, inking, or painting.

anodizing—The process of preserving metal by adding a protective oxide film by an electrolytic process.

answer print—The first positive print of a movie film made from the rough edited negative.

antidiscrimination law—A law that protects individuals from job discrimination; includes any reference or demands made by the employer that do not directly relate to the job description and that are in violation of the law.

antipasto—Italian appetizers that include olives, salami, peppers, marinated vegetable salads, sliced meats, cheeses, and other similar foods.

anti prost—Lighting instruments hung in front of the proscenium.

antistat for carpets—A spray that helps reduce static electricity in carpets.

antistat wax—A solution applied to plastics to minimize dust accumulation.

antitrust laws—United States legislation designed to promote competition and prevent unfair practices that may lead to monopolies or suppression of competition.

A1—The first-class condition.

APCOSA—See **Association for Professional Conference Organisers in South Africa.**

aperture width/height—The dimensions of a slide or film frame.

APEX fare (advance purchase excursion fare)—A special fare at a lower rate for an airline.

appetizer—The first course of a meal, such as salad, soup, or fruit cup.

application to present a demonstration—A form requesting authorization to give a demonstration.

application to present a film—A form for submission of a film or video for presentation in a film program for assessment and screening by a selection committee.

application to present a paper—A form for submission of an article for assessment and screening by a selection committee.

application to present a poster—An application form to present a poster for assessment and screening by a selection committee.

appliqué—Any applied item to fabric or other surfaces for the purpose of décor.

apprentice—An individual who works in the theater for the learning experience, usually not paid.

approximate calculation—See **estimate.**

apron—The part of a stage in front of the main curtain.

arbitrage—The process of buying foreign exchange, stocks, bonds, and other commodities in one market and immediately selling them in another market at higher prices.

arch—An exhibit display that spans two points, such as a ceiling or entryway.

Archie—A service on the Internet for gathering, indexing, and displaying information (such as a list of files available through anonymous file retrieval and transfer services).

architectural cuisine—Menu items where food is stacked, such as endive boats filled with salad greens; also known as **vertical cuisine.**

arc light—A light source providing high-intensity light utilizing a positive and negative metal rod (instead of a light bulb) for large screens or long projection distances; also used in follow spotlights. Replaced by xenon lamps in the 1980s.

area of rescue assistance—An area that is located out of harm's way, providing protection from smoke, fire, and heat, where an individual can retreat until help arrives.

argon—An inert, colorless, odorless gas that creates a blue-green color inside a laser tube.

Armorply—A term for plywood or lumber with a metal veneer.

arrangement background—Determines the shape—height, width, and breadth of décor for an event set or floral design.

arrangement focal point—The center or heart of a floral design; also known as feature focal point of arrangement in Australia.

Arri—The film industry designation for an Arriflex camera. The 16mm versions are used for news gathering, industrials, commercials, and documentaries, whereas 35mm models are used for commercials, high-budget documentaries, industrials, and feature motion pictures.

arrival pattern—The anticipated dates and times of arrival of group members.

arrival time—The anticipated time guests are expected to arrive at a facility.

art—Any materials (drawings, photographs, type) used in preparing camera-ready art; also known as **artwork.**

art principles—An accepted principle encompassing line, form, color, texture, and pattern.

artwork—See art.

ASA—See Advertising Standards Authority.

ASAE—See American Society of Association Executives.

ASCAP—See American Society of Composers, Authors, and Publishers.

ASCII—See American Standard Code for Information Interchange.

ash can—See ash stand.

ash stand—A receptacle for tobacco ashes; an ashtray. Also known as **ash can.**

aside—A dramatic device in which an actor speaks directly to the audience while other individuals onstage supposedly do not hear him or her.

ASM—See assistant stage manager.

aspect ratio—The ratio of image width to height; pertaining to audiovisual, video, and slides.

assembly—A general or formal meeting of an organization for the purpose of deciding legislative direction, approving policy, electing committee members, approving balance sheets, budgets, etc. Rules of procedure as prescribed in an organization's articles and by-laws are observed.

assist animal—See dog guide.

assistant director/associate director (AD)—A person who assists the director in supervising other workers.

assistant stage manager (ASM)—A person who assists the stage manager by taking responsibility for the stage area only.

associate director—See assistant director/associate director (AD).

association—An organization of people with a common purpose.

association agreement—1. A union contract covering companies and unions that bargain on an area-wide basis. 2. A union contract negotiated by a group of employers through an employer's association with the union representing their employees.

association booth/stand—An exhibit booth or stand at which an association provides information about its purpose and services to members and prospective members.

Association for Professional Conference Organisers in South Africa (APCOSA)—A professional organization comprised of Professional Congress Organizers (PCOs) throughout South Africa.

Association of Cable Television and Radio Artists (ACTRA)—An organization for artists who perform on audiotape, radio, and cable television.

Association of Collegiate Conference and Event Directors-International (ACCED-I)—An organization whose members work in colleges and universities as conference and event managers.

Association of Theatrical Press Agents and Managers (ATPAM)—
A union for theater publicists and house managers.

assortment—The variety and combination of products or services offered for sale by an organization.

ASTA—See **American Society of Travel Agents.**

ASTD—See **American Society for Training and Development.**

ATA—See **Air Transport Association of America.**

at-a-glance program—See **pocket program.**

ATC—See **Air Traffic Conference of America.**

athletic event—An event that involves athletes, guests, or attendees in competition or demonstration.

at liberty—Euphemism used by actors, consultants, and others for unemployed or available for work.

atmospheric—A term used to describe a lighting effect created by laser light projected through the air, often enhanced with theatrical fog; also known as **aerial beams.**

ATPAM—See **Association of Theatrical Press Agents and Managers.**

at sight—A phrase indicating that payment on a draft or other negotiable contract is due upon demand.

at-site—At the location of an event or exhibit; also known as **on-site.**

attendance—The total number of people attending an event.

attendee—An individual person attending an event.

attender—An individual person attending event sessions, although not officially involved with the event; also known as an **observer.**

attraction—A natural or man-made facility, location, or activity that offers items of specific interest. An attraction can be a natural or scenic wonder (the Grand Canyon), a man-made theme park (Disneyland), a cultural or historic exhibition (the World's Fair), or a wildlife/ecological park (a zoo or aquarium).

audience count—The number of people in an audience. In a controlled situation, this number is most accurately found through ticket sales, turnstile counts, or established seating capacities. In a noncontrolled situation, estimates from law enforcement agencies, park and recreation departments, or other organizations involved in crowd control are usually reliable.

audience left or right—The stage direction as seen from the audience perspective; see **camera left and right; screen/audience left and right;** and **stage left, stage right.**

audioconference—A conference using only voice transmissions between two or more sites; also known as **conference call.**

audio monitor—A loudspeaker used for listening to the playback of tapes or records and by musicians to hear themselves or other musicians onstage.

audiovisual (AV)—Equipment, materials, and teaching aids used in sound and visual presentations, such as television monitors, video, sound equipment, etc.

audiovisual aids—Audio and visual support for meetings, usually taking the form of film, slides, overhead projection, flip charts, sound equipment, and blackboards.

audit—1. A certified count of attendance. 2. An official review of finances by a certified public accountant.

audition—A tryout performance before producers, directors, casting directors, or others for the purpose of obtaining a part in a production.

auditorium lens—A projection lens used for long distances.

auditorium lights—See **house lights**.

auditorium setup—An arrangement of chairs in rows facing a head table, stage, or speaker; the rows may be straight or semicircular; also known as **church seating** or **theater setup**; see **V-shaped setup**.

au gratin—Foods sprinkled with crumbs and/or cheese and baked until browned.

au jus—Served with natural meat juices or gravy without thickening.

au lait—With milk, as in café au lait.

Australian Federation of Travel Agents (AFTA)—An organization whose members work as travel agents and are from Australia or service Australia.

Australian Incentive Association (AIA)—An Australian professional association comprised of individuals who organize or supply incentive programs.

authorized signature—A signature of a person with authority to: 1. Sign checks and contracts on behalf of an organization. 2. Charge to an organization's master account. 3. Guarantee payment. 4. Contract for space, services, and supplies; also known as **signatory**.

author's guideline/kit—The instructions regarding the required format for the written presentation of a speech; also known as **preparation of paper**.

automated lighting—See **intelligent lighting**.

automatic advance—A feature on a slide projector that mechanically inserts the next slide.

automobile liability insurance—An insurance coverage that protects the owner or operator of a motor vehicle from financial risk due to accidents caused by the driver; also known as **third-party policy**.

auxiliary services—Services, such as stewards, technicians, interpreters, tour guides, valet parking, or other additional services that support an event.

AV—See **audiovisual**.

AV contractor—A supplier of audiovisual equipment, including projectors, screens, sound systems, video, staging, and technical staff.

average room rate—The total guest room revenue for a given period's occupied rooms divided by the number of rooms occupied for the same period. Since it can be related to investment, this statistic is frequently used as a measure of economic feasibility.

awards banquet/celebration—An event, usually formal, to honor outstanding performance.

awning—A monopitch tent structure made up of legs, trusses, and purlins, and clad with PVC.

B

baby spot—A small spotlight in a booth or stand, usually 100, 250, or 400 watts.

backbone—A high-speed line or series of connections that forms a major pathway in a computer network.

back curtain—Swagged tent curtains, approximately 30" wide, used for decorative purposes on side poles; also known as **backdrop.**

backdrop—1. A drape, curtain, or fabric panel at the back of a stage, speaker's table, or exhibit booth or stand; also known as **back curtain.** 2. Decorations in theme events.

backing light—Illumination behind a set used to give a lighting effect on a backdrop.

backing unit—Any piece or pieces of scenery placed behind an opening, door, windows, etc., to limit the view of the audience from the offstage areas.

backlight—A light source that illuminates any transparent or translucent material from behind.

backline equipment—Equipment required by performers, such as amplifiers, microphones, or other instrumentation.

backloader—A truck that loads from the back opening door.

back of house—An area of an event used as a boneyard, that is, not accessible or visible to guests; for example, a kitchen, storage, or work area.

back projection—The process by which an image is projected on the back of a stage or screen that is placed between the viewer and the projector; also known as **rear-screen projection** or RP.

backstage—The portion of the stage behind the main curtain, including the stage, dressing rooms, and wings.

back-to-back—A travel program operating on a continuous basis so that as one group arrives another soon departs.

back-to-base—Communication means for event staff and security officers to contact headquarters.

backup facilities—Substitute event space that is booked as part of the planning strategy and used should planned space be insufficient.

backwall—A panel arrangement at the rear of a booth.

backwall booth/stand—An exhibitor's booth or stand that is located on the perimeter or rear wall and not considered premier booth space; also known as **perimeter booth/stand.**

backwall exhibit—An exhibit that is back-to-back with another exhibit or against a building wall.

badge—Identification worn by event participants; also known as a **name tag.**

badge holder—A pocket that the badge stock slides into that attaches to the exhibition or conference visitor by pin, clip, or lanyard.

badge stock—The paper or plastic on which an exposition or conference visitor's badge is printed. Different sizes and styles are available to use.

baffle—A partition to control light, air, sound, or traffic flow.

baguette—A long loaf of French bread with a crunchy crust.

baked Alaska—Brick ice cream on a cake, covered with meringue and browned quickly in the oven; sometimes served flaming.

baklava—Russian, Greek, or Turkish pastry made of flaky dough, honey, butter, and chopped nuts.

balance sheet—A statement that reflects the financial position of an event or operation by revealing the assets, liabilities, and owner's equity as of a given date.

balcony front spotlights—Spotlights that are mounted on the front of the balcony or related locations to light the acting area.

bale ring—A means of raising tents by raising center poles and securing them with guy ropes. The peak at the center poles is secured to a bale ring (a metal ring), which in turn is raised (along with the roof of the tent) by block and tackle to its ultimate or ideal height on the center poles.

ball—A formal social dance.

bandwidth—The amount of information one can send through a connection, usually measured in bits per second.

banjo (fabric)—A type of lightweight cloth used for backdrops, draping, and linen; also known as **calico.**

bank draft—A written authorization by an individual or agency for the transfer of money into another account; a bank check.

bank guarantee—The guarantee on the part of a bank that it will pay in the event of default, so that no inquiries regarding the solvency of the individual in question are needed.

bank remittance—A deposit forwarded to a bank by mail, personal, or electronic means.

bank transfer—A movement of funds from one bank account to another.

banner—A suspended rectangular piece of fabric or paper used for decorations or signs.

banquet—A formal or ceremonial dinner held during an event, including speeches, music, etc.

banquet captain/banquet manager—The person responsible for all food service; for larger functions may be responsible for a specific area of the dining room; also known as **captain, supervisor, manager,** or **maître d'.**

banquet check—A check or bill issued to a client for food and beverage orders for an event based on the banquet event order.

banquet event order (BEO)—A form providing detailed instructions prepared by an event facility; provides details such as food and beverage, and room setup to facility personnel concerned with a specific area of the function dining room. Also known as **résumé, function sheet, event order, running order,** or **running schedule.**

banquet room—See **function room.**

banquet round—A circular table used for meal service; depending on the diameter, can comfortably seat up to 12 people.

banquet services manager—See **convention services manager.**

barbeque—Roasting meat over direct flame or under direct heat similar to broiling, but basted with well-seasoned barbeque sauce.

bargaining agent—A union recognized by the employer or designated by a government agency to act as the exclusive representative of employees in a bargaining unit.

bargaining unit—A group of employees designated by a government agency or accepted by the employer as constituting an appropriate unit for representation by a union.

bar mitzvah—A Jewish religious ceremony on a male's thirteenth birthday, marking his entry into maturity and often accompanied by a social celebration.

barn doors—Movable, hinged flaps used to control the beam spread of stage lights.

barratry—Negligence or fraud on the part of a ship's officers or crew resulting in injury or loss to the ship's owners.

bar reading—A detailed written record of liquor consumption during an event.

barrier-free—Absence of obstacles that prevent handicapped persons from moving freely to all public areas.

barter—A type of trade in which merchandise or service is exchanged directly for other merchandise or service without the use of money. Barter can be an important means of trade with countries using currency that is not readily convertible. Barter may also have tax liabilities.

base—A steel floor support piece designed to support an upright post.

base plate—1. A large empty plate in the center of each place setting. It is usually removed prior to the entrée course; also known as **place plate** or **service plate.** 2. A plate that a tent or pipe (as in pipe and drape) is fixed to in order to spread the load onto the floor or ground to provide stability and prevent the tent from sinking into the ground.

basic elements—Accepted elements that encompass dominance, scale, rhythm, harmony, and space.

basic life support (BLS)—First aid provider at an event.

basic life support (BSL)—A term used in South Africa for medical service. See **medical service.**

bas mitzvah/bat mitzvah—A Jewish religious ceremony on the thirteenth birthday of a female, marking her entry into adulthood and often accompanied by social celebrations.

batten (bat)—A length of pipe from which scenery, curtains, and lights can be hung; also known as **timber batten.**

bay—The number of storage or tent bays multiplied by the length of the bays equals the length of a structure.

B&B—See **bed and breakfast.**

BBB—See **Better Business Bureau.**

BBS—See **bulletin board system.**

BDI—Both date inclusive.

B/E—See **bill of exchange.**

bead—A metal edge of lath or framing that finishes corners or openings and gives plaster finish continuous, smooth corners.

beaded screen—See **glass-beaded screen.**

beam, ceiling—A beam in the ceiling of an auditorium in which spotlights are concealed; also a beam of light is the ray of light that is projected from a lighting instrument.

beam front spots—Spotlights mounted high in the beams of the auditorium ceiling for the purpose of lighting the stage area from above.

beams, or beam sculptures—A designed array of high-power laser beams, which can be sent directly from the laser source into infinity or bounced off carefully aligned mirrors to create complex compositions. Beam sculptures can be static or kinetic; if kinetic, they can be sequenced through reconfigured positions or scanned (swept) across space; also known as **mirrors.**

béarnaise sauce—A derivative of the hollandaise mother sauce. It is prepared by adding a tarragon reduction to hollandaise. Béarnaise must be kept on or near heat or it will separate and break down. Often served on filet mignon.

Beaulieu—The trade name for a lightweight professional motion picture camera that is used extensively for news and documentary coverage.

bed and breakfast (B&B)—A room rate that includes a sleeping room and breakfast, often in homes or inns and in small intimate locations; also known as **continental plan (CP)** or **Bermuda plan.**

bed hook—Metal hardware in pairs (male and female) that are attached onto a panel edge, permitting an easy coupling of panels.

beef Wellington—Tenderloin coated with liver pâté and baked en croûte.

beep—An audio signal used in cueing and editing.

beignet—1. A square-shaped French doughnut, minus the hole, lavishly sprinkled with powdered sugar. 2. Foods dipped in batter and deep fried.

Bell and Howell—An early motion picture equipment manufacturer of cameras, projectors, and accessories.

bell captain—A hotel employee who supervises the work of the bell staff.

bell end—A South African term for the half-circle shape with a pitch to the end of a tent structure.

bell staff/bell stand—Hotel personnel charged with escorting guests to rooms, carrying luggage, and running errands.

below-the-line advertising—Media other than above-the-line; includes exhibitions, direct mail, point-of-sale displays, sales literature, give-aways, and sponsorships, but not public relations.

Ben Day—The technique of photographing continuous tone art through a screen to break up the subject for reproduction.

BEO—See **banquet event order.**

Bermuda plan—See **bed and breakfast (B&B).**

best price available—A venue's or hotel's best price indicating time available, for example, off-season.

best time available—A request to schedule an advertiser's commercial, at the broadcast station's discretion, in the best available commercial occasion; a scheduling instruction for television or radio advertising.

Beta—See **VHS.**

Better Business Bureau (BBB)—An agency supported by a local business community to detect and prosecute frauds and to correct misleading advertising.

B/G—Background, as in background music.

bid document—A proposal with rates submitted by a destination or a venue inviting a group to meet in their venue.

bid manual/specifications—A written document sent to vendors and issued by an organization that contains requirements for their future events and outlines primary selection and decision procedures; also known as **request for proposal (RFP)** or **job tender.**

billboard—1. A flat, upright structure for the display of outdoor advertising. 2. A brief announcement identifying the sponsor of a program (in television or radio).

billed on consumption (BOC)—Postbilling based on actual usage, usually for beverages.

billing cycle—A period of time in which creditors regularly submit bills to customers.

bill of exchange (B/E)—An absolute order in writing from one person (the drawer) to another person (the drawee), addressing the drawee to pay a specified amount to a named payee at a fixed or determinable future date; also known as **draft.**

bill of lading (B/L)—A document that establishes the terms of a contract between a shipper and a transportation company under which freight is to be moved between specified points for a specified charge. Usually prepared by the shipper on forms issued by the carrier, it serves as a document of title, a contract of carriage, and a receipt of goods.

bill of sight—A customhouse document that allows a cosignee to see the products before paying duties.

binder—A temporary evidence of insurance to the insured before the insurance policy is actually issued.

binding—The process of joining sheets of paper into a completed book.

bipole—A bidirectional loudspeaker with zero degrees of phase difference between its front and rear acoustical output.

bisque—Soup thickened with a vegetable puree; usually a shellfish soup.

Bitnet—A network of mostly IBM mainframes connected to the Internet.

bit part—A small role in a dramatic or event production, rarely with more than two or three lines.

B/L—See **bill of lading.**

blackboard—A hard, smooth, dark surface for drawing or writing with chalk; also known as **chalkboard.**

black light—Ultraviolet lighting that when applied causes phosphorescent colors (paint, dye, fabric) to glow.

blackout—Dates that airlines or hotels cannot offer certain fares.

black out—1. Usually refers to painting out portions of a photo negative on-screen. 2. Close off area to light. 3. Dates that airlines or hotels cannot offer certain fares.

black powder—A chemical mixture of potassium nitrate, sulfur, and charcoal used as the propellant for fireworks shells.

black tie—A term that indicates a tuxedo or dinner jacket, bow tie, and cummerbund for men and formal evening dress for women is required. In the United States and Canada, black tie indicates tuxedo; also known as **formal dress.** In South Africa a black suit or dark suit is also acceptable.

black tie optional/black tie preferred/black tie invited/black tie requested—Terms that indicate formal dress, that is, tuxedo or evening dress, is preferred but not required.

blanket contract—A general agreement between an advertiser and a medium of communication covering all products advertised, regardless of the agencies involved; also known as **master contract.**

blanket wrap—Noncrated freight shipped via van line and covered with protective blankets or padding.

blanking—A momentary diversion of laser light into a light trap within the laser optics, creating a discontinuity, or black space, within the laser graphic, which may be fast, slow, clean, wiped, accurate, or approximate, depending on the equipment.

bleachers—A tiered seating space, usually without cover, for spectators of events; also known as **grandstand.**

bleed—Printing beyond the cutting edge of paper.

blending color—A gradual merging of one color into another.

B lights—A string of 35 to 100 half-watt miniature lights spaced 8" apart; also known as **mini-Italian, bud,** or **fairy lights.**

blintz—A thin pancake rolled around a filling of cream cheese and chopped meat or fruit.

block—A number of rooms held for a group for a specified period of time.

block and tackle—Ropes and pulleys used to lift and to pull out stress points where greater leverage is required; for example, used to lift and stretch tents.

block booking—See **blocked space.**

blocked space—A term that indicates that a group of sleeping rooms, exhibit, meeting, or other function space has been reserved by an organization holding a future event; also known as **block booking.**

blocking—A rehearsal, during which the director sets up all the action or movements for the scene.

blocking notation—Movement of actors in the acting area.

bloom—1. A flower or blossom of a plant. 2. A powdery substance seen on the surface of freshly picked fruit.

blower—The general term for a device to circulate or remove warm air from restricted areas.

blowup—An enlargement of a photo, a piece of art, or typography.

BLS—See **basic life support.**

blueline/blueprint—A final proof copy for the client's approval before printing; also known as **brownline, silverprint,** or **proof.**

blue sky—A term for extreme design, thinking, or abstract value used during the brainstorming process in the design phase.

BMI—Broadcast Music, Incorporated.

BO—Bad order; buyers option.

boarding card—See **boarding pass.**

boarding pass—A permit to board a ship, train, plane, or other form of transportation; also known as **boarding card.**

board meeting—A meeting of the governing body of an organization.

board of directors setup—A configuration of tables in a meeting room set in a rectangular or oval shape with chairs placed on both sides of the tables and at the ends; also known as **conference-style setup** or **boardroom setup.**

board of trustees—Official members who manage the affairs and administer the funds of an organization.

boardroom—A meeting room set up permanently with a table and suitable seating; also known as **committee room.**

boardroom setup—See **board of directors setup.**

bobbinet—A transparent curtain of silken texture.

BOC—See **billed on consumption.**

body type—The type size used for the main text; also known as **typeface.**

boeuf à la bourguignonne—Traditional beef stew with vegetables in Burgundy wine sauce.

boldface—In printing, a type with a heavy face.

bombe—A molded dessert of ice cream, whipped cream, and fruit.

bonbon—Any sweet candy.

bonded warehouse—A warehouse authorized by customs authorities for the storage of goods on which payment of duties is deferred until the goods are removed.

bonding—The purchase, for a premium, of a guarantee of protection for a supplier or a customer. In the travel industry, certain bonding programs are mandatory. Air Traffic Conference of America (ATC) insists that travel agents be bonded to protect the airlines against defaults. Some operators and agents buy bonds voluntarily to protect their clients and for promotional purposes.

bone china—A type of china that contains animal bone ash (up to 40 percent) for added translucency and whiteness of dinnerware.

boneyard—An equipment storage area at an event site such as an exposition; also known as **warehouse.**

bonus—See **perquisite** or **gratuity.**

book—To commit, ahead of time, meeting space, sleeping rooms, speakers, entertainers, or services on a definite basis; also known as **reservation.**

booking agent—See **talent agent/booking agent.**

booking form—A document that the applicant must complete to give the operator full particulars about who is buying the tour. It states exactly what is being purchased (including options) and must be signed as acknowledgment that the liability class has been read and understood.

book of abstracts—A collection of articles available to meeting participants for use in selecting sessions.

book on payment (BOP)—A payment guaranteed by a travel agency for a package reserved within a cancellation period.

boom arm—An adjustable support for positioning microphones, lighting fixtures, or video cameras.

boom microphone—A microphone attached to a long, movable arm and used in stage production.

booth—A specific area assigned by management to an exhibitor under contractual agreement; also known as **stand.**

booth/stand area—The amount of floor space occupied by an exhibitor; also known as **exhibition area** or **exhibition space.**

booth/stand contractor—A company that constructs or assembles exhibit booths/stands under contract with the organizing committee.

booth/stand number—A number designation to identify each exhibitor's space.

booth/stand personnel—The staff assigned to represent the exhibitor in an assigned space; also known as **booth/stand representative.**

booth/stand representative—See **booth/stand personnel.**

booth/stand sign—1. An identification stating the name, city, state, and booth/stand number of an exhibitor. 2. A sign, behind a desk, indicating the service provided at that point; also known as **fascia board.**

booth/stand size—The dimensions of an exhibitor's space.

bootleg wages—The wages above those at the prevailing rate or union scale that an employer may pay in a tight labor market to hold or attract employees.

BOP—See **book on payment.**

bordelaise—Cooked with Bordeaux wine.

border—A curtain across the top of a stage with two vertical legs left and right to hide flying scenery and other offstage elements, also known as **teaser.**

border chaser—Programmed lighting around signs or other displays.

borscht—Chilled soup made of chopped beets, onions, lemon juice or vinegar, salt and pepper, and water or soup stock, topped with sour cream. Sometimes cabbage is added.

bouillabaisse—Wine-flavored mixed seafood stew.

bouillon cup and saucer—A two-handled cup used for serving clear soups.

boundary microphone—See **plate microphone.**

bourgeois—Plain; cooked family style.

boxed—Draped linen usually around buffet or presentation tables that is folded, pinned, and creased at the corners.

box framing—A perimeter frame with lumber on the edge.

box lunch—A light lunch in a box.

B/P—Bills payable.

brainstorming—A group technique for stimulating creative ideas that are not initially judged for merit; also known as **collection of ideas.**

brain trust—A group of expert advisers assembled to answer questions of current interest.

brand—A name, phrase, design, symbol, or a combination of those elements that associates a product or service to an advertisement and differentiates it from other similar products.

brand loyalty—Loyalty of a customer to a particular brand of goods.

bread-and-butter plate—A plate used for bread, rolls, and butter; also used at receptions for buffet items that do not need silverware.

break—A short interval between sessions when coffee, tea, and other refreshments are served; also known as **coffee break** or **refreshment break.**

break a leg—The traditional wish of good luck exchanged between theatrical people prior to opening-night curtain instead of "good luck."

breakaway—Scenery or props that disappear, break, or change form in full view of the audience.

break character—To say or do anything, as an actor, during a rehearsal or performance, that is not consistent with what the character portrayed would say or do.

breakdown—The time required to dismantle the structure of an event; see **move-out.**

break-even analysis—1. The total fixed costs divided by the contributions margin percentage. 2. A formula for analyzing income and expenditures in order to find the profit at various levels of quantity sold.

breakfast plate—A standard dinner plate used for breakfast.

breakout session—A small group formed within a meeting to discuss topics related to the general session.

breakpoint—The level at which discounts are allowed for volumes of freight.

break terminal—The location at which common carriers separate consolidated freight.

breakup—An image or audio distortion.

bridge lights—The lights that are mounted on the bridge.

bridgeway—See **aisle** and **gangway.**

brief—See **summary/brief.**

briefing—A meeting shortly before the start of the event.

brilliance—The degree of intensity of colors; also known as **vibrancy.**

bring a bottle—See **bring your own (BYO).**

bring up—See **dim in/dim up.**

bring your own (BYO)—A term that refers to the practice of bringing alcoholic beverages to restaurants and establishments that charge a corkage fee for that privilege; also known as **bring a bottle.**

broadcast equipment—High-caliber video and audio equipment used by television stations, production companies, and other broadcasting professionals who require a high-quality visual product.

broadcast production—The process of creating television or radio spots as a form of advertising.

brochure—A pamphlet describing and promoting a particular event or product; also known as **pamphlet** or **leaflet.**

brownline—See **blueline/blueprint.**

browser—A client program (software) that is used to view various kinds of Internet resources.

brunch—A midmorning meal that includes breakfast and luncheon food selections.

brushed finish—A finish primarily on aluminum or steel achieved by rubbing with a wire brush or steel wool to achieve a matte quality.

Brussels Tariff Nomenclature—The customs tariff used by many countries, including most European nations, but not the United States; also known as **nomenclature of customs cooperation council** or **customs duties.**

brut—Dry, as in wine; not sweet.

budget—A financial statement of estimated income and expenditure for a specific time period. Also known as **cash flow chart** or **phased budget.** See **budget chart.**

budget chart—The estimated total revenue and expenditure, divided into subject categories, projecting cash needed to meet expenses over a specific time frame; also known as **cash flow chart, phased budget,** or **budget.**

bud lights—See **B lights.**

buffer zone (Canadian)—The zone in Canada, 225 miles from the border, dividing the two tax structures applied to Y class fares.

buffer zone (PRS)—A section of airplane seats located between smoking and nonsmoking sections allowing for variance in the smoking and nonsmoking boundary.

buffet—An assortment of foods offered on a table and self-served.

buffet service—A presentation of food, offered on a table from trays, chafing dishes, and other similar equipment.

build—The process of adding lines or changes to a series of sequential slides; also known as **multiple disclosure.**

buildup—A system of programming a flasher to light lamps in cumulative sequence with time intervals between.

bulk carrier—A vessel engaged in the carriage of such bulk commodities as petroleum, grain, or ores that are not packaged, bundled, bottled, or otherwise packed.

bulkhead—The seats at the front of an airplane cabin and facing a wall.

bulk mailing—A mailing of third-class matter in large quantities of identical pieces at a special rate.

bullet/bullet point—A large, heavy dot used in printing for emphasis or enumeration.

bullet catch—A device for holding a hinged door closed.

bullet hit—A pyrotechnic device used to simulate the effects (visual or audio) of a rifle or gun shot.

bulletin board system (BBS)—A computer system used by various special interest and discussion groups to communicate electronically on an ongoing basis.

bullnose—A technique for finishing a raw edge with half-round molding, or shaping to half-round.

bump-in—See **move-in.**

bumping—The process of removing a confirmed airline passenger from a full flight to make room for a passenger with higher priority.

bump-out—See **move-out.**

bums in bed—The Australian term for the number of persons in sleeping rooms in a hotel/motel. See **heads in beds.**

bunting—1. Linen gathered together in loose folds on top of a table and suitable seating. 2. Flags, banners, or swagged strips of cloth hung as festive decorations. 3. A decoration of colored flags or streamers strung on a line.

burned-in copy—Written copy appearing on photographs.

burn units—See **smoke generation.**

bus—1. A motor-driven vehicle for transporting groups of people; also known as **coach.** 2. Generally refers to the physical connection used on the motherboards or backplanes within an electronic equipment enclosure, such as a personal computer, to cross connect two or more circuit boards so that electronically coded messages can pass back and forth between the individual components that make up the overall system. May take the form of either a multiconductor cable with connectors attached or a printed circuit board with edge connectors to accommodate plugging in other circuit boards.

business agent—A political, elected position within a union. Salary is not paid by the service contractor, but the union itself; also known as **steward** or **foreman.**

business attire—Business suits or jackets with shirts and ties for men and day dresses or suits for women; usually taken to mean office and not recreational wear; can include informal forms of national dress; also known as **informal dress.**

business center—An area in a hotel or meeting facility offering office equipment and services; see **communication center.**

business class—A transportation service priced between first and economy class and offering special amenities.

business manager—A person responsible for the finances and elements of the production for the client and for the public.

business market—Companies that purchase catering services. There are three levels: shallow (low budget), midlevel (customarily includes a sit-down meal), and deep (fancy meal function).

business occurring—A phrase referring to the number of groups and attendees meeting in a city during a specific time frame.

busy—A cluttered image on the screen.

butler service (American)—A method of serving in which waiters move amongst the guests and serve food and drinks; also known as **tray service** in Australia and **silver service** in the United Kingdom.

butler service (Australia)—A personalized method of serving in which the waiter holds a platter as the guests serve themselves; also known as **formal dining service.**

butterfly nut—See **wing nut.**

butt joint—A joint in carpentry achieved by nailing and gluing square ends of lumber together at a right angle.

buying agent—See **purchasing agent.**

buying team—Two or more people from the same company who jointly evaluate a product or service and either make or influence the buying decision.

buzz session—A method used to increase participation by dividing event participants into smaller discussion groups that then report their findings and opinions in plenary session.

BX cable—Flexible armored electrical cable accepted as insulated by most codes; has two, three, or more wires.

by-laws—The rules by which an organization is governed.

BYO—See **bring your own.**

by the bottle—Liquor served and charged for by the full bottle.

by the drink—Liquor served and charged for by the number of drinks served.

by the person—A fixed price that covers food consumption within a given time frame; sometimes includes snacks or hors d'oeuvres or canapés.

by the piece—Food purchased by the individual item, usually for a reception.

C

cabana—A hotel room adjacent to a pool area, with or without sleeping facilities.

cabaret table—A small round table, 15" to 30" in diameter, used for cocktail parties; also known as a **club table, cocktail table,** or **cocktail round.** In Australia known as **le café table** in off-premise catering and in the United Kingdom as **poseur table.**

cabled interpreting system—The system for the transmission of interpreting by cable or wire; also known as **wired system interpreting.**

cable ramps—Steel, plastic, or wood structure to provide protection for electrical cable and to provide a safe method for large numbers of people to cross over cables, wires, pipes, and to alter ground impediment.

CAC—See **Canadian Association of Caterers.**

cacciatore—Chicken casserole cooked with olive oil and vegetables.

CAD—See **cash against documents.**

CAD/CAM—Computer-aided design/computer-aided manufacturing.

CAEM—See **Canadian Association of Exposition Management.**

cafeteria service—A form of service in which counter attendants serve guests in a buffet line.

calamari—Italian fried squid.

calico—See **banjo.**

call board—A theater bulletin board for announcements of rehearsals, work calls, and general theater information.

call boy—An individual who gives calls to the actors.

call brand—A specific brand of liquor selected by a client according to personal preference for serving at an event; see **house brand** and **premium brand.**

call for papers—A document containing detailed instructions for the submission of papers that are assessed and selected by a review committee; often referred to as abstract forms; also known as **abstract** and **conference papers.**

calligraphy—See **computer-composed script.**

call-out—A notation on drawings or exhibits of special significance, such as finish, edge, color, detail, or features.

cam—A metal disk, commonly used to open and close flash switches and other mechanical devices.

camera chain—Television cameras, cables, video controls, and power supply working together.

camera left and right—The direction from the camera's (or audience's) perspective, as opposed to from the stage or the performer's perspective.

camera-ready art—Material that is ready for photographic reproduction.

Canadian Association of Caterers (CAC)—A professional association comprised of caterers and suppliers to the catering industry in Canada.

Canadian Association of Exposition Management (CAEM)—An organization providing information and resources to its members, who work for hotels or convention centers as exposition managers.

Canadian Centre for Philanthropy (CCP)—A professional organization providing education and resources about philanthropy in Canada.

Canadian Hotel and Motel Association (CHMA)—A Canadian organization providing information, education, and resources to its members, who work in hotel and motel operations in Canada.

Canadian Society of Association Executives (CSAE)—The Canadian association whose members are association executives and their suppliers. The organization provides education and other resources to its members.

Canadian Tourism Human Resource Council (CTHRC)—The Canadian organization promoting and enhancing professionalism in the Canadian Tourism Industry through industry standards, training, and professional certification.

canapé—A hot or cold appetizer with a bread or cracker base.

cancellation clause—1. A contract provision that outlines penalties for both parties for cancellation or failure to comply with terms of the agreement. 2. A contract provision in the entertainment industry that allows an artist to cancel a performance within a specified time prior to the play date.

cancellation insurance—A policy that protects the financial interests of the event sponsor or event organizer in the event of a cancellation.

cancellation or interruption insurance—Insurance that protects an event organizer from financial loss or expenses incurred when contractually specified perils necessitate canceling or relocating an event or cause a reduction in attendance.

candelabra—An ornamental, branched candlestick.

canopy—A drapery, awning, or other rooflike covering that provides overhanging shelter.

cantilever—A horizontal member extending well beyond its vertical support.

canvas—A heavy cloth used for outdoor banners, tents, and sails. In South Africa, the material used for cladding tents (see **cladding**). Vinyl is commonly used in Australia.

capacity—A maximum number of people who can be contained in any given event area.

capacity control—A restriction on the number of seats available for a particular fare or event.

caper—The pickled green bud of a Mediterranean bush.

capital—The money or assets contributed to an organization by the owners or stockholders to be used in the conduct of the business.

capital expenditure—An expenditure for property or for equipment rather than operating expenses.

capital letter—See **uppercase**.

cap nut—A decorative nut, usually plated, to secure the end of a threaded bolt where a finished appearance is desired; sometimes called acorn nut.

cappuccino—A hot beverage of one-third espresso, one-third steamed milk, and one-third foamed milk.

cap strip—A piece of finished material used to cover end framing.

captain—The person responsible for food-related services at banquet functions; see **banquet captain/banquet manager.**

carbonated (sparkling water)—Naturally carbonated water is water whose carbon dioxide comes from the water's source; carbonated water is water with added carbon dioxide.

cardioid microphone—A unidirectional microphone often used on lecterns that picks up sound in a heart-shaped pattern; see **lectern microphone.**

cargo ton/freight ton—See **measurement ton.**

car hire—The facility to hire a car.

carnet—A customs document that permits its holder to carry or send merchandise into a designated foreign country for a defined period of time for the purpose of display or demonstration without paying customs fees or posting bonds.

carousel projector—A 35mm slide projector using a carousel tray.

carousel tray—A circular holder used for projecting 35mm slides; also known as **round slide tray.**

carpenter—A person skilled in the building and repair of wooden objects and used to fabricate and install booths, stands, exhibits, and environmental designs.

carpet tape—Tape used to adhere the edge of a carpet to the floor.

carriage bolt—A bolt with a square shank next to the head to allow tightening in wood without tools.

carrier—A company employed to transport passengers or freight. Uses all or some space on an airplane, bus, ship, or other vehicle during a special period of time and for a specific itinerary.

carrying capacity—The maximum amount of people a room or area can hold before violating regulations or policies or endangering the individuals that are contained in the area.

cartage—Short-haul moving of exhibits; often incorrectly referred to as drayage; also known as **transport** or **freight.**

cart service—A method of service in which foods are prepared at tableside, and servers design individual plates for each guest. Sometimes used as a dessert cart; also known as **English service.**

carver—An in-room attendant who carves and serves meats during a reception or buffet.

cascade fold napkin—A napkin fold that is underscored with decorative edging on the napkin.

CCAE—See **Canadian Council for the Advancement of Education.**

CASE—See **Council for the Advancement and Support of Education.**

cash—Cash includes cash on hand, demand deposits, and temporary cash investments such as short-term certificates of deposit.

cash against documents (CAD)—Payment for goods in which a commission house or other intermediary transfers title documents to the buyer upon payment in cash.

cash bar—A private bar setup where guests pay for drinks.

cash flow—Monies available to meet daily operating expenses as opposed to equity, accounts receivable, or other credits not immediately accessible.

cash flow chart—See **budget** and **budget chart.**

cash in advance (CIA)—Payment for goods in which the price is paid in full before shipment is made. This method is usually used only for small purchases or when the goods are prepared to order.

cash registration—The full payment of estimated room charges at the time of hotel guest registration; credit for incidentals, such as room and laundry services and telephone charges, is not extended.

cash reservation—A payment made at the time of reservation for anticipated charges.

cash with order (CWO)—Payment for goods in which the buyer pays when ordering and in which the transaction is binding on both parties.

cassette—A self-enclosed two-reel audiotape or videotape module.

cast—Players in a play.

casual attire—A term used to designate a sport shirt, possibly with a jacket, for men and dressy casual wear, such as slacks outfits, fashionable casual dresses, or resort-type outfits for women.

CAT—See **computer-assisted translation.**

catenary arch—The curve made by a flexible, nonelastic chain or cord when it is suspended freely between two points of the same height as referring tents.

Caterers Guild of South Africa (CGSA)—A professional association of caterers and their suppliers in South Africa. The association provides education and networking for its members.

catering manager—A person who maintains client contacts and is responsible for servicing accounts.

catering sales manager—1. The hotel or facility staff person responsible for servicing group and local food and beverage functions. 2. The staff person responsible for selling the catering services to potential clients.

catwalk—1. A narrow walkway above an auditorium used for hanging lights and sound equipment; also known as **stage**. 2. A narrow walkway in an overhead or roof structure to reach equipment suspension points. 3. A modeling runway.

cause-related marketing—A type of marketing that promotes donations for a charity or nonprofit organization in conjunction with sales of a product.

caviar—Sturgeon roe (eggs); lightly salted. The lighter the color, the better quality and the more expensive.

CC—**Current cost.**

CCP—See **Canadian Centre for Philanthropy.**

CD—See **compact disc.**

CDRG—See **Center for Devices and Radiological Health.**

ceiling décor—Suspended decorations to enhance the appearance of the venue.

ceiling height—Maximum height of the ceiling of a venue. Dimensions quoted by halls and hotels often do not take into account the lowest ceiling points or any light fixtures hanging from the ceiling.

CEIR—See **Center for Exhibition Industry Research.**

cel—1. A sheet of transparent plastic whose width and height accommodate screen ratios; used to paint, ink, or draw on directly, mainly for animation and titling. 2. A single frame of film.

cel animation—A succession of rapidly changing drawings, or cels, that create the sense of movement, as in film; see **animation (slides).**

celastic—A material formed to shape by using treated fabrics, resins, and adhesives.

celebrate—1. To mark an event or milestone. 2. To observe with ceremony and ritual.

Celotex—The manufacturer of a material composed of compressed paper and adhesives.

CEM—See **Certified Exposition Manager.**

center channel loudspeaker—A single loudspeaker that sits in front or on top of a television screen and reproduces the dialogue of a movie in a surround sound system.

Center for Devices and Radiological Health (CDRG)—A division of the U.S. Food and Drug Administration that regulates the use of lasers in the United States, including those used for display purposes.

Center for Exhibition Industry Research (CEIR)—An organization that conducts research for the exposition industry for the purpose of determining economic impact and other market research.

Center for Exhibition Industry Research (formerly known as the Trade Show Bureau)—A membership organization representing the entire exhibition industry, whose mission is to promote the growth of the exhibition industry through research, information, and communication, and to position exhibitions as primary marketing tools.

centerpiece—A decorative object placed at the center of a dining table; also known as **table center.**

center poles—Solid or telescopic poles of wood or metal used to support the center and highest part of a tent.

center sections—The sections of a tent that form the roof between the two end sections.

center stage—The area in the center of the acting area.

central console—The desk from which the technicians operate microphones, lighting, and audiovisual equipment; also known as **operator desk.**

central staging—Placing the audience area on all four sides of the acting or event area.

CEO—See **chief executive officer.**

ceramics—Pottery, earthenware, china, glass, and other products that are made from a mixture of natural materials processed by firing.

certificate of inspection—A document certifying that merchandise (such as perishable goods) was in good condition immediately prior to its shipment.

certificate of insurance—A document that serves as written evidence of insurance.

certificate of insurance currency—A document proving an organization has public liability insurance.

certificate of manufacture—A statement (often notarized) in which a producer of goods certifies that the manufacturing has been completed and the goods are now at the disposal of the buyer; also known as **guarantee.**

certificate of origin—An official government document stating the origin of foreign goods.

Certified Exposition Manager (CEM)—An exhibit industry professional, as officially designated by the International Association for Exposition Management.

Certified Manager of Exhibits (CME)—An exhibit industry professional, as officially designated by the Trade Show Exhibitors Association.

Certified Meeting Professional (CMP)—A designation offered by the Convention Liaison Council (CLC) that certifies competency in 25 areas of meeting management.

Certified Special Events Professional (CSEP)—A designation signifying competency in event management, administered by the International Special Events Society (ISES). The CSEP is considered the hallmark of professional achievement in the event industry.

Certified Tour Professional (CTP)—A designation conferred upon tour professionals who complete prescribed academic study, professional service, escorted travel employment, and evaluation requirements. The CTP program is administered by the National Tour Foundation located in Lexington, Kentucky, and is open to individuals employed in any segment of the group travel industry.

CEMEs—See **continuing event management education units.**

CESSE—See **Council of Engineering and Scientific Society Executives.**

CEUs—See **continuing education units.**

C&F—See **cost and freight.**

CFO—See **chief financial officer.**

CGSA—See **Caterers Guild of South Africa.**

chai—Spiced tea with cream and sweetener.

chain drive—A power transmission chain device for animation.

chain lock—A security device that uses a chain that can be attached to the door jamb to limit the opening of the door; also known as **security lock.**

chair cover—A tailored, stretch cover to fit a classic chair; see **snug banqueting.**

chairperson—A person selected to preside over a session, meeting, committee, board, or conference.

chalkboard—See **blackboard.**

chamfer—The technique of reducing a sharp corner of lumber or timber by sanding or machining the edge.

change order—A facility form used to advise departments of changes in reservations or functions.

channel—Any material milled or extruded in a continuous U shape.

character generator—An electronic device that displays words or characters within a television image.

charge per square meter—The basic charge for a square meter of exhibition space.

charger—1. Another name for a larger plate used as a base plate in catering. 2. Home for electrical fitting to provide power; also known as showplate in Australia.

charitable contribution—The contribution of money, securities, etc., to organizations engaged in charitable purposes; see **donation.**

charitable corporation—A not-for-profit corporation organized for charitable purposes.

charitable deduction—A contribution to a qualified charity or other tax-exempt institution for which a taxpayer may claim a deduction on his or her tax return.

charitable foundation—An organization dedicated to education, health, or relief of the poor.

charity—1. A gift for an individual or institution. 2. An organization engaged in public benevolent purposes.

charter—The exclusive use of all or some space on an airplane, bus, ship, or other vehicle for a special period of time and fare and for a specific itinerary.

charter flight—A flight booked exclusively by a single host or a specific group of people who generally belong to the same organization.

charter operations—As used in motor carrier certificates. The term contemplates the transportation of preformed groups, that is, groups organized by someone other than the carrier, and that are sold the exclusive use of the vehicle. An operator authorized to arrange transportation in charter operations, however, is not limited to dealing with preformed groups, but can itself form the tour group.

charter party—A written contract, usually on a form, between the owner of a vessel and a "charterer" who rents use of the vessel or a part of its freight space. The contract generally includes the freight rates and the ports involved in the transportation.

charts—Music books, sheets, or scores.

chaser—A mild drink that is consumed following hard liquor.

chaser flasher—An electrical device to accomplish rapid sequential lighting.

chaser lights—A system of lights wired so that a mechanical or computerized device can control different lights and their pattern (forward, reverse, alternating, random, or cascade).

chaser music—See **walk-in/walk-out music.**

chateaubriand—Thick tenderloin steak, cut from the center or "barrel" of the loin.

cheat—To vary the positions of actors to create a better television or stage picture.

check-in—A registration procedure for guests at the time of arrival.

check-in time—The time at which a guest may check in and occupy rooms.

checkout—A procedure at the time of guest departure, including account settlement.

checkout time—The time set by a facility when guests are required to vacate rooms.

cheddar cheese—White to orange-colored cheese with a flavor ranging from mild to sharp depending on the amount of aging.

chef's choice—The selection by the chef of food items that best complement the entrée or main course and that can demonstrate the chef's culinary ability.

chemise—With skins, as in boiled potatoes in their skins.

cherry picker—A piece of heavy equipment used to lift a person or equipment to a given height; also known as **high jacker.**

chevron—1. A type of room setup with the chairs and/or tables arranged in a V-shaped pattern; also known as **herringbone setup** or **V-shaped setup.** 2. A type of cloth used for backdrops.

chief executive officer (CEO)—The principal officer responsible for the overall administration of an organization.

chief financial officer (CFO)—The individual in an organization responsible for the financial management of the company; also known as **financial controller.**

chief information officer (CIO)—The individual in an organization responsible for the information of the company.

chief operating officer (COO)—The executive responsible for day-to-day operations of an organization.

chiffonade—Food served with shredded vegetables, such as lettuce salad with shredded carrots and/or red cabbage.

china—A nonporous type of dinnerware made of white clay and fired at an exceptionally high temperature.

chinagraph pen/pencil—A special pen/pencil used for marking on print overlays and acetates because it rubs off easily.

chopping—In laser presentations, a form of blanking that is not often used to create discretionary blank spaces (such as spaces between letters in a word), but is used to lace abstract graphics with a wave-form pattern of black, to create an attractive interference pattern.

chrome finish—The electrolytic process of achieving a bright finish on a metal surface.

church seating—See **auditorium setup.**

C&I—See **cost and insurance.**

CIA—See **cash in advance.**

CIC—See **Convention Industry Council.**

CIF—See **cost, insurance, freight.**

CIF&C—See **cost, insurance, freight, and commission.**

CIF&E—See **cost, insurance, freight, and (currency) exchange.**

cinema style—Rows of seats behind one another.

Cinemoid—A colored plastic sheet used for producing color in light.

CIO—See **chief information officer.**

cioppino—An Italian fish stew made from tomatoes, white wine, clams, shrimp, crab, calamari, swordfish, and fresh basil and garnished with a garlic crouton.

circle trip—A journey with stopovers that returns to the point of departure without retracing its route; also known as **round-trip.**

circline—A circular fluorescent fixture.

city central—The association of AFL-CIO local unions in a city or metropolitan area.

city tour—A sightseeing trip through a city, usually lasting a half day or full day, during which a guide points out that city's highlights.

civic celebration—An event that celebrates civic pride through parades, festivals, and other annual traditional programs; also known as **public event** in South Africa.

cladding—A South African term for the clothing of the walls and roof of a tent structure to keep the weather out.

claim—1. An assertion used in an advertisement, regarding a product's or service's performance in providing benefits to purchasers. 2. A report submitted to an insurance carrier to document a loss. 3. The demand for payment for a loss coming under the terms of an insurance policy.

clamp-on fixture—An electrical fixture with a C-clamp device for attaching to a display or other surface.

claque—Paid members of an audience hired to applaud.

class action—A lawsuit brought by a class of people on behalf of themselves and others in a similar class.

classified advertising—Newspaper and magazine advertising subdivided according to the types of products and services offered or sought.

classroom seating—See **classroom setup** and **schoolroom setup**.

classroom setup—A configuration of tables set in rows, one behind the other, with chairs facing the stage front; also known as **schoolroom setup**.

clean bill of lading—A receipt for goods issued by a carrier with an indication that the goods were received in apparent good order and condition, without damages or other irregularities; also known as **advice note** in the United Kingdom.

clean draft—A draft to which no documents have been attached.

clearance—1. Permission obtained to use restricted property. 2. The space between a passing object and the roof of a passageway.

clear span—An aluminum portal frame structure with PVC cladding; see **polyvinyl chloride (PVC)** and **cladding**.

clear-span tent—A tent with an aluminum frame support structure that eliminates the need for center pole support.

cleats—Wood strips on the sides of a shipping container for sliding and handling purposes; also known as **wedges**.

climax—The part of the central action, usually near the close, in which tensions are greatest and in which the theme is finally and fully revealed.

clinic—A workshop-type educational event where students learn by experiencing; see **workshop**.

clip microphone—See **lavaliere microphone**.

cloakroom/coatroom/coat check—The room in which an outer garment or other article may be stored temporarily.

cloakroom attendant/coatroom attendant/checkroom attendant—An individual who is employed to take care of coats, hats, and luggage in the cloakroom.

clogged head—The accumulation of oxide on the head of a videocassette recorder, which results in noise, breakup, or loss of picture.

closed/fully booked—See **full house**.

closed-end—The number of incentive or travel winners limited by a predetermined amount.

closeout—The finalization of a tour, cruise, or other similar group travel project after which time no further clients are accepted. Any unsold area or hotel space is released, and final lists and payments are sent to all suppliers.

close-talking microphone/transmitter—A microphone designed particularly for use close to the mouth of the speaker; also known as **radio mic.**

close-up—A picture composition in which only a small portion of the person, place, or object being filmed, photographed, televised, or videotaped fills the frame.

closing address—See **closing speech.**

closing ceremony—The final activities at an event that occur during the closing session; also known as **wash-up** in the United Kingdom.

closing date—1. The final date for contracting for an advertisement. 2. The final date for supplying printing material for advertising.

closing session—The final gathering of an event in which the meeting topics are summarized and conclusions are announced.

closing speech—The speech that is given to close a meeting and that includes the results of the meeting or recommendations; also known as **closing address.**

clothes rail—See **garment rack.**

club manager—A specialist who manages events, food and beverage, and business activities for a club.

club table—See **cabaret table.**

cluster—1. Enclosed lights used to illuminate the top of film and stage sets. 2. A group of loudspeakers mounted in auditoriums, arenas, and theaters.

clutch mechanism—A friction device to reduce the tension on gear drives when the gear is interfered with or jammed.

CME—See **Certified Manager of Exhibits.**

CMP—See **Certified Meeting Professional.**

CNYT—See **Current New York Time.**

coach—1. A trainer, instructor, or teacher who develops special skills such as public presentation. 2. See **bus.**

coach fare—Economy fare.

coated stock—Paper manufactured with coatings of clay or other materials to give the base paper a smooth, often glossy, surface.

coaxial cable—1. Cable used to carry audio and television signals. 2. A type of transmission line, used for high-frequency television, telegraph, and telephone signals.

COBRA—See **Consolidated Omnibus Budget Reconciliation Act.**

cochairperson—One of two or more persons appointed as chairperson on an equal footing.

cockscomb fold napkin—A napkin fold that is used to keep a hot roll warm.

cocktail music—See **walk-in/walk-out music.**

cocktail table/cocktail round—See **cabaret table.**

COD—Cash on delivery; collection on delivery.

code of accounts—See **account codes.**

coexhibitor—An agent or main exhibitor sharing the same stand or booth.

coffee break—See **break** or **refreshment break.**

coherent light—Light waves that stay almost parallel and are in sync with each other, working together to produce a concentrated and very bright beam like that of a laser.

coinsured—Legally no such term exists, but informally it represents an additional insured.

cold call—A sales call made without an appointment.

collateral—The activities, events, or handout material that are presented or provided in direct or indirect support of the event's primary function.

collection of ideas—See **brainstorming.**

collective agreement—A written agreement between an employer and a union specifying the terms and conditions of employment for workers, the status of the union, and the procedure for settling disputes arising during the contract term; also known as **union contract.**

collective bargaining—The process of negotiation between an employer and employees to reach agreement on the terms and conditions of employment for a specified period.

collective ring—A metal ring used to make continuous contact with electrical power, while permitting constant rotation, as on turntables.

collimator—A device that makes rays of light more parallel; used to reduce the divergence of laser light for very long throws (the long length that light must reach from origin to destination) and at the output of transmission fibers.

colloquium—An informal participatory discussion, usually of an academic or research nature, held irregularly to identify areas of mutual interest through the exchange of ideas; also known as **academic conference/seminar.**

colocate—To hold two related trade or consumer shows at the same time and in the same venue.

color frame—See **gel frame.**

color key proof—A medium to view color images and copy.

color wheel—A motorized, revolving metal disk, approximately 18" in diameter, with five or six holes cut around the perimeter, each covered with a color filter, and mounted to a light source. As the disk rotates, the filters pass through the light beam creating a changing pattern of color.

column—A pillar that supports the roof or other structures of an exhibition facility. Usually denoted on the floor plan as a solid square.

combo—1. A small jazz or dance band. 2. A plate made up of two or more food selections.

comet—In pyrotechnics, a star formation that is round (the size of a quarter and manufactured in the Far East) or square (the size of a pool chalk and manufactured in Italy). A large pellet of powder, either round or cylindrical, ignites, propels the star, and leaves a cometlike tail.

command center—See **nerve center**.

commencement/graduation—An event that celebrates graduation from the highest grade in a particular school or college.

commercial general liability—A broad form of liability insurance providing protection from liability claims for bodily injury and property damage resulting from the use of products or services or from completed operations, excluding automobile liability; also known as public liability insurance.

commercial invoice—A document specifying the content of a shipment of goods.

commercial rate—See **corporate rate**.

commissionable—A type of sale in which a fee, or percentage of the amount of sale, is to be paid to the agent or purchaser.

commissionable tour—A tour available for sale through retail and wholesale travel agencies that provides for a payment of an agreed-upon sales commission to either the retail or wholesale seller.

commission agent—See **purchasing agent**.

commitment—An agreement between a client and a facility to reserve function and guest room space; also known as **contract** or **letter of agreement**.

commitment authorization—See **purchase order**.

commitment ritual—A religious or spiritual event in which two individuals proclaim their lifelong commitment to one another. Popular in alternative lifestyles such as gay and lesbian.

committee—A group of people elected or appointed to perform specific functions.

committee of honor—The individuals in a related field whose names are lent to an event by way of endorsement.

committee on the verification of credentials—See **credentials committee**.

committee room—See **boardroom**.

commodity—1. A raw material, especially a food product, bought and sold in bulk. 2. A product category in which it is difficult to differentiate a brand from its competition.

common carrier—A transportation company that handles crated or any materials.

communication center—An area in an event venue for telephone, fax, telex, teleconferencing facilities, and other business equipment; see **business center**.

commuter airline—An air service providing connecting flights between small communities and larger airports.

comp—An abbreviation for complimentary.

compact disc (CD)—A device that stores large amounts of information, including music, video, and electronic data as in a CD-ROM.

compact disc player—A digital source component that reads and converts the binary information from a compact disc and sends this bitstream into an external device for analog conversion.

compact disc transport—A component that reads the binary information from a compact disc and sends this bitstream into an external device for analog conversion.

compère—See **master of ceremonies (MC).**

complete meeting package—An all-inclusive plan offered by conference centers.

complimentary—A service, space, or item offered without charge; also known as **comp.**

complimentary registration—A service provided where the fee has been waived.

complimentary room—An occupied guest room for which no charge is made.

component—The number of tasks that are planned to support the program for the success of an event; also known as **element.**

composite—Several pictures showing an actor in various costumes and poses that is part of the actor's résumé.

comprehensive general (public) liability insurance—An umbrella insurance policy that the event manager or event sponsor must maintain in full force to cover injuries, fire, theft, and other potential liabilities; covers lawsuits brought forth by event participants; also known as **public liability.**

comprehensive layout—An artist's precise rendering of a proposed piece, showing paper and color selection, size and placement of type, illustrations, and photographs.

comp rooms—Complimentary rooms that a facility provides without charge based on the number of paid rooms occupied by a group.

computer-aided translation—See **computer-assisted translation (CAT).**

computer animation—The creation and/or manipulation of moving artwork with a computer program; see **animation (slides).**

computer-assisted drawing—An electronic system for designing an event diagram or floor plan via computer.

computer-assisted translation (CAT)—A translation technique that uses the computer as a tool for the solution of problems; also known as **computer-aided translation.**

computer card (registration)—See **registration card key.**

computer-composed script—The lettering generated by a computer; also known as **calligraphy.**

computer-controlled stereophonic conference system—The sound balance control assisted by computer.

computer-generated animation—A sequence of graphics giving the sense of movement and generated by computer; sometimes can interact with the audience.

computer graphic—A special effect using computer-generated animation mixed with live action.

computerized registration—Automated registration records.

con carne—With meat, as in chili con carne.

concentrated marketing—A marketing strategy in which the marketing message is created for and directed toward one specific market segment.

concept—A briefly stated idea of a benefit that an event, product, or service could provide to customers.

conceptual art—An artist's impression or drawing of a proposed event.

concert rider—See **rider.**

concessionaire—A firm, under special contract rights from another party, that operates food, beverage, lodging facilities, and/or services on-site at an attraction.

concessions—The sale of promotional items, such as albums, posters, or T-shirts, by an artist's representatives; usually set up in conjunction with the artist's engagement.

concierge—1. A facility staff person who arranges information and services for guests, including tickets, transportation, and tour arrangements. 2. A designated area providing special amenities and services to guests in a facility.

conclave—A private meeting or assembly for a group with shared or special interests; also known as **special interest group** in South Africa.

concrete weights—Heavy weights used for anchoring a tent.

concurrent sessions—Event meetings that are held during the same time period.

condensed type—A narrow or slender type that permits a greater number of characters per line than regular type does.

condenser microphone—A microphone with an electronically charged element that allows a fuller frequency response but is a more delicate device; used to amplify piano or string music and soprano singers; also known as **electret.**

conditions—The section or clause of a transportation or tour contract that specifies what is not offered and may spell out the circumstances under which the contract may be invalidated in all or in part.

conducted tour—See **escorted tour.**

cone—1. A pencil-thin laser beam that is scanned very quickly in a circle, to which fog is introduced, producing a solid cone of light. 2. A part of a sound speaker.

conferee—A registrant who signs up for conference sessions or classes.

conference—1. A participatory meeting designed for the discussion of subjects related to a specific topic or area. May include fact-finding, problem solving, and consultation. 2. An event used by any organization to meet and exchange views, convey a message, open a debate, or give publicity to some area of opinion on a specific issue. No tradition, continuity, or specific period is required to convene a conference. Although not generally limited in time, conferences are usually of short duration with specific objectives. Conferences are generally on a smaller scale than congresses and/or conventions. 3. An assembly of a large number of individuals to discuss items of mutual interest or engage in professional development through learning.

conference administrator—The chief administrator of the entire conference.

conference call—See **audioconference**.

conference handbook—A manual that provides information about a conference, including the schedule of events, the agenda, the description of programs, information on participants, and logistical information.

conference interpreter—An individual who interprets into another language the oral presentation made during a meeting; see **simultaneous interpretation**.

conference officer/organizer—A title conferred upon the chief administrator of the entire event; also known as **professional congress organizer (PCO)**.

conference pack/kit—A comprehensive collection of conference documentation within a binder or envelope; also known as **information kit** or **registration packet**.

conference papers—A collection of abstracts of lectures to be presented during a conference compiled in the book of abstracts; see **call for papers**.

conference report—An official summary of conference events.

conference secretariat—An office responsible for administration, clerical, and secretarial affairs surrounding planning and management of a conference.

conference-style setup—See **board of directors setup**.

conference terminologist—An individual who conducts terminology work specifically in the context of a meeting.

conference tour—See **meeting tour/conference tour**.

conference translator—An individual who translates meeting documents into other languages.

confidential tariff—A schedule of wholesale rates distributed in confidence.

configuration—1. The arrangement of seats within an aircraft. 2. A sleeping berth in a day/night compartment on a European train.

confirmation—A written acknowledgment of a reservation request.

confirmation of order—The written authority for an exhibitor or vendor to proceed.

confirmed letter of credit—A letter of credit, issued by a foreign bank. An exporter whose payment terms are a confirmed letter of credit is assured of payment even if the foreign buyer or the foreign bank defaults; see **letter of credit (LC).**

confirmed reservation—An oral or written agreement to provide accommodations on a particular date, at a particular rate, and of a particular type for a specified number of guests. An oral agreement may require a credit card number to guarantee availability.

conflict of interest—A situation in which a member has opposing obligations.

confirmation letter—See **joining instructions.**

conform date—See **date protection.**

congress—1. A scheduled, periodic meeting of delegates or representatives of interested groups to discuss some subject. 2. The European term for convention.

congress auxiliaries—The individuals who have been identified by the organizer and whose names are clearly stated in a previously prepared register.

congress card—An admission card confirming a booking and registration to an event; also known as **admission card, entrance card,** or **ticket.**

congress travel agent—A travel agent specializing in handling incoming or outgoing meeting participants and all their future travel arrangements including pretours and post-tours.

connecting canopy—An awning between two tents or buildings that provides a protected passageway or walkway.

connecting rooms—Two or more adjoining rooms with private connecting doors.

consecutive interpretation—The oral translation of conversation or speeches from one language to another as the speaker pauses between phrases to allow for interpretation; see **simultaneous interpretation.**

consensus—General opinion reached by the members of a group; also known as **general agreement.**

consignee—The person or agency to whom goods are shipped.

consignment—Delivery of merchandise from an exporter (the consignor) to an agent (the consignee) under the agreement that the agent will sell the merchandise for the account of the exporter. The consignor retains title to the goods until the consignee has sold them. The consignee sells the goods for commission and remits the net proceeds to the consignor.

console—An electronic device with multiple inputs and outputs, used to combine, modify, and distribute the audio and video signal; the control point of the sound in a production; also known as **mixer, mixing board, preamp desk, sound board,** or **lighting desk.**

consolidate—To ship freight to a central depot where several loads bound for the same destination are put together before being shipped to the destination.

Consolidated Omnibus Budget Reconciliation Act (COBRA)—The United States legislation that allows employees to continue insurance benefits after termination.

consommé—Clear soup, served hot or chilled.

consular declaration—A formal statement, made to the consul of a country, describing goods to be shipped.

consular invoice—A document certified by a consular official that describes a shipment of goods and provides information on the consignor, consignee, and value of the shipment and used by customs officials to verify the value, quantity, and nature of the shipment.

consular security manager—See **regional security officer (RSO).**

consultant—An individual who provides business, professional, or expert advice for a fee.

consultative committee—A committee consisting of honorary members that can be called upon for advice as necessary; also known as **advisory committee.**

consumer advertising—Advertising directed at the public as a whole rather than to a profession, industry, etc.

consumer affairs—An organization that controls and protects business names, trading hours, and practices.

consumer profile—The demographic, geographic, and psychographic characteristics of the users of a product, especially as they differ from the total population.

consumer-quality equipment—Equipment designed for use by nonprofessionals, appropriate when the quality of the final product is not critical; used often for social events.

consumer/trade show—An exhibition open to the public and usually requiring an entrance fee; also known as **gate show** or **public show.**

contact cement—A bonding agent usually used for cementing plastic laminates to wood.

continental breakfast—A morning meal consisting of pastries, juices, hot beverages, and fruit.

continental buffet—A buffet consisting of pastries, juices, hot beverages, and fruit.

continental plan (CP)—A room rate that includes a continental breakfast; see **bed and breakfast (B&B).**

contingencies—1. Promises made in agreements or contracts that can be affected by future uncertainties. 2. Allocated funds reserved in budgets for uncertainties.

contingency contract—A contract, part of the performance of which at least is dependent on the happening of a contingency.

contingency planning—The process of formulating strategies or detailed plans to deal with possible and unanticipated problems.

continuing education units (CEUs)—Requirements of many professional groups by which members must certify participation in formal educational programs designed to maintain their level of ability beyond their original certification date.

Continuing Event Management Education (CEMEs)—Awarded by the International Special Events Society for completion of approved education programs.

continuity—A smooth flow of action and narration from scene to scene.

contract—A legal agreement between two or more persons that creates an obligation to perform some act and establishes a mutual binding promise with a penalty for failure to perform; also known as **commitment** or **letter of agreement.**

contracting—A system in which all or part of the product or the work to be done is sublet to contractors.

contractor—A person who contracts to supply certain products or services for a stipulated fee.

contractual liability—Liability of another party assumed under contract or agreement as opposed to direct liability, as in tort.

contrast—An opposition of intensity between light and dark areas of a scene.

contributed paper—A written manuscript, provided after acceptance of the abstract, that becomes the basis for a speech or presentation; also known as **paper contribution.**

contribution margin percentage—The total revenue minus the variable costs divided by total revenue.

contributor—One who presents a paper or contributes to the project.

controllable net per capita—The net profit excluding deductions for fixed expenses divided by total attendance.

control room—1. The communication center for an event. 2. The soundproofed enclosure within a radio or TV studio, wherein the director, producer, and technicians supervise the logistics of taping or live broadcasting.

control track—A section of videotape used as a reference to control the speed of the tape.

convener—A person charged with welcoming and gathering participants; see **host.**

convention—A general and formal meeting of a legislative body or social or economic group to provide information on a particular situation and to establish consent on policies among the participants. Usually of limited duration with set objectives, but no determined frequency.

convention and visitors bureau (CVB)—A not-for-profit umbrella organization that represents a city or geographic area in the solicitation and servicing of travelers to that city or area whether they visit for business, pleasure, or both; also known as **tourist information board.**

convention bureau—A service organization that provides destination promotion and may offer personnel, housing control, and other services for meetings, conventions, and other events.

convention center—A facility for events and expositions, without sleeping rooms.

Convention Industry Council (CIC)—An organization whose members represent many convention industry organizations. The CIC conducts research, administers the Certified Meeting Professional (CMP) program, and discusses issues of common interest.

convention résumé—A summary of function-room use for a convention or meeting.

convention services manager—An employee of a facility or hotel who is responsible for the facility-related details of an event; also known as **banquet services manager.**

conversation piece—A comedy in which there is much talk and little action.

converted in plant—See **near-plant.**

convertibility—A currency is usually described as convertible if the holder can exchange it for another currency freely.

COO—See **chief operating officer.**

cookie—A piece of information sent by a Web server to a Web browser that the browser software is expected to save and send back to the server whenever the browser makes additional requests from the server.

cooperative advertising—An agreement where two or more companies share the cost of advertising when their products are presented together.

coordinating committee—A committee created by the hosting organization(s) to plan, oversee, and ensure the creation of a successful event.

copresident—One, two, or more people appointed to serve jointly as president on an equal footing with the official president.

copy—1. Original text material being prepared for reproduction. 2. Duplicate.

copyfitting—The process of determining the space required and the type size for copy to fit the allotted space; also known as **typesetting.**

copy negative—A film negative made from a glossy print for the production of additional prints.

copyrights—A written or other work-protected document signed by the creator when the work is created.

cordial—1. An aromatic, syrupy liqueur often served after dinner. 2. In Australia, a fruit-flavored, nonalcoholic syrup.

cordless microphone—A portable microphone that operates on its own power source, connected to a radio transmitter; also known as a **Vega, wireless microphone,** or **radio microphone.**

core competencies—An event organization's or product's elements or knowledge that are competitively superior to those of similar organizations or products.

corkage—A charge placed on beer, wine, and liquor that is brought into a facility but purchased elsewhere; may include glassware, ice, and mixers.

corner booth/stand—An exhibit space with aisles on two sides. Larger trade shows may add an additional charge because of the advantageous position.

cornucopia—1. A pastry roll shaped like a horn, filled with whipped cream and nuts. 2. A large paper or plastic horn filled with fresh fruits spilling over onto the table.

corporate event—An event sponsored by a corporation for the purpose of achieving specific goals and objectives such as entertaining customers, introducing and promoting new products or services, or providing incentives or training for employees, as well as other activities.

corporate exhibit—An institutional exhibit telling the story of a company without intentionally marketing its product or service.

corporate identification—The organization logo signifying sponsorship of an event to ensure visibility.

corporate meeting—An officially sanctioned and required gathering of employees, with travel, room, and meal expenses paid by the organization.

corporate picnic—A business-sponsored picnic used to motivate employees through the fostering of goodwill. For associations, goals are to entertain existing members and solicit new memberships.

corporate planner—An event manager employed by an organization to manage its events.

corporate public relation—An open two-way communication between a company and its stakeholders that promotes a climate of goodwill for the company without specifically influencing marketing efforts.

corporate rate—A special room rate, lower than rack rate, for corporations that have made prior arrangements with the facility. Usually based on a certain commitment of rooms to be used in a period of time; also known as **commercial rate.**

corporate show—A private exhibition produced by a corporation. Exhibits are limited to products and services of that corporation or its marketing partners; no competitors participate.

corporate special event manager—An individual who plans, researches, designs, coordinates, and evaluates company events.

corporate theater—The use of actors to dramatize a company's image, a new product, or the history of an organization; also known as **industrial theater** in South Africa.

corporate travel—A market segment of business travelers paid at company expense.

COS—Cash on shipment; cancel on site.

cost and freight (C&F)—A pricing term indicating that these costs are included in the quoted price.

cost and insurance (C&I)—A pricing term indicating the insurance costs are included in the quoted price.

cost box—The cost of printing indicated on a certain area of printed publications.

cost charge per square meter/foot—A basic charge for a particular unit of measurement.

costing—The process of itemizing and calculating all costs on a given event; usually the function of the operations manager.

cost, insurance, freight (CIF)—A pricing term indicating that these costs are included in the quoted price.

cost, insurance, freight, and commission (CIF&C)—A pricing term indicating that these costs are included in the quoted price.

cost, insurance, freight, and (currency) exchange (CIF&E)—A pricing term indicating that these costs are included in the quoted price.

cost of products sold/cost of sale—The total costs incurred, including product cost, freight, packaging, paper products, sales taxes on inventory, and other costs related to the transaction but not including employee, payroll, or operating supply cost for each area.

couchette—A sleeping berth in a day/night compartment on a European train.

council—See governing board.

Council for the Advancement and Support of Education (CASE)—An organization whose members work in higher education or supply products and services for the higher education field.

Council of Engineering and Scientific Society Executives (CESSE)—An organization providing education, information, and resources for engineering and science professionals who work for societies in an administrative, legislative, or advisory position.

counselor—See adviser.

count—1. The total number of attendees for a given period. 2. The total number of exhibitors for a given period.

counter—1. A cabinet for display, demonstration, or registration. 2. A wooden or metal board fixed horizontally either on legs or on a wall with display material and the possibility of making purchases.

countermount—A technique for mounting material to the rear of a panel equal to the weight and consistency of face-mounted material to prevent warping.

countersink—The technique of recessing heads of screws and nails below the surface.

countervailing duty—An extra duty imposed by the Secretary of the Treasury to offset export grants, bounties, or subsidies paid to foreign suppliers in certain countries by the governments of those countries as an incentive to exports.

country-style table service—A method of serving large groups of guests in a short time, which reduces the chance of cold food; also known as **family-style buffet.**

coupe soup—A shallow, flat, round bowl without handles.

courier—1. A European term for a travel professional who supervises arrival details and escorts tours. 2. A person who delivers products.

cover—1. A table setting for one person. 2. A term often used for the number of waiters per person.

cover charge—A fee, usually a flat amount per person, charged to patrons to cover the cost of music and entertainment.

cover footage—A series of generic filmed or videotaped scenes shot during a particular event and shown primarily during general script dialogue.

cover plate—A protective, removable panel used with self-contained exhibits in transit.

covers—The actual number of meals served at a catered meal function or in a food-service facility.

cover shot—1. A single, wide-angle shot giving a broad view of the location and action of a filmed or televised event. 2. A safety shot taken to ensure a proper image is captured. 3. A photo taken for the front of a magazine, newspaper, or book.

cover stock—A heavyweight paper used for protective and decorative purposes in binding a document.

CP—See **continental plan.**

C-print—A type of color reproduction print.

CR—Carrier's risk.

craft person—A skilled individual who provides actual services on the exhibit show floor.

craft union—A labor organization, the membership of which is restricted to individuals possessing or working at a specific skill or trade, such as die makers, electricians, carpenters, or plumbers; see **union.**

crane—See **animation stand.**

crash box—A box filled with broken glass or small metal parts and used for sound effects.

crash cloth—A name for a plain weave of coarse and uneven yarns, such as cotton, linen, or a mixture of fibers, that is often used for luncheon cloths, place mats, and napkins.

crate—A large box that holds booth or stand equipment for secure shipment.

crating list—A list of the contents of a crate, such as exhibit pieces, carpet, and other items.

crawl—A text that moves horizontally across the bottom of a video screen.

crazing—Fine cracks appearing in the glaze of dinnerware that is caused by different rates of expansion between the body and the glaze.

cream cheese—White cheese, usually foil-wrapped in rectangular portions.

cream-soup bowl and saucer—A two-handled low bowl to serve bisques and cream soups at informal meals.

credentials—Evidence of identity and qualification; also known as **laminate.**

credentials committee—The committee that is formed to verify that individuals have the necessary qualifications to attend an event or become a member of an association; also known as **committee on the verification of credentials.**

credit line—The amount of money or merchandise that a banker, merchant, or supplier agrees to supply to an individual on credit.

credit memorandum—A document used by a seller to inform a buyer that the buyer's account is being credited because of errors, returns, or allowances.

creditor—An individual to whom a debt is owed by another person, who is the debtor.

credit rating—The evaluation of an individual's or organization's ability and past performance in paying debts.

credit report—A document from a credit bureau setting forth a credit rating and financial data concerning an individual or an organization and used by banks, merchants, and suppliers in evaluating a credit risk.

credit-risk insurance—Insurance designed to cover risks of nonpayment for delivered goods.

credits—The names of the individuals who created, performed in, or contributed to an event, recording, film, or video.

credit sale—A sale in which the buyer is permitted to pay for the products or services at a later time.

crème brûlée—A pudding of cornstarch, eggs, milk, sugar, and whipped cream served in a cassoulet.

crepe—A very thin pancake, used to roll up anything from meat to dessert.

crew—Stagehands, technicians, truck loaders, and others responsible for the technical setup of a show.

crime reports—Police files that can be requested to view documentation of criminal activity and may be used to assess a venue's degree of threat to an event.

crisis management—When a situation is unplanned, dangerous, and/or unpredictable a person can take control of the circumstances and is given exceptional or temporary authority to eliminate or manage the distress and pose as a representative of the event.

croissant—Crescent-shaped French bread that is very tender due to a lot of butter.

crop—A cutting technique that reduces the area of a photograph, artwork, or video.

crop mark—An indication on original art or photo defining the area that is to be reproduced.

cross aisle—An aisle at a right angle to a main aisle.

crossbar—A rod used in draping or as a support brace.

cross brace—A tent component that is designed to prevent a tent from collapsing.

cross-cultural marketing—Marketing that is directed toward people of multiple cultures.

cross-fade—1. A change from one color, image, or track to another. 2. A technique used to change scenes or images by fading out as another fades in; see **dissolve unit**.

crossover—A frequency that divides an electrical network and splits an incoming audio signal into ranges best suited to a loudspeaker's various drive elements.

cross parallel session—A session that is similar to another session involving the exchange of information.

crossroads cuisine—See **fusion cuisine.**

crosstalk—An undesired sound emanating from another channel or track.

crumbdown—The process of a waiter removing table crumbs before the next course is served.

CSAE—See **Canadian Society of Association Executives.**

CSEP—See **Certified Special Events Professional.**

CTHRC—See **Canadian Tourism Human Resource Council.**

CTLO—Constructive total loss only.

CTP—See **Certified Tour Professional.**

cubic content—The use of exhibit properties in the airspace over the entire leased area above a height of eight feet or more.

cue—A visual or audio signal to elicit a response or action. 2. A signal in dialogue, action, or music for an actor's action or speech or a technician's duty backstage.

cue card—An off-camera card containing text used by performers to read lines; also known as **idiot card.**

cueing—The process of assigning cue numbers to various elements of a production; also known as **lining-up.**

cultural services—A service concerned with organizing activities that are mainly related to the artistic and intellectual side of civilization.

currants—Small piquant berries used for jellies or dried like raisins.

current assets—The accounts that are to be converted to cash or used in operations within 12 months of the balance sheet date.

current liabilities—See **notes payable.**

Current New York Time (CNYT)—A standard of time used in broadcast television to coordinate time differences for booking broadcasting facilities.

curtain—A hanging drapery that conceals the stage or scene from the audience.

curtain line—An imaginary line that marks the position of the front curtain when it is closed across the stage.

customer service—Assistance that a company provides for its customers when they buy or use its product.

custom exhibit—An exhibit created to be a unique solution to the specific requirements of the user.

customhouse/customhouse broker—An individual or firm licensed to enter and clear goods through customs.

customized marketing—Specialized marketing programs that are tailored to each individual event, customer, organization, or market segment.

customized tour—A tour designed to fit the specific needs of a particular target market or group.

customs—1. The established social conventions of a country or region. 2. A government agency that controls entry of people and products into that country and is charged with the collection of duties.

customs broker—A person or company that provides customs-clearing services to shippers of goods to and from another country; see **Brussels Tariff Nomenclature.**

customs duties—A fee paid to a government agency for importing, exporting, or consuming goods; see **Brussels Tariff Nomenclature.**

cut—1. An instantaneous change from one scene to another without a fade or dissolve. 2. A visual or auditory signal to interrupt or cancel.

cut and lay—The installation of carpet other than normal booth/stand or aisle size.

cutline—The text identifying a photograph.

cutoff date—The designated day that a facility will release to the general public a block of guest/sleeping rooms that had previously been reserved.

cutoff time—The hour at which a nonguaranteed reservation must be filled or may be canceled.

cutout—A profile-cut display item, such as letters, photos, etc.

cut rate—Cost per hundredweight.

cut-rate—A lowered price given to assist or get something in return.

cuts-only editing—The video editing with basic cut transitions between shots.

cutting sheet—A drawing made by a carpentry shop, detailing the size and shape of raw material to be cut; see **template.**

CVB—See **convention and visitors bureau.**

CWO—See **cash with order.**

CWT—Abbreviation for hundredweight. This is the unit of measure used in drayage.

cyberspace—The whole range of information resources available through computer networks.

cyc, or cyclorama—1. A stage background scene that gives the illusion of depth. 2. A curved, continuous background for theatrical staging or dioramas.

cycles—The amount of "movement" in electrical current. The international standard is 50 cycles; in the United States, 60 cycles.

D

DA converter (digital-to-analog converter)—A device that accepts an incoming digital bitstream and converts it to an analog electrical signal.

daily newsletter—A daily information sheet for participants during an event.

dais—A raised platform for seating prominent people at the head table; also known as **podium** or **rostrum.**

damages—Pecuniary compensation (money) or indemnity that may be recovered in the courts by any person who has suffered a loss, detriment, or injury, whether to his person, property, or rights through the unlawful act, omission, or negligence of another.

damages, punitive—Punishment for negligent or outrageous conduct and intended to deter from future transgressions. It does occur that actual damages are trivial and those punitive damages can be quite substantial. Some insurance policies exclude coverage for claims or lawsuits for punitive damages.

damask—Woven silk or linen fabric used for tablecloths and napkins.

dance floor—1. An area for dancing that can be carpeted when not in use. 2. A portable surface for dancing that can be rented and assembled for events.

Danish candle fold napkin—An easy three-dimensional folded napkin often used for the candlelight dinner party theme.

dark day/period—A day on which a venue has no events booked.

dark night—A period when a theater is not open to the public.

DAT—See **digital audiotape.**

database—A collection of historical information to be used for current or future planning.

Data on Meetings and Events (DOME)—An on-line database of reports and research for the meetings, incentives, convention, and exposition-events industry.

data-mining—A method of analyzing the data within electronic databases to find out trends and buying habits that can be used as a basis of targeted direct marketing.

date selection—The date of an event is chosen based on availability of participants, facilities, etc.

date draft—A bank document that matures a specified number of days after the date it is issued without regard to the date of acceptance.

date protection—A guarantee that the dates an event organizer has selected for an event in a specific facility are reserved for that organizer; also known as **conform date.**

day rate—A reduced rate granted for the use of a guest room during the daytime, not overnight occupancy.

dead area—A space in the event facility where sound is muffled or absent.

dead time—Time during which an employee is unable to work due to factors beyond his or her control and for which he is paid. Also known as **allowed time, down time, idle time,** or **waiting time.**

debate—A discussion of opposing arguments or positions.

debit—An entry made on the asset side of the ledger or account that represents an asset or potential asset to an organization.

deboarding—The process of removing a confirmed airline passenger from a full flight, bus, train, or other transportation to make room for a passenger with higher priority.

debriefing—A meeting shortly after an event to review what went right or wrong, what to do for the next time, and other information.

debt—A specified amount of money owed to an individual from another.

debt adjustment—The settlement of a dispute regarding a debt obligation by compromise and adjustment; also known as **adjustment of debts.**

debt capacity—The optimal amount of debt in an organization's capital structure.

debtor—An individual who owes a debt to another, who is called the creditor.

declared value—The shipper's stated value of an entire shipment in terms of dollars.

decorating—The planning and furnishing of an exhibition or function with carpet, drapes, plants, stage sets, props, florals, etc., to create a pleasant, attractive environment.

decorator—A general contractor or service contractor, usually hired to set up an exhibition and/or to design and implement "the look" of an event; also known as **designer.**

deductible—1. The amount of money paid by an insured for a loss. This can be a specified amount or a percentage of the loss, or it may be determined in some other way. Deductible may apply to all losses covered under a policy or only to certain losses. 2. The amount that a facility must pay for any claim against it before an insurer becomes responsible.

deductibles, aggregate—All of the deductibles applicable to the total loss.

defendant—The party being sued, usually the company or manager in an employment case.

deferred airfreight—Long-haul airfreight that waits for available cargo space (usually one to two days) at a reduced rate.

deferred charge—A payment made for a long-term service that will be received in future accounting periods.

definite booking—Space reservations confirmed in writing.

delegate—A voting representative at a meeting.

delegate card—An admission card confirming a booking and registration.

delegate profile—The age, gender, title, and other demographic and psychographic descriptions of a delegate.

delegation—The representatives of a particular country or organization at a meeting.

delft—A type of earthenware recognized by its blue-and-white designs.

deluxe—Presumably "of the highest standard."

demipension—A rate that includes a room, breakfast, and dinner; in the United States and Canada: modified American plan (MAP), which includes room, breakfast, and one other meal (usually dinner); also known as **half board.**

demitasse—A small-size cup and saucer for after-dinner coffee.

demographics—Age, income, gender, title, and other qualitative factors describing individuals.

demonstration—An active display showing a product or service in use or being consumed.

demonstrator—A person hired to work in a booth demonstrating or explaining products or services.

demux (demultiplexer)—Combining multiple signals into one signal, which can be separated again by a demultiplexer.

denied-boarding compensation—A refund of airfare or a payment to a passenger when an airline fails to honor a confirmed reservation within two hours of scheduled departure.

Department of Transportation (DOT)—The United States federal, provincial, state, county, or local department of transportation.

departure date—The date when a majority of an event's participants check out of a facility.

departure tax—A fee collected from a traveler by the host country at the time of departure.

deposit—A partial payment to secure a product or service.

deposit policy—A policy that requires a specified amount or a percentage of the total bill due on a specified date prior to arrival.

depreciation—The decline in value of a tangible asset, such as a building, tool, machine, ride, game, etc., due to age and the normal wear and tear of use.

deputy stage manager—The assistant to the production stage manager.

design—An artist's conception or rendering of how a printed piece or event should look.

designer—See decorator.

dessert plate—See pie plate.

dessert tray—See pastry cart.

destination controls—Any of various statements that the United States government requires to be displayed on export shipments and that specify the destinations for which the shipment has been authorized.

destination management company (DMC)—A company, based in the city, county, or state in which an event is being held, that handles service contracts, tours, ground transportation, decorations, props, and theme events; similar to professional congress organizer (PCO).

destination management system (DMS)—A computer system used by destination marketing organizations to provide all the business processes.

destination manager—A local on-site coordinator.

destination marketing organization (DMO)—A category of membership of the National Tour Association that includes state or provincial tourism offices, convention and visitors bureaus, and chambers of commerce that promote a city, region, or state as a travel destination.

destination marketing organization (DMO)—An organization that promotes its destination within its responsibilities.

DET—See domestic escorted tour.

detail drawing—A drawing that shows the method of construction for a specific element.

devaluation—The official lowering of the value of a currency.

deviation—The departure of an individual traveler from the established group itinerary.

DFWA—See Drug-Free Workplace Act.

diabetic—An individual suffering from diabetes, in which sugar and starchy foods cannot be properly absorbed.

dialogue—A discussion of ideas and opinions between two or more persons.

die cutting—A process of cutting shapes into a sheet of printed paper stock; used for cuts not following a straight line on the paper.

differential amplification—The method of amplifying a signal whereby the output signal is a function of the difference between two input signals.

differentiated marketing—A marketing strategy in which different marketing methods are used for each market segment.

differentiation—The process of incorporating unique features that add value to a product and are not included in other competitive products.

diffraction grating—A series of fine grooves that break down light into its component frequencies, as a prism does. It may also produce step-and-repeat patterns of scanned images.

digital audiotape (DAT)—A product that uses digital instead of analog audio signals; similar to a videotape.

digital recording—1. The process of sampling analog video or audio programs using an analog-to-digital (D/A) processor to produce a stream of binary-coded electronic signals numerically representing the content of the programs, which are then stored on an appropriate device for retrieval at some later time. Once the video and audio programming material has been converted to a digital media format, the programs can be easily transmitted to other locations or copied to other media without further degradation to the quality of the recorded image or sound. 2. Refers to a video or audio program that was previously processed through an analog-to-digital processor and then stored for later playback using any one of a variety of media that employ binary recording techniques. Examples of commonly used digital recording media that can be used to store video and audio programs are compact discs (CD), compact disc read-only memory (CD-ROM), digital audiotapes (DAT), and digital video discs (DVD).

digital video effects—The special graphics and special effects produced by a programmed computer control unit based on a numerical system to enhance and manipulate a video image.

dim—To decrease the intensity of the light on the stage by means of rheostats or dimmers; also known as **take down.**

dim in/dim up—To increase the intensity of the light; also known as **bring up.**

dimmer—An electronic device used to control light intensity.

dimmerboard—See **switchboard.**

dine around—A restaurant term that indicates the use of a number of restaurants in a destination with reservations and billing arrangements for one particular event organization.

dinner—The evening meal for an individual or a group, not usually ceremonial; also known as **supper.**

dinner plate—A plate used for the main course at dinner; usually 8" diameter.

dipole—A bidirectional loudspeaker with 180 degrees of phase difference between its front and rear acoustical output.

direct billing—Account receivables mailed to individuals or firms with established credit.

direct channel—A marketing channel in which the marketer exchanges information about the product directly with the customer.

direct flight—A flight between two points that occurs on the same aircraft. There may be stops but no plane changes.

direct mail advertising—The use of mail as the medium for delivering an advertising message to a target audience.

Direct Marketing Association (DMA)—An organization based in New York City comprised of national and local providers of direct mail advertising, formed to further their members' interests and to promote this advertising medium.

direct marketing—A type of marketing with communication between the marketer and the buyer without contact from other channel partners.

director of catering (DOC)—The person who assigns and oversees all catering functions and is responsible for marketing, production, and service.

director of sales (DOS)—The person in charge of the operation and sale of sleeping rooms for a hotel; also known as **sales manager.**

directory/directory board—The board or video screen listing the day's events; also known as **function board** or **reader board.**

direct selling—Promoting a product directly to a customer, face-to-face, without other channel partners.

direct-view television—A television that uses a cathode ray tube (CRT) to display a picture.

dirty rice—A Cajun dish of panfried cooked rice sautéed with green peppers, onions, celery, stock, and giblets.

disability—A physical or mental impairment that substantially limits a person's ability to participate in normal daily activities.

disclaimer—See **hold harmless.**

disco effects—A variety of techniques used to light the dance floor with movable beams and changing color; less expensive than intelligent lighting.

disconnect—1. A device to permit easy and rapid separation of electronic components. 2. The gap when an event plan does not consistently track with the goals and objectives desired.

discount—Any deduction from the customary price of products, services, or admission.

discovered at rise—Onstage when the curtain goes up.

discussant—A member of a meeting audience who participates in discussion during a meeting; also known as **floor speaker.**

discussion form—An application to put a question to a particular speaker on a specific subject and submitted in advance of the conference session.

discussion group—A group of participants in separate debates; similar to a working group but with no expectation of reports or papers.

discussion leader—The person who introduces topics of discussion and mediates group discussion; also known as **moderator.**

dismantle—To disassemble and remove exhibits, sets, or props.

dismantling deadline—A designated day and time by which exhibits, sets, or props must be dismantled and removed from an exhibition area.

dispatcher—A person responsible for scheduling and routing freight, labor, etc.

display builder—A company that fabricates displays.

display case—A showcase used to display and protect exhibit articles.

display fibers—See **fiber optics.**

display material—Articles exhibited for participants at meetings and conventions; may be insured or have value stated in writing for insurance purposes.

display place—An exhibit booth or stand.

display rules and regulations—A set of specifications for exhibit construction endorsed by all major exhibit industry associations.

display screen—A physical computer device, usually based on a cathode ray tube (CRT) or liquid crystal display (LCD), on which information is displayed.

display type—1. In printing, a type larger than body type. 2. A type of fireworks used for exhibitions and displays.

dissolve—In a slide or multimedia presentation, to change from one scene to another by blending visual images together as one image fades out and another fades in.

dissolve unit—A device that creates fade-out and fade-in of slides between two projectors; see **cross-fading**.

distance interpreting—See **teleinterpreting**.

distant-talking microphone/transmitter—A microphone that is designed for use at a substantial distance from the mouth of the person speaking; also known as **rifle mic** in South Africa.

distributed sound—Low to midlevel sound produced by locating a large number of loudspeakers around a central listening area and used for background music, soundscaping, or to keep the sound level from being too loud.

distributor show—A show produced by a distributor at which exhibitors are the manufacturers of products sold by the distributor and attendees are the distributor's customers.

district sales manager—The person responsible for hotel room sales in a designated territory.

divergence—The angle at which a laser beam widens, which has design implications for the user. For long throws, beam width at the final target may be critical. Low divergence is a plus but can be traded off sometimes to increase other assets, such as getting higher power from the same laser.

divider—See **air walls**.

diving walls—See **air walls**.

DMAA—See **Direct Mail Advertising Association**.

DMC—See **destination management company**.

DMO—See **destination marketing organization**.

DMS—See **destination management system**.

DNS—See **domain name system**.

DOC—See **director of catering**.

docent—A tour guide in a museum or art gallery.

dock—A location where freight is loaded onto and taken from vessels or vehicles.

dock receipt—A receipt issued by an ocean carrier to acknowledge receipt of a shipment at the carrier's dock or warehouse facilities.

document distribution—Handing out or mailing out documents.

document duplication—The reproduction of documents.

document for acceptance—Instructions given by a shipper to a bank indicating that documents transferring title to goods should be delivered to the buyer (or drawee) only upon the buyer's payment of the attached draft.

dog guide—A trained dog that provides assistance to an individual who is blind, deaf, or mobility-impaired; also known as **assist animal.**

Dolby AC-3—Surround sound standard from Dolby Laboratories that incorporates six discrete channels of information for the playback of video soundtracks.

Dolby Pro Logic—Surround sound standard from Dolby Laboratories that utilizes five loudspeakers (two main, two rear, and one center) and a decoder to properly steer the signal to its appropriate channel; used for the playback of movie soundtracks in the home.

dolly—A low, flat platform on wheels, used for carrying heavy loads.

domain name system (DNS)—A multipart naming system devised to avoid the crisis of naming hosts (individual computers) on the Internet. Host names are a string of words separated by dots (periods).

domestic beer/wine—A beer or wine produced in the country where it is served.

domestic escorted tour (DET)—A packaged, preplanned itinerary (including services of an escort) within a traveler's own country.

domestic meeting—1. Domestic/national: A meeting of an organization with membership from a single nation available to meet in only that nation. 2. Domestic/subregional: A meeting of an organization with membership from a single nation available to meet in only a given subregion of that nation.

Donahue—A style of event presentation wherein the moderator moves with a microphone among audience members and seeks questions and comments for a group of panelists.

donation—A sum of money or items of value received as gifts for charity.

DOS—See **director of sales.**

DOT—See **Department of Transportation.**

double bed—A bed measuring 53" x 75".

double booking—The practice of reserving space for two or more groups for the same dates when only one group can be accommodated.

double cloth—The use of two tablecloths on a banquet table for decorative purposes.

double-decker—1. A two-storied exhibit; also known as **multiple-story exhibit.** 2. A British-style bus.

double-double room—A room with two double beds, suitable for two to four persons.

double-faced/double-sided—1. An exhibit panel that is finished on both sides. 2. Tape with adhesive on both sides.

double lock—The use of two locks, one of which is often a dead bolt, on a door for extra security.

double-occupancy rate—The price of a room for two people, to be shared with another person.

double room—A room occupied by two persons; may have a king, queen, or double bed, or two single beds.

double room for single occupancy—A twin or double room occupied by one person, often charged at a lower rate than if occupied by two people. In Australia the room rate is normally based on room type, not the number of guests.

double room rate—The full price of a room for two people, but be careful: some people say double when they mean double occupancy.

doubling—The playing of more than one instrument by a musician during an engagement.

downgrade—To move to a lesser accommodation or class of service.

downline space—The remaining flights on an itinerary.

down-linking—The reception of a satellite-transmitted signal.

download—The transfer of electronic data from a third-party computer to one's own.

downstage—The front of the stage, closest to the audience.

down time—See **dead time.**

draft—See **bill of exchange (B/E).**

dram-shop laws—The United States laws that protect individuals who are injured due to negligence not only of the person intoxicated by alcohol but also the supplier or server of the alcohol.

draper—A person who installs drapes, pleats, and special décor.

drapery—Table linen arranged decoratively.

drapes/theatrical curtains—A decorative material hung to partition an area, adorn a room, or provide privacy.

draping—A fabric hanging used to create exhibit booths or stands, to finish or surround an area such as an audiovisual screen, or to provide a backdrop for a stage or wall; also known as **pipe and drape.**

drawback—A refund of duties paid on imported goods that is provided at the time of their reexportation.

draw curtain—A type of curtain suspended from an overhead track and that opens from the center to each side; also known as **traveler curtain.**

drayage—The transfer of exhibit booths or stands, equipment, material, and properties from decorator storage to exhibit site.

drayage contractor—A company responsible for handling exhibit materials.

drayer—The official exhibit show handler designated to move exhibits from the truck dock to the booth space. Usually coordinated by the general service contractor.

dress—1. Clothing worn by talent. 2. Dress rehearsal; final camera rehearsal. 3. Set dressing; necessary set properties. 4. To neatly arrange cables lying on the floor.

dress code—Suggested acceptable dress.

dressing the exhibit—Placing graphics, plants, and literature and applying any finishing touches to the display.

drinking water—Water from a government-approved source.

drop—1. A large, painted piece of cloth used for stage background or scenery. 2. A term used to describe the height of a curtain.

drop curtain—See **olio curtain.**

dropout—The momentary loss of a recorded audio or video signal during playback, due to imperfections in the tape.

Drug-Free Workplace Act (DFWA)—The United States legislation that requires an antidrug policy within the workplace.

dry lease—The rental of an airplane without crew, supplies, fuel, or maintenance service.

dry run—The rehearsal or trial run-through of a program.

dry snack/nibbles—Finger foods, such as peanuts, pretzels, potato chips, corn chips, etc., usually served at receptions.

dual capacity—The legal principle that a business may stand in relation to its employees not only as employer but also as supplier of a product, provider of a service, owner of premises, etc.

dual setup—An arrangement of duplicate meeting room setups in two different locations.

dub—1. To transfer recorded sound, video, or film from one unit to another. 2. A copy of a recording, video, film, or photo.

dub (dubbing)—Synchronization to on-camera lip movement that replaces the existing voice, whether the actor's own voice or for another actor.

duchess potatoes—Potatoes mashed with eggs and squeezed through a pastry tube; can be served as a side dish, or used as piped decoration around a serving platter.

du jour—Of the day.

dummy—1. A paper mock-up of a proposed printed piece. 2. A mannequin.

duo—Two performers or musicians.

duotone—A photograph prepared for two-color reproduction.

dupe—See **duplicate.**

duplex outlet—A double electrical outlet.

duplicate—A film or tape that is printed from the original; also known as **dupe.**

dutchman—A strip of material, usually muslin, about 3 inches wide, that is used to cover cracks where flats meet.

duty—A tax imposed on imports by the customs authority of a country. Duties are generally based on the value of the goods (ad valorem duties), some other factors such as weight or quantity (specify duties), or a combination of value and other factors.

duty-free imports—Item amounts and categories specified by a government that are free of tax or duty charges when brought into the country.

duty manager—See **manager on duty.**

duvetyne—A soft, flexible fabric with a thick nap used for table covering and skirting.

dynamic loudspeaker—A loudspeaker that uses conventional cone and dome drive elements exclusively.

E

EAP—See **employment assistance program.**

early arrival—1. Guest arrival before the confirmed reservation date and/or time. 2. Arrival prior to the majority of the group.

early-bird rate—A special room rate for early registration.

earthenware—A type of clayware that is opaque, somewhat porous, and not as strong or as thin as china.

EASA—See **Exhibition Association of South Africa.**

easel—A tripod stand with a rack used to hold a magnetic board, poster, sign, chart, or flip chart.

eaves—1. The perimeter of a tent roof where the side walls are attached with a wall rope. 2. The top edge of a valance curtain.

eaves troughing—Canvas used to channel rainwater away from a tent roof to the outside edge, like gutters on a building.

EBDIT—Earnings before depreciation, interest, and taxes.

EBIT—Earnings before interest and taxes.

EBITDA—Earnings before interest, taxes, depreciation, and amortization.

éclair—1. A chocolate French-style pastry with a cream filling. 2. The prime camera for shooting synch sound documentaries in the new lightweight portable style.

economic strike—A work stoppage to compel changes in wages, hours, or working conditions, as distinguished from a strike to protest unfair labor practices.

ecotour—A tour designed to focus on preserving the environment or on environmentally sensitive areas, such as "Rebirth of Yellowstone" or greenhouse tours.

ECU—See **European Currency Unit.**

EDAC—See **Exhibit and Display Association of Canada.**

edit—1. To prepare or revise final copy before publication. 2. To arrange and assemble film or tape, prepare it for TV playback or projection, and set it up for final sound mix.

editorial alteration—Any alteration made by a publisher other than one made at an author's request or one to correct a printer's error.

EDPC—See **Exhibit Designers and Producers of Canada.**

educational credit—A credit earned for continuing professional education that acknowledges participation and is recognized by an accredited authority.

educational event—1. An event sponsored by a school, college, or other educational institution. 2. An event comprised of people employed or working within the education industry. 3. An event for the purposes of training and development.

educational program—The total educational selection offered during an event.

educational session—A time period during an event in which information or instruction is presented.

educational tour—A tour designed to promote education, such as studying Renaissance art.

educational visit—See **study mission.**

effect—The impression of a particular thing given to an audience by a technical achievement, such as a rainbow produced by lights, wind produced by a wind machine, and/or pyrotechnics.

effects device—An electronic device placed in an audio system and used by the mixer to create special effects and control sound level and quality; also known as **limiter, reverb,** or **equalizer.**

efficiency—1. A guest room with kitchen facilities. 2. A self-contained or self-serviced apartment. 3. The ratio of a loudspeaker's acoustical output to a given electrical input.

EFP—See **electronic field production.**

eggs Benedict—Poached eggs on an English muffin with Canadian bacon or ham and hollandaise sauce.

electret—See **condenser microphone.**

electrical codes—The national and local rules that are used to control the quality as well as the safety of permanent and temporary electrical operation.

electrical contractor—A company contracted by event management to provide electrical services.

electric cart—An electric-powered vehicle used by crew and staff at large events and in convention halls; also known as **scooter.**

electrician—A skilled craftsperson who handles the installation of all electrical equipment, which may include headers and signs, depending on the jurisdiction.

electricity connection—The temporary supply of electricity to a booth or stand to which electrical products can be connected.

electric pointer/laser pointer—An electric device used by a speaker to cast an illuminated spot of light to draw attention to a particular feature being demonstrated.

electronic blackboard—A system for sending handwriting and hand-drawn graphics over a telephone line so that the appropriate image will appear on a television monitor at the remote location.

electronic editing—A process by which program elements are inserted and assembled on audiotape without physically cutting the tape.

electronic field production (EFP)—On-location production that utilizes lightweight portable video gear.

electronic mail—See **e-mail.**

electronic news gathering (ENG)—On-the-spot news coverage employing highly portable videotaping systems in place of motion picture cameras; the standard practice for television stations.

electronic payment—A payment by electronic funds transfer.

electronic pour—An electronic system of dispensing an exact amount of liquor per drink.

electronic whiteboard—A system of controlling multimedia presentations by displaying computer-generated images onto a whiteboard, which copies all information written or taped onto it and saves, publishes, or prints out the notes.

electrostatic loudspeaker—A planar loudspeaker that incorporates a charged transducer suspended between two oppositely charged electrodes.

element—See **component.**

elevated table—A counter-height table used in a registration area to provide a writing surface.

elevation—The front and side views of an item in a drawing.

elevator stage—A stage floor with sections that may be lowered and raised by a hydraulic process.

elite—A type size that produces 12 typed characters per inch.

ellipsoidal spotlight—A lighting instrument containing shutters and allowing for the use of a gobo to project patterns or text.

e-mail (electronic mail)—Messages, usually text, sent from one person to another via computer.

embossing—Impressing letters or artwork in relief to produce a three-dimensional effect. Blind embossing is an inkless impression on blank paper.

E-MEAT—See **event management entrepreneur assessment tool.**

emergency exit—A door with clear instructions that is designed to be used in the event of a fire or other evacuation; also known as **fire exit.**

employers' association—An organization of employers who band together mainly to deal as a unified group with labor unions.

employment assistance program (EAP)—A United States program that is provided voluntarily by some employers to counsel employees about substance abuse and other personal problems.

endorsement—To give approval or agreement to a certain subject matter or event.

end sections—The roof sections forming the ends of a sectional tent; for example, a sectional 60' x 120' tent has two end sections that, when put together, form a 60' x 60' tent. Adding three 20' center sections results in the full 120' length.

energy break—A refreshment break where nutritious foods and beverages are served, occasionally including exercise.

ENG—See **electronic news gathering.**

engineering—A department responsible for keeping a building in physical working condition, including repair and maintenance of the electrical system, lighting, temperature control, and general repair.

English breakfast—A morning meal consisting of hot cereal, eggs, meat, pastries, preserves, juices, hot beverages, and fruit; also known as **full breakfast.**

English service—A style of banquet service where an elaborately prepared main course is first displayed on a rolling cart before it is served; also known as **cart service.**

engraved glass—Glass that is cut by a small abrasive wheel.

enhancement—See **tour option.**

entertainment—An activity performed for the enjoyment of others.

entertainment provider—A specialist who assesses entertainment needs and provides talent-booking services for events.

entrance canopy—An awning from a permanent building or from a main tent to the driveway or street that enhances the visual effect and provides shelter for guests.

entrance card—See **congress card.**

entrée—1. A dish served as the main course of a meal. 2. The appetizer in Europe and Australia.

Environmental Protection Agency (EPA)—The United States government agency that enforces the clean air and water acts.

EO—See **event order.**

EP—See **European plan.**

EPA—See **Environmental Protection Agency.**

epergne—A vertical pedestal, with attached vases or bowls, to hold floral arrangements and serve as a centerpiece for a table.

epilogue—A scene that follows the end of a play.

EPO—See **pay own.**

equalizer—An effects device used to compensate for undesirable sound system characteristics or room acoustics; see **effects device.**

equal opportunities—See **affirmative action.**

equity—1. The net investment a person has in some enterprise, business property, etc. 2. The difference between the total assets of a business and the total liabilities.

erase—The electronic removal of program elements from a recorded tape.

erection—The assembly of exhibits and displays or tents on-site.

errors and omissions insurance—A liability coverage that protects event management consultants from financial risk due to mistakes or oversights they have made that cause physical, financial, or other injury to additional parties.

ESCA—See **Exposition Service Contractors Association.**

escargots—Snails cooked in broth.

escort—1. A person, usually employed or subcontracted (or independently contracted) by the tour operator or destination management company (DMC), who accompanies a tour from departure to return, as a guide, troubleshooter, etc. 2. A person who performs such functions only at the destination. Also referred to as an on-site courier, conductor, host, manager, director, or leader.

escorted tour—1. A prearranged travel program, usually for a group, escorted by a tour guide. In a fully conducted tour, escort and/or guide service is provided throughout. 2. A sightseeing program conducted by a guide, such as a city tour.

escrow account—Funds placed in the custody of a licensed financial institution for safekeeping. Many contracts in travel require that agents and tour operators maintain customers' deposits and prepayments in escrow accounts.

E-shaped setup—A configuration of tables in a meeting room arranged in the shape of an E with chairs placed on the outside of the closed end and on both sides of each table leg.

estimate—A preliminary calculation of the cost of work to be undertaken; also known as **approximate calculation.**

est. wt.—The estimated weight of freight and other components of an event.

ETA—Estimated time of arrival.

etched glass—A type of glass whose design is etched out by acid.

ETD—Estimated time of departure.

Ethernet—A very common method of networking computers in a local area network (LAN).

ethical conduct—Setting and maintaining the highest ethical standards to ensure the professionalism of the event industry.

ethnic tour—A tour designed for people of the same heritage traveling to their native origin or to a destination with ethnic relevance.

E-ticket—An electronic ticket that has no physical coupon; used by transportation and other agencies.

Euro—The common currency adopted in 2000 by several countries in Europe.

Eurodollars—United States dollars placed on deposit in banks outside the United States.

European Currency Unit (ECU)—The currency unit of the European community.

European plan (EP)—A room rate that does not include meals; also known as **room only.**

evaluation—1. A process used to critique and rate the overall success of an event. 2. A process used to develop an event profile gathered from accurate event statistics at the completion of the event.

event management—1. A function requiring public assembly for the purpose of celebration, education, marketing, and reunion. 2. The process that includes research, design, planning, coordinating, and evaluation of events.

event management entrepreneur assessment tool (E-MEAT)—A tool used to evaluate the personal characteristics, abilities, and qualifications of a professional as an event entrepreneur.

event manager—The individual responsible for researching, designing, planning, coordinating, and evaluating an event.

event marketing—The process that integrates a range of marketing elements around a central event sponsorship or lifestyle-themed activity. This process incorporates advertising, employee and consumer programs, sales promotion, public relations, causes, business to business, television property, and trade promotion with a specific event.

event order (EO)—Detailed instructions for an event; also known as **banquet event order, function sheet, résumé, running order,** or **running sheet.**

event specification—The compilation by organizations of all function sheets, scripts, instructions, room setup diagrams, directory of key personnel, forms, and other material relating to the event; also known as **schedule of services** or **outline of services.**

event sponsorship—A process in which an organization provides funds or in-kind support to underwrite some or all of an event in return for marketing exposure at the event; a commercial transaction between a seller (the event) and a buyer (the sponsor).

event stewards—Security service employed to protect the building, people, event, etc.

event team—The individuals working together or associated in some joint action; also known as **production team** or **production crew.**

example—See **scenario.**

excess baggage—Luggage that exceeds the allowance set by the airline and requires a fee.

excess insurance—Additional insurance coverage above the limits imposed by the primary insurance.

exchange rate—The value of a currency in relationship to the value of the currencies of other nations.

exciter lamp—A lamp that projects illumination through the optical sound track on 16mm film. Light patterns are read by the projector sound head, converted to electronic signals, and fed to an audio amplifier.

exclusion—An insurance policy provision that stipulates specific prohibitions (hazards, circumstances, and property) to coverage.

exclusive—1. Any agreement that limits who may provide services to an exhibition or in a facility, meaning that no other contractor is allowed to work in that building. 2. Private, for members only.

exclusive contractor—A contractor appointed by show or building management as the sole agent to provide services.

exclusive use—1. A form for an exhibitor requesting handling materials. 2. The rental of an entire truck or van by one shipper; may be used only by the designated person or company.

exclusivity—Freedom from competing advertising within a given communications medium enjoyed by one advertiser; requires major space or time purchases.

excursion—1. A journey made with the intention to return to the original point of departure. 2. A recreational trip provided as a scheduled portion of an event program; also known as **tour.**

executive board—The members appointed by the governing board to manage the affairs of a society or association on a daily basis.

executive coach—A luxury motor coach with seating for 25 or less, which can include such amenities as TV, galley, wet bar, card tables, etc.

executive committee—A committee created to decide policy and strategy for the organization of an event; also known as **management committee.**

executive secretary—A person appointed to handle organizational functions and given certain administrative authority and responsibilities.

exhibit—Although the terms *exhibit, booth,* or *stand* are often used interchangeably, an exhibit is actually all of the display materials and products housed in a booth or stand.

Exhibit and Display Association of Canada (EDAC)—An organization for exhibitors at conferences and events in Canada.

exhibit booth/stand—A display area constructed for exhibitors to showcase their products or convey a message.

exhibit designer/producer—An individual or company responsible for designing and constructing an exhibit booth or stand.

Exhibit Designers and Producers of Canada (EDPC)—A Canadian organization whose members are designers and producers of exhibits of events in Canada.

exhibit directory—1. A program or catalog listing exhibitors and exhibit booth or stand location. 2. The complete alphabetical list of exhibitors, their products, their headquarters, and sales points that incorporates a floor plan and advertising; also known as **exhibition catalog.**

exhibit hall—The area within a facility where an exhibition is located.

exhibition—A display for public view of products or promotional materials for the purpose of public relations, sales, and/or marketing; also known as **exposition, industrial show,** or **trade show.**

exhibition area—See **booth/stand area.**

Exhibition Association of South Africa (EASA)—The professional association providing education and networking for exhibitors and their suppliers in South Africa.

exhibition catalog—See **exhibit directory.**

exhibition contractor—The organizer or promoter of an exhibition responsible for the letting of space, financial control, and management.

exhibition cooking—See **action station.**

exhibition manager—An individual responsible for coordinating an exhibition; also known as **exposition manager** or **show manager.**

exhibition plan—A plan showing the space occupied by exhibitors, including the areas for booths or stands, passageways, and services.

exhibition space—See **booth/stand area.**

exhibit manager—1. The person in charge of an individual exhibit booth or stand. 2. The show management staff member in charge of an entire exhibit area.

exhibitor—A company or organization sponsoring an exhibit booth or stand.

exhibitor advisory committee—Representatives of a show's exhibiting companies who act as advisers to show management on rules and procedures and also update show management on industry trends and issues.

exhibitor appointed—Any company other than the designated "official" contractor providing a service to an exhibitor. Can refer to an installation and dismantle business, photographer, florist, or any other type of contractor.

exhibitor lounge—An area either on or adjacent to the exhibit floor where exhibitors may relax or meet with customers. Show management sometimes provides special services in this area, such as translators for a show that has international attendees.

exhibitor retention—Persuading current exhibitors to participate in subsequent events. Exhibitor retention rate is the percentage of exhibitors that renew.

exhibitor's kit—A kit prepared and sent by the exhibition organizer to all registered participants, containing information and supplier request forms or names of local contractors; also known as **service kit** or **exhibitor's manual.**

exhibitor's manual—See **service kit** or **exhibitor's kit.**

exhibitor's newsletter—A newsletter sent by show management to exhibitors prior to a show. It includes updates on deadlines, show rules and regulations, events, marketing opportunities offered by show management, and educational articles to improve exhibitors' effectiveness.

exhibitor's pass/badge—An identification card or badge to enable exhibitors to gain access to an exhibition.

exhibit prospectus—A pamphlet for potential exhibitors and other interested parties, containing the conditions, technical points, cost of exhibition space, floor plan, and application for participation.

expedited service—A service offered by a transportation company to assure prompt delivery.

exploder—An electrical apparatus used to ignite fireworks.

export—To send or transport products out of one country for sale in another country. The exporter is usually the seller or the seller's agent.

export broker—An individual or firm that brings together buyers and sellers for a fee, but does not take part in actual sales transactions.

export license—A government document that permits the licensee to engage in the export of designated goods to specified destinations.

export management—A private firm that serves as the export department for several manufacturers, soliciting and transacting export business on behalf of its clients in return for a commission, salary, or retainer plus commission.

export merchant—A company that buys products directly from manufacturers, then packages and markets the merchandise for resale under its own name.

export trading company—A firm that purchases international goods for resale in its own local market.

exposition—1. An event at which products and services are displayed for public view; also known as **exhibition.** 2. An assembly of a large number of individuals to discuss items of mutual interest or engage in professional development through learning activities.

exposition manager—The person responsible for all aspects of planning, promoting, and producing an exposition. Also known as **exhibition manager, show manager,** or **show organizer.**

exposition service contractor—A supplier of booth or stand equipment, including rental furnishings and floor coverings, labor, drayage, and signs for expositions and trade shows.

Exposition Service Contractors Association (ESCA)—An organization whose membership provides services and products within the exposition industry.

exposure—The state of being subject to loss because of some hazard or contingency.

extended type—A type that is wider than standard type, allowing fewer characters per line.

extension—A full arranged subtour offered optionally at extra cost to buyers of a tour or cruise. Extensions may occur before, during, or after the basic travel program; also known as **side trip.**

exterior—A film or video set painted to represent an outdoor scene.

external exhibit—See **outside exhibit / external exhibit.**

extinction—The removal of unwanted portions of a laser graphic by blanking.

extra-man—See **manpower agency.**

extranet—Two or more intranets connected across the Internet.

extraordinary session—A special session for activities, needs, or situations that are different from those normally and originally scheduled.

extra overnight stays—All extra nights spent by a participant other than overnight meeting stays.

extra section—An aircraft or bus added to accommodate a group's planned transportation needs.

F

FAA—See **Federal Aviation Administration.**

fabrication—The construction of an exhibit or display.

FAC—See **Federal Airports Corporation.**

facilitator—A trained mediator who guides discussion and decision making in small group meetings.

facility—See **convention center.**

facility manager—The manager of a venue.

facsimile machine/fax—See **telefax.**

fade in—To change gradually from a dark screen to a visual image; also known as **dissolve.**

fade out—See **go to black.**

fader—A device used to control all dimming circuits.

fair—A public celebration that includes commercial and civic activities.

Fair Labor Standards Act (FLSA)—The United States federal overtime and minimum wage law.

fairy lights—See **B lights.**

false bow—A staged bow and exit by the artist with a planned return pending audience response.

FAM—see **familiarization trip.**

familiarization trip (FAM)—A program designed to acquaint participants with specific destinations or services and to stimulate the booking of an event offered to potential buyers of an event site; also known as **inspection trip.**

family name—The preferred term for "last name" for international registration documents; see **given name.**

family plan—A discount price offered by hotels and resorts to families consisting of two or more members traveling together.

family-style buffet—See **country-style table service.**

family-style service—A style of serving in which guests serve themselves from platters and bowls of food placed on the table; also known as **family table service.**

family table service—See family-style service.

fan—A laser effect in which a pencil-thin laser beam is moved rapidly from side to side creating the appearance of a sheet of light. By mixing up and down motion with the side-to-side motion, laserists can create a variety of fan effects.

FAP (full American plan)—See American plan.

fare—The transportation charge paid by a passenger.

FAS—See free alongside.

fascia—1. A panel displayed at the top of an exhibit, indicating company name. 2. A hard skirting applied to a stage.

fascia board—A hard panel used to display information or screen a stage or event area.

fashion show—A choreographed display of garments by models.

fax—See telefax.

FDIC—See Federal Deposit Insurance Corporation.

featherbedding—A trade practice of creating additional jobs or spreading work by placing limits on production, requiring more people than necessary to do a job, or requiring the performance of superfluous work.

feature—An important characteristic of a product or service.

Federal Airports Corporation (FAC)—An Australian organization responsible for creating and enforcing the rules and regulations for flying.

Federal Aviation Administration (FAA)—The United States federal agency responsible for creating and enforcing the rules and regulations for flying.

Federal Deposit Insurance Corporation (FDIC)—The United States independent agency that insures deposits up to the statutory limitation in qualified banks and savings associations.

fee—1. A charge for registration and permits. 2. A sum paid for admission. 3. A payment for a professional service.

feedback—A regeneration of sound from audio speakers back through a microphone, causing a squealing sound.

feeder space—Reservations for passengers from their home city to a gateway city for international flights or flights to Hawaii; see stub space.

festival—A public celebration that conveys, through a kaleidoscope of activities, certain meanings to participants and spectators.

festoon—Decorations or fabric hanging in the form of garlands or loops.

feta cheese—Soft, flaky white cheese with a salty pickled flavor.

fete—An outdoor festival.

fete stall—A 2m x 4m tent used as a booth or stand.

FHC—A notation on floor plans indicating the location of fire hose cabinets.

FI—See free in.

fiber optics/fibre optics—Very thin, transparent glass or plastic fiber encased in a material with a lower index of refraction that transmits light through internal reflections. Transmission fibers move laser light from its source to a remote location without showing a light path. Display fibers glow, like neon wire, when laser light is passed through them.

FidoNet—A large, electronic worldwide Internet bulletin board system (BBS).

field camera—A lightweight camera used in news coverage and documentaries; also known as **portable camera.**

field production—The shooting of rough footage early in film production. At this point the storyboard is established during preproduction and followed to ensure all bases are carefully covered.

filed—How a lawsuit begins. The legal complaint is filed in court.

filet mignon—The most expensive cut of the beef tenderloin.

file transfer protocol (FTP)—A program on the Internet that allows users to transfer files between computers. Many Internet nodes (individual computers) contain files that are available to the general public through anonymous FTP.

fill light—Light used to fill shadows created by key light.

film chain—A series of projectors and video equipment transmitting projected materials through a television system.

film clip—A brief piece of film shown from a larger film production to elicit interest.

film projector—Equipment for projecting motion picture film.

film report—A conclusive summary of conference events.

filmstrip—A series of slides reproduced on one continuous strip of film.

filter—1. A coated glass used to separate or combine colors within the optical section of a laser projector, by transmission or reflection. 2. A paper cartridge used to strain particles of dirt from laser-cooling water. 3. Special equipment used in still and motion picture photography and video to create specific optical effects. 4. A color filter or gel used in front of light.

final account—The statement of income and expenditure following the end of an event; also known as **final statement of account.**

final program/blueprint—A document containing the definitive conference program, distributed to participants prior to or at the commencement of an event.

final report—The final summary of the outcome of an event.

final statement of account—See **final account.**

finance committee—The individuals responsible for budgeting, cash flow, accounting, and controlling finances and whose chairperson is generally the treasurer of the event.

financial controller—See **chief financial officer (CFO).**

financial procedures—An outline of accounting and banking techniques.

financial report—A document incorporating the statement of income and expenditure and the budget at a given date.

financial responsibility law—A statutory provision requiring owners of automobiles to provide evidence of their ability to pay damages arising out of automobile operation.

fine china—A thin, translucent china that is very strong and made of top-quality clays fired at high temperatures that cause them to fuse into a hard nonporous body.

Finger—A service on the Internet that can provide information about the person associated with a particular user identification.

finger bowl—A dish of hot water, sometimes scented and accompanied by fresh linen, presented after or during a meal or course, to cleanse the hands and lips.

FIO—See **free in and out.**

fire exit—A means of egress regulated by local regulations to ensure safe exit during an emergency; also known as **emergency exit.**

fire insurance—The insurance that covers loss or damage attributable to fire, smoke, explosion, or forces of nature; can also cover related water damage.

fire retardant—A finish (usually liquid) that coats materials with a fire-resistant cover that does not render the material fireproof.

fire wall—A combination of hardware and software that separates a local area network (LAN) into two or more parts for security purposes.

first aid—1. Emergency care or treatment given before a doctor arrives. 2. The location where emergency health care is provided by licensed medical personnel.

first announcement—An initial notification of an event outlining the basic framework of a meeting and widely circulated to potential participants; see **preliminary announcement.**

first option—See **option.**

fish pole—A long pole with a microphone often used in question-and-answer sessions.

FIT—See **foreign independent tour/free or fully independent traveler.**

fixed assets turnover—The total revenue divided by average total fixed assets.

fixed costs—All of the expenditures that remain the same regardless of the quantity of products sold; see **variable costs.**

fixed expenses—1. Event expenses that do not vary with the number of guests, such as promotional costs, tour manager's expense, charters, etc. 2. Expenses that are set and cannot be controlled, such as depreciation, interest, and income taxes; see **variable expenses.**

fixed seating arrangement—An arrangement in which the chairs in a meeting room are permanently mounted to the floor.

fixed theater—The permanent, nonmovable seats in a meeting room or amphitheater.

flag carrier—1. An airline carrier designated by a country to serve international routes. 2. An individual carrying a flag or banner in a procession.

flambé—A meat dish or dessert item flamed with spirits, for show.

flameproof—A material used to retard flammability in clothing and construction materials.

flaming—The use of derogatory language on the Internet or through e-mail.

flash—A technique of blinking a slide on and off to add emphasis.

flash box—A smoke-producing device for special effects.

flasher—A device to activate one or more lamps by intermittently interrupting current.

flash pot—A pyrotechnic device that simulates a flash.

flat—A covered frame to construct partitioning or theatrical décor.

flatbed editing—An editing machine with a horizontal bed instead of an upright working area, consisting of matching pairs of circular plates, with one for feed-out and one for take-up.

flat rate—One price based on average cost, for all guest/sleeping rooms in a hotel, exclusive of suites; may be flat rate single or flat rate double; also known as **run-of-the-house rate.**

flip chart—A large pad of paper placed on an easel and used by a speaker for illustrative purposes.

floater/casual—A temporary worker used to assist permanent workers for a short period of time.

floodlight—A light fitting with a reflector to aim a wide beam of light in one direction.

floor language—The language from which a speech or document is translated; also known as **source language.**

floor load/loading—The maximum amount of weight per square foot a floor can support.

floor manager—1. A person retained by management to supervise the exhibit area. 2. A television technician who directs and cues the talent during studio operations.

floor marking—A method of marking booth or stand space.

floor order—Products or services ordered on-site.

floor plan—A schematic drawing of a room, including its dimensions and design, used to develop event plans.

floor port—A utility box, recessed in the floor, containing electrical, telephone, and/or plumbing connections.

floor setup diagram—A detailed floor plan drawn to scale showing the specific setup requirements for a meeting or function, including the dais, tables, and chairs; also known as **setup plan.**

floor speaker—See **discussant.**

flop—To reverse a photo or illustration so that it conforms to the basic design.

floppy disk—A diskette on which a computer file or program is created or stored.

floral designer—A professional who specializes in designing with floral materials and décor.

Florentine—Served with spinach.

FLSA—See **Fair Labor Standards Act.**

flush—A style of typesetting with even right, left, or both margins; also known as **justified margin** or **justified type.**

fly curtain—A curtain that is raised and lowered.

flyer—A one-piece printed announcement or advertisement of a special event, distributed as a handbill or by mail.

foam core—Two sheets of lightweight specially coated paper sealed on either side of a foam center; used for signs, decorating, and exhibits.

FOB—see **free on board.**

focal length—1. The distance from the center of a lens to the film plane. 2. The size of a lens required to obtain a specific-size picture.

focus—1. The proper sharpness of the outline of an image. 2. The pointing of lights to a specific area.

FOH—See **front of house.**

foil-stamping—Metallic or colored foil leaf used in stamping printed matter. Heat and pressure are used to print the design on a surface.

folio—A form on which all charge transactions incurred by a registered guest are recorded.

follow spotlight—A spotlight mounted to a yoke that can be swiveled, allowing an operator to pan and tilt the beam to follow the movement of a performer. It generally contains an adjustable iris, shutter, and color changer for further alteration of the beam.

font—A typeface of one style and size.

food and beverage director—An individual in a hotel who manages all activities related to food and beverage.

food cost percentage—The total cost of food sales divided by food revenue.

food cover—A unit of food service provided to a customer.

food inventory turnover—The cost of food sales divided by average food inventory.

food station—See **action station.**

force majeure clause—A contract clause that limits liability should the event be prevented due to disruptive circumstances beyond the sponsor's control, including war, strikes, or catastrophic weather; see **act of God.**

forecast—1. To predict a hotel's occupancy situation on any given date. 2. The projected revenue of a facility for a given period of time.

foreign flag—Any airline or other transportation carrier not registered in the United States and not flying the American flag.

foreign independent tour/free or fully independent traveler (FIT)—A custom-designed prepaid tour for an individual traveler.

foreign meeting—A meeting comprised of attendees from other nations; also known as **international meeting** or **institute.**

foreign/national—Membership of meeting participation available to organizations or individuals from one nation, but able to meet in another nation.

foreman—See **business agent.**

forklift—A vehicle with a power-operated pronged platform for lifting and carrying loads; also known as **lift truck** or **tow motor.**

formal dining service—See **butler service (Australia).**

formal dress—See **black tie.**

for-profit show management company—A management company whose owners, or stockholders, share in its net proceeds.

forum—An open discussion between the audience, panel members, and moderator.

forward business—Any business transaction that can be expected in the future; also known as **projected business.**

forward contract—A financial instrument guaranteeing a specific rate of exchange in a foreign currency for a future transaction.

foul bill of lading—A receipt for goods issued by a carrier with an indication that the goods were damaged when received.

four-color separation—A photographic process utilizing four-color screened patterns from which printing plates can be engraved.

four-hour call—A minimum work period for which union labor must be paid if called to work.

foyer—A public or prefunction area in a hotel or hall for assembly or registration.

fragmentation—The use of a great variety of types of media for a single advertising campaign, with no single medium used predominantly or heavily.

fraises—Strawberries.

framboises—Raspberries.

frame—An individual picture in a filmstrip, motion picture, or video.

frame tent—A professionally installed tent consisting of a canvas or vinyl top stretched over a metal frame and containing no center poles.

framework decision—The preliminary decision setting out a framework within which detailed provisions may be established by means of later individual decisions; also known as **outline decision.**

franchise—The right to market a service and/or product, often exclusive for a specified area, as granted by the manufacturer, developer, or distributor in return for a fee; prevalent in the fast food service industry.

fraternal—A group associated by common personal interests rather than common job or career responsibilities.

free alongside (FAS)—A price quotation under which the exporter quotes a price that includes delivery of the goods to the vessel's side and within reach of its loading tackle. Subsequent risks and expenses are for the account of the buyer.

free-form—Self-supporting and independent exhibit material.

free in (FI)—A pricing term indicating that the chartered operator of a vessel is responsible for the cost of loading and unloading goods from the vessel.

free in and out (FIO)—A pricing term indicating that the chartered operator of a vessel is responsible for the cost of loading and unloading goods from the vessel.

freelance—A production worker, crew person, escort, tour guide, etc., who does not limit his or her employ to one organization, but instead is free to work for a variety of event organizations, hourly, daily, or on a project basis.

free on board (FOB)—A price quotation under which the exporter includes delivery of the goods on board the vessel. Subsequent risks and expenses are for the account of the buyer.

free paper—A presentation of a written transcript given after acceptance of the abstract on a subject chosen by the author.

free paper session—Reports on topics that don't strictly relate to the meeting theme, but are closely related and are held in a separate session.

free port—An area such as a port city into which merchandise may legally be moved without payment of duties.

free pour—The preparation of alcoholic drinks by hand without the use of a shot glass or other measuring utensils.

free-rider—A union term for a nonunion worker who receives the benefits of the union's collective bargaining activity without sharing in the costs.

freestanding—Self-supporting and independent display material for an exhibit.

free trade zone—A port area designated by a government for duty-free entry of nonprohibited goods, which may be stored, displayed, or used for manufacturing within the zone and exported without paying duty. Duties are imposed on the goods and manufactured items only when the goods pass from the zone into an area subject to customs.

freeze-frame—A motion picture or video frame that is supported so that the single frame is displayed; see **stop motion.**

freight—See **cartage.**

freight desk—A shipping company that typically handles international freight shipments.

freight forwarder—1. A business that handles export shipments for compensation. 2. A company transporting goods from one site to another (interstate, international).

freight ton—See **measurement ton.**

French action—A curtain that opens from the center.

French service—A method of banquet service in which each food item is served by the waiter from a platter to an individual plate; also known as **butler service (American)** and **silver service.**

frequency—The number of times that an individual is exposed to an advertising message during the period that it is run.

frequency response—The measurement of an audible signal's amplitude and phase characteristics relative to a given absolute level.

Fresnel—A lighting instrument that uses a Fresnel lens to produce a diffused, soft-edged beam. The spacing between the lamp and the lens can be adjusted to alter the beam spread from spot to flood.

frit—Fried.

froid—Cold.

fromage—Cheese.

frontages, front—Refers to dimensions across the front of an exhibit.

front booth/stand—The booth or stand at the head of a row.

front desk—1. An area in a hotel where guests check in and out, room assignments are made, and the final guest bill is paid. 2. The center of a meeting facility activities, including registration and cashier services.

front of house (FOH)—Anything in the house that the guests will see.

front-projection television—A television that forms an image by projecting a picture from in front of a screen.

front-screen projection—The projection of an image onto the front surface of a light-reflecting screen from a projector placed within or behind the audience.

frosted glass—A glass that is exposed to acid.

FTP—See **file transfer protocol.**

full American plan (FAP)—See **American plan.**

full board—An inclusive fee for room, all meals, and tax and service charges; see **inclusive rate.**

full booth/stand coverage—A carpet covering the entire area of a booth or stand.

full breakfast—A full morning meal; see **American breakfast** or **English breakfast.**

full coverage—Any form of insurance that provides payment in full of all losses caused by the perils insured against to the limits of the policy.

full house—A term that indicates that guest rooms are occupied or committed; also known as **closed/fully booked.**

full-service restaurants—This category includes coffee shops, dinner houses, fine dining establishments, and theme restaurants with several menu selections and table service.

full stage—The entire stage area that can be used as the acting area.

full text—The complete version of a text.

fully equipped booth/stand—A stand equipped with all services and facilities such as electric, carpet, lighting, etc.

fumé—Smoked.

function—A prearranged, catered group activity, usually held in a private room or area. It may be a cocktail party only, or it may be a banquet, which includes food service.

function bill (account)—An itemized invoice prepared by a hotel stating the charges for each function of an event.

function board—An area where announcements are listed with the day's events; also known as **directory/directory board** or **reader board.**

function book—A journal used to record the assignment of event space within a venue.

function room—A special room that is used primarily for private parties, banquets, and meetings; also known as **banquet room.**

function sheet—A document that records the details of an event's needs, including sleeping rooms, billing arrangements, food, beverages, and audiovisual equipment, and is distributed to all hotel departments and the event organizer; also known as **résumé, banquet event order,** or **event order.**

function space—A facility area where private functions, meetings, or events can be held.

fund-raising—The activity or profession of obtaining money for charitable organizations.

fund-raising event—An event whose purpose is to raise funds for a charitable cause and to identify new sources of support.

funnel flight—An air trip requiring a change of planes at an intermediate stop while maintaining the same flight number.

fuse head—See **squib head.**

fusion cuisine—A menu that includes a blend of foods from several cultures; also known as **crossroads cuisine.**

future bookings—An event or meeting that is reserved during a specific time period and scheduled for a future date in a specific location.

G

gable end—A South African term for the squared end shape of the roof at the end of a tent structure.

gaffer's tape—A vinyl, impregnated fabric tape used to anchor cables and fabrics.

gagging—Slang for unauthorized improvisation or revision of lines by an actor.

gain—The level or degree of audio volume; also known as **level**.

gala dinner—The outstanding social event of an event, including a formal meal, speeches, and entertainment.

galantine—Boned meat, pressed into a symmetrical shape, that usually includes truffles.

galley proof—Typeset copy for an author's review and correction before printing.

galvo/galvanometer—See **scanner (laser)**.

gang box—See **trouble box**.

gangway—1. See **aisle**. 2. A connecting bridgeway between two points.

gap analysis—An analytical tool used to identify gaps in the design of an event. For example, an outdoor event planned during the rainy season would produce a gap that could be closed with either a tent or an indoor location.

Garcy Strip—The trade name of a manufacturer who produces brackets and standards for the mounting of materials, usually shelves.

garment rack—A metal frame or rail that holds apparel; also known as **clothes rail**.

garni—To adorn or decorate food.

garni, hotel—A hotel without dining facilities.

garnish—A food decoration, usually edible, that adds color and form to food presentation.

gate show—See **consumer/trade show** or **public show**.

gateway—1. A city, airport, or area from which a flight or tour departs. 2. A hardware or software setup that translates between two Internet protocols.

gateway city—A city with an international airport.

GATT—See **General Agreement on Tariffs and Trade.**

gauge—When tariffs refer to gauge, they mean the U.S. Standard Gauge for determining the thickness of sheet or plate steel; Brown & Sharpe Gauge for rods and sheets of aluminum, copper, brass, and bronze; U.S. Steel Wire Gauge for iron and steel wire.

gear drive—The technique of transferring motion from a motor shaft to an object by use of one or more interlocking gears.

gel—A colored transparent material placed in front of a lighting instrument to color the light.

gelatine (gel)—A thin, transparent sheet of material for producing colored light.

gel frame—A metal, wood, or cardboard holder for the color medium that is placed in front of a lighting instrument; also known as **color frame.**

general agreement—See **consensus.**

General Agreement on Tariffs and Trade (GATT)—A multilateral treaty whose purpose is to help reduce trade barriers between the signatory countries and to promote trade through tariff concessions.

general assembly—The general and formal meeting of an association, club, organization, or company attended by its members for the purpose of deciding legislative direction, policy matters, the election of internal committees, and approval of balance sheets, budgets, etc.

general contractor—A company that can provide all services to exhibition management and exhibitors.

general export license—Any of various export licenses used to export commodities requiring formal application or written authorization.

general session—A meeting open to all event participants; also known as **plenary session.**

general strike—A strike by the organized workers in all companies in a geographic area.

geographic segmentation—The arbitrary division of a market by country, region, state, zone, district, standard metropolitan statistical area (SMSA), or city.

gerb/fountain—A pyrotechnic device that displays a 2" to 2' flame, depending on its diameter; see **lance.**

get-together—An informal social gathering; also known as **informal meeting.**

ghost image—See **afterimage.**

GIT—See **group inclusive tour.**

giveaway (or novelty)—1. An advertising specialty item, imprinted with a logo or an event theme, freely given as a keepsake; see **amenity.** 2. A gift or item for sale imprinted with an event's logo and theme; also known as **merchandise gift.**

given name—The preferred term for "first name" for international registration documents; see **family name.**

glacé—1. Ice. 2. Ice cream. 3. Iced.

glass, plate—Sheets of glass commonly available in thicknesses of ⅛", ³⁄₁₆", or ½".

glass, single thick—One-eighth-inch-thick glass, such as is used for windowpanes.

glass, solar—Glass that has been treated to transmit light but reflects infrared solar rays.

glass, tempered—Hardened glass, usually plate.

glass, wire—Plate glass with embedded wire reinforcement.

glass-beaded screen—A type of screen surface used for front-screen projection; also known as **beaded screen.**

glass-ceramic—A comparatively new type of dinnerware body that begins as glass, then undergoes special treatment that causes it to take on the appearance of white ceramic.

glaze—A glasslike coating that is applied to pottery and dinnerware by either dipping or spraying.

glide—Hardware used to support or permit sliding movement.

global marketing strategy—The standardization of all marketing activities so that they can be used in multiple countries.

glossy—Common term for photographs reproduced on high-gloss paper.

GMT—See **Greenwich Mean Time.**

gnocchi—1. Pasta made from potatoes. 2. Potato dumplings served in a red tomato-based sauce.

goals—Measurable accomplishments that contribute to an exhibit's objectives.

goblet—A drinking glass with a stem and foot.

gobo—A metal or glass template inserted into a focusable lighting fixture used to define projected light patterns. It does for a lighting designer what a stencil does for a sign maker.

gofer—A person hired to act as a runner or messenger.

goodie bag—A container for gifts given to guests at the end of an event; see **amenity.**

good one side/surface quality—A piece of plywood or decorative material whose face side is free of blemishes.

good standing—An association member who is not under suspension because of some ethical or other infraction of the membership rules or regulations.

good theater—A business that communicates easily with the audience.

Gopher—A distributed service on the Internet that can organize and provide access to hierarchically related information. The information can be in various forms, such as library catalogs, databases, news groups, etc.

gopher/gofer—A production assistant who gets his title from the fact that he is frequently sent to "go fer" something.

gorgonzola cheese—White cheese, marbled with blue-green mold, with a spicy flavor.

go to black—1. An entertainment term meaning to turn off the room light or change the light gradually from an image to a black screen; also known as **black out.** 2. The situation where room lights are turned off or a video screen becomes black; also known as **fade out.**

gouda cheese—Creamy yellow cheese with or without a red wax coating and with a nutlike flavor.

governing board—A group of members who are responsible for establishing and enforcing the rules and regulations of a society or association; also known as **council.**

governing statutes—The laws of a country, state, province, or other jurisdiction as they relate to the operation of an incorporated association.

government event—A public function to acknowledge significant community change, including ground breaking, inaugurations, and dedications of public buildings.

government meeting—A gathering of groups of civil servants, elected officials, or service providers to governmental entities.

graduation—See **commencement/graduation.**

grain of wheat—A general term for miniature lamps, usually the 4-volt, snap-in type.

grand opening—A celebration marking a new place of business or first day of operations of a public venue to which potential customers and important contacts are invited.

grandstand—See **bleachers.**

grants—The money obtained from bodies or authorities to underwrite expenditures; also known as **subsidies.**

graphics—1. Illustrations, photographs, and layouts, combined with type style and copy. 2. Simple line images, which can be abstract patterns, drawings, or words.

gras—Fat.

gratuity—The amount paid as a reward for special service, sometimes obligatory in the form of a service charge, but often optional in the form of a tip; see **perquisite** or **bonus.**

greenfield—A flexible metal conduit, used where code allows.

green room—A room, stocked with refreshments, for an artist, honored guest, or speaker and entourage to relax or meet guests and media representatives.

Greenwich Mean Time (GMT)—The mean solar time determined at the prime meridian at Greenwich, England, and used as the standard basis of time throughout the world; also known as **Zulu Time.**

gridlock—See **shoehorn.**

grid system—A technique of providing a system of structural supports, electrical conduit, etc., on a pattern of centers.

grievance—An employee's or employer's stated dissatisfaction with some aspect of the employment relationship.

grille—Grilled or broiled.

grip—1. A stagehand who assists a master carpenter. 2. A general assistant in the film industry.

grits—Ground hominy (corn).

grommet—A rubber, metal, or plastic element for reinforcing holes in weaker materials.

gross per capita—The revenue before discounts divided by total attendance of an event.

gross profit—The net revenue minus total cost of an event.

gross revenue—The total revenue of an event.

gross square feet—A measurement of area determined by multiplying the width by the length.

gross weight—The full weight of a shipment, including products and packaging.

ground arrangements—Services after reaching the destination that are provided by a destination management company (DMC); also known as **land arrangements.**

ground breaking—The ceremonial turning of the first piece of earth at a construction site to promote the project and the product or service to be produced.

ground operator—A company or person in a destination city who handles local transportation and other local travel needs; see **destination management company (DMC).**

ground plans—A layout of the stage showing the location of set properties and lights for a production.

groundrow—Freestanding, low scenery, or a painted cutout that provides an illusion of depth and masks unsightly views.

ground transportation firm—A service contractor that transports people, baggage, and/or equipment from an airport, railway station, or bus terminal to event sites and other locations.

group booking—A reservation for a block of rooms specifically for one group.

group inclusive tour (GIT)—A travel program with special fares and specific requirements, for example, a minimum number of persons traveling as a group throughout the tour.

group leader—An individual, acting as liaison to a destination management company (DMC) and client.

group of experts—The group of specialists in a particular field.

group rate—A negotiated guest/sleeping room rate for a group.

group tour—A prearranged, prepaid travel program for a group, usually including transportation, accommodations, attraction admissions, and meals; see also **package tour.**

Gruyère cheese—A Swiss cheese used to make fondue.

GT—Gross ton.

guarantee—1. See **certificate of manufacture.** 2. The number of food and beverage servings to be paid for regardless of whether they're actually consumed. Usually the number of servings must be relayed by the host to the caterer 48 hours in advance of the event.

guaranteed late arrival/guaranteed arrival—A guest room secured by credit card or advance payment to ensure the reservation is not canceled for the evening.

guaranteed number—Servings, meals, or rooms requested and paid for whether actually consumed or occupied.

guaranteed payment—A hotel reservation secured by the guest's agreement to pay for the room whether it is used or not. Payment is usually guaranteed by a company, destination management company (DMC), travel agent, or tour wholesaler who has an established credit rating with the hotel.

guaranteed reservation—A prepaid reservation held until an agreed-upon arrival time or checkout time the next day, whichever occurs first, making the guest responsible for payment if the reservation is not cancelled.

guaranteed tour—A tour guaranteed to operate unless cancelled before an established cutoff date (usually 60 days prior to departure).

guest account—An itemized record of a guest's charges and credits, which is maintained in the front office until departure. Also referred to as **guest bill, guest folio,** and **guest statement**.

guest list—A list of peoples' names invited to and/or attending a function.

guest room/sleeping room—A sleeping room for an event attendee or participant.

guest speech—A speech submitted on a specific topic at the request of a committee; also known as **invited paper.**

guide—A person accompanying a tour who provides detailed knowledge of places of interest.

guided tour—A sightseeing trip conducted by a guide.

guidelines for authors—The instructions regarding the required format to be used for the version of the paper to be published; also known as **instructions for the preparation of papers.**

gusset—In construction, a triangular reinforcement or brace in corners of panels or framing.

guy ropes—Ropes that extend from the eaves of a tent to each side pole and then to anchors in the ground, providing support for the roof.

H

half board—See **demipension** or **modified American plan (MAP)**.

half-moon table—Two quarter-round tables attached to make a half circle.

half-round step—A 60" to 72" round table with seating only around the half of the table facing the speaker or stage.

halftime spectacle—Events designed to entertain spectators midway through a sports event.

halftone—A photograph that has been prepared for single-color reproduction.

hall—A large room for public assembly.

hallmark—A onetime or recurring event of limited duration; see **mega event**.

handbill—A written circular flyer intended for distribution by hand, either to persons encountered on the street or to homes, offices, etc., also known as a **flyer**.

handblown glass—A hot molten glass that is blown into shape on a rod.

handout—Information provided during sessions that pertains to the subject being discussed.

hand service—A method of service in which one banquet server is designated for two guests. The servers wear white gloves. When serving, they stand behind guests and hold two created plates. When the motion is given, all guests are served at the same time.

hand truck—A small hand-propelled implement with two wheels and two handles used for transporting small loads.

happenings—All nonintellectual-oriented meetings.

hard disk—A disk within a computer that serves as its permanent memory.

hardwall booth/stand—A stand or booth constructed with plywood or similar material, as opposed to a booth formed by drapery only.

hardware—Computer equipment.

HCCEA—See **Health Care Convention and Exhibitors Association**.

HDCD—See **high-definition compact disc**.

93

HDTV—See **high-definition television.**

head—1. A pan-tilt device on which a camera is mounted. 2. The part of a laser that includes the tube and emits the beam; the other part of a laser is its power supply, connected to the head by an umbilical cord. 3. The XY scan output of a laser; a laser projector may support one or more of these heads. 4. The video or audio device that records or reads the electronic signals from the videotape or audiotape.

head count—The total number of people attending an event.

header—1. A sign or other structure across the top of an exhibit; usually displays the company name. 2. The top of each page of a document.

headline—The phrase at the top of a newspaper or magazine article indicating the subject of the article.

headquarters hotel—A facility that serves as the center of operations where registration, general sessions, and the conference staff office are located.

headset—Headphones with a built-in microphone.

heads in beds—A term that refers to sleeping-room reservations in places of accommodation; also known as **bums in bed** in South Africa.

head table—1. The most visible area to seat VIPs and the master of ceremonies at a function. 2. The seating location for honored guests and/or presenters at events.

head tax—A fee charged to arriving and departing passengers in some foreign countries.

Health Care Convention and Exhibitors Association (HCCEA)—An organization whose members exhibit health care products and services or provide products and services to health care exhibitors.

HeNe (helium-neon)—A mixture of the two gases helium and neon inside a laser tube, which creates a warm red color.

herringbone setup—A configuration of tables and chairs angled in a V shape facing the head table, stage, or speaker; see **V-shaped setup** or **chevron.**

hidden charge—Unbudgeted expense.

highball glass—A tall glass used to serve an alcoholic mixed drink.

high-definition compact disc (HDCD)—An encode-decode process attempting to improve upon the sound quality provided by the original compact disc standard. CDs recorded in HDCD can be played back in a conventional CD player, and likewise, a CD player incorporating an HDCD decoder can play back non-HDCD-encoded discs.

high-definition television (HDTV)—A high-definition television standard developed in the United States as a digital system of high bandwidth and high resolution.

high jacker—A piece of equipment capable of elevating one or several people to a given height; also known as **cherry picker** or **scissor lift.**

high-key lighting—A lighting technique in which picture intensity creates limited dark areas.

high season—The period or season when traffic or volume is highest; also known as **peak season.**

hip—The external angle formed by two sloping sides of a tent roof when quarter poles are used as supports.

hipped end—A South African term for a pitched-roof shape at the end of a tent structure.

hiring cost—The price paid by the organizer to the owner of the meeting facilities.

historical report/guest history report—A report that gives the history of a group attending an event.

history—The record of an organization's previous meetings, usually containing information pertaining to the room block, actual room pickup, meeting space required, and food and beverage revenues generated.

hit—A single request from a Web browser for a single item from a Web server. Thus, in order for a Web browser to display a page that contains three graphics, four hits would occur at the server: one for the HTML page and one for each of the three graphics.

hold harmless—A contract clause that ensures a group or company will not be responsible in the event of a claim; also known as **disclaimer.**

holding-down bolts—A threaded brad that is cast into a concrete pad foundation and designed by a structural engineer to secure a tent to the concrete pad foundation with nuts and washers.

holiday event—A celebration marking an annual civic, religious, or legal holiday such as Independence Day or Christmas.

hollandaise sauce—A sauce of egg yolks, clarified butter, lemon juice, and spices. Served on vegetables or on eggs Benedict.

hollow circular setup—A circular configuration of tables with chairs placed at the perimeter and the center remaining empty.

hollow square setup—A configuration of tables in a square or rectangle with chairs at the perimeter and the center remaining empty.

hollowware—All sterling or silver-plated serving and decorative items that add to the ease of service and total look of the table.

hologram—A photographic effect using lasers to obtain a three-dimensional image on a flat surface.

homard—A lobster that has two front claws. Most lobster tails come from rock lobster or spiny lobster, which are actually a large variety of crawfish.

home page—The starting page a user "visits" on a World Wide Web local site on the Internet.

honorarium—A payment made to recognize an individual who has played a key role without the expectation of a fixed fee.

honorary—An appointment made without the expectation of full participation or payment of dues, often in recognition of expertise or past work.

honorary secretary—The member of a committee who is responsible for recording decisions and keeping records of discussions voluntarily.

horizontal bar—See **crossbar.**

horizontal show—A show in which the products or services being displayed represent all segments of an industry or profession.

horn loading—An acoustical effect achieved by placing the diaphragm of a driver element at the throat of a horn, producing a driver of greater efficiency.

hors d'oeuvres—Appetizers.

horseshoe setup—A configuration of tables in a U shape, with chairs placed outside and sometimes inside; also known as **open-U setup** or **U-shaped setup.**

hospitality desk/hospitality room—A meeting, registering, or gathering point for information.

hospitality suite—A room or suite used to entertain guests in which refreshments are served and exhibitor personnel and visitors socialize.

host—1. An organization, association, corporate body, city, country, or other such party that initiates an event to take place within or under its jurisdiction and its financial responsibility. 2. An individual or organization that issues an invitation for persons to attend an event. 3. Any computer that is a repository for services available to other computers on the network. It is quite common to have one host machine provide several services, such as the World Wide Web and Usenet.

host/hostess—An individual employed on a temporary basis to work on staff registration and information desks or in meeting rooms and to assist delegates in general.

host bar—A private bar at which drinks are paid for by a sponsor; also known as **open bar.** The opposite is a **cash bar.**

host country—The country that invites an event to take place within or under its jurisdiction.

host interview setup—See **Johnny Carson setup.**

hotel accommodation form—A hotel booking form provided for event participants, showing arrival and departure dates and types of rooms and rates; also known as **hotel reservation form.**

hotel classifications—The ranking of a hotel in terms of its amenities, facilities, level of service, and cost. Classifications include deluxe, luxury, first class, superior, standard, economy, and budget. Qualifications and terms may vary by country.

hotel reservation form—The booking form for reservation in a hotel for use by participants; also known as **hotel accommodation form.**

Hotel Sales and Marketing Association International (HSMAI)—An organization providing information and resources to its members, who are international sales marketing persons of hospitality firms and agencies, and those who provide products and services for hospitality sales and marketing professionals.

hot microphone/camera—A microphone or camera that is open and working.

hot spot—An undesirable concentration of light on one area of a slide or film.

hot-tag VIP—Luggage tagged for special handling.

house account—An expense account used for miscellaneous incidental expenses that are not chargeable to an event or another hotel account.

house board—A switch panel that controls all electrical fixtures.

house brand—A medium-priced or lower-priced brand of liquor used when a particular brand is not specified; also known as **well brand.**

house count—1. The number of sleeping rooms actually occupied during a particular night. 2. The number of individuals attending a specific event.

housekeeping—A facility department that provides daily maid and cleaning service in addition to irons, ironing boards, hair dryers, laundry, and other items as requested by guests.

housekeeping announcement—An announcement about schedule changes, locations of functions, or similar program information.

house lights—1. Electrical fixtures that provide light for the audience; also known as **auditorium lights.** 2. Room lighting that operates separately from stage lighting.

houseman—Service-staff member who handles function-room setup and teardown.

house manager—An individual in charge of the auditorium or the entire facility but not the stage production.

house plan—A diagram depicting the function space in a facility.

house specialty—See **signature dish.**

house wines—The standard wines offered by a facility usually at lower cost.

housing—The process of assigning hotel sleeping rooms to attendees.

housing bureau—A reservation office within a convention bureau that coordinates housing for groups.

HSMAI—See **Hotel Sales and Marketing Association International.**

HTML—See **hypertext markup language.**

HTTP—See **hypertext transport protocol.**

hub and spoke tour—A tour that utilizes a central destination with side trips of varying length to nearby destinations.

hue—A color or gradation of color.

human resources event—A conference or session used to motivate, educate, or develop human resources within an organization.

hummingbird—In pyrotechnics, a short tube packed with an explosive that propels the device, creating a strong jet flame in a straight pattern while emitting a buzzing sound.

hush puppies—Small, round, fried cornbread with onions and spices, usually served with fish.

HVAC—Heating, ventilation, and air-conditioning.

hybrid loudspeaker—A loudspeaker that utilizes both dynamic and planar components.

hypercardioid (car-di-oid) microphone—A unidirectional microphone with a tight, long-reaching pattern that accepts only a narrow angle of sound, enabling the pickup of distant voices for question-and-answer sessions, as well as for choirs; also known as **shotgun microphone.**

hypertext—A computer technology that can handle text, graphics, and sounds.

hypertext markup language (HTML)—The coding language used to create hypertext documents for use on the World Wide Web.

hypertext transport protocol (HTTP)—The protocol for moving files across the Internet.

Hz (hertz)—A unit of frequency equal to one cycle per second.

I

IAAM—See International Association of Assembly Managers.

IAB—See Internet Architecture Board.

IACC—See International Association of Conference Centers.

IACVB—See International Association of Convention and Visitors Bureaus.

IAEM—See International Association for Exhibit Management.

IAMC—See Institute of Association Management Companies.

IANA—See Internet Assigned Numbers Authority.

IATA—See International Association of Travel Agents.

IATSE—See International Alliance of Theatrical Stage Employees.

IBEW—See International Brotherhood of Electrical Workers.

ICC—See Interstate Commerce Commission.

ICCA—See International Congress and Convention Association.

ice carving—Decorative carving from large blocks of ice used to enhance a buffet or reception table.

ICPA—See Insurance Conference Planners Association.

I&D—See installation and dismantle.

idiot card—A handwritten placard that displays script to performers; see **cue card**.

idle time—See dead time.

ID sign—A placard that identifies a booth's or stand's exhibitor.

IEA—See International Exhibitors Association.

IFEA—See International Festival and Events Association.

IFSEA—See International Food Service Executives Association.

ILDA—See International Laser Display Association.

illumination—The lighting available in a hall, built into an exhibit, or available on a rental basis.

immigration—The process by which a government official verifies a person's passport, visa, or birth certificate.

Immigration Reform and Control Act (IRCA)—The United States law that prohibits employers from hiring people not legally entitled to work in the United States.

impact—The effect of a communications medium upon the audience.

impaired-vision seating—See **obstructed view.**

import—To bring international goods into a country. In international sales, the importer is usually the buyer or an intermediary who accepts and transmits goods to the buyer.

imported liquor—Beer, wine, and spirits not produced in the country where they are served.

import license—A document required and issued by governments authorizing the importation of goods.

Impressionism—The theory that productions should be concerned with artistic interpretation rather than with reality.

imprimatur—See **ready for press;** also known as the official identity of an organization or individual.

inaccessible—Design that does not meet the ADAAG minimum requirements and is either inappropriate, hazardous, or unusable by most people with disabilities.

inauguration ceremony—An official ceremony marking the induction of officers that often includes an address by a dignitary or a symbolic gesture.

inbound tour—A group of travelers whose trip originated in another city or country.

inbound tour operator—See **receptive operator/reception agency.**

incentive—A reward offered to stimulate greater effort.

incentive event—1. A corporate-sponsored meeting or trip to reward performance, motivate work effort, and create company loyalty; often built around a theme. 2. A celebratory event intended to showcase persons who meet or exceed sales or production goals.

incentive meeting/trip—A corporate-sponsored event that is offered to reward outstanding performance.

incentive travel—A corporate-paid trip offered as a prize to stimulate productivity.

incentive travel company—An agency that designs, sells, and coordinates incentive travel programs.

incident—A term used in liability coverage to describe any negligence, accident, or omission that may later result in a claim or lawsuit.

incidental entertainment—1. All expenses other than room charge and tax billed to a guest's account, such as room service and telephone calls. 2. See **sight act.**

incident report—See **accident report.**

in-city transport—The means of traveling within a city.

inclusive—Catering or accommodation rates that include gratuities and taxes.

inclusive cost—A quoted cost, often for food and beverage functions, to which no extra costs are to be added.

inclusive rate—1. The amount charged for a room, meals, and service charge; see **full American plan (FAP), full board,** or **modified American plan (MAP).** 2. Charges for food and beverages, including taxes, gratuities, and/or service charges.

inclusive tour—A group trip that includes costs, such as admission fees, transfers, and most gratuities.

indemnification—Insurance protection from a loss under stated circumstances or a reimbursement for liabilities.

indemnify—To pay the legal expenses of another because the payer caused the injury or expense.

indemnity—The replacement, repair, or payment of value of a loss. It is an agreement by which one party agrees to indemnify a second party for losses suffered by the second party.

indentured apprenticeship—Apprentice training under a contract that establishes the type and length of training and the compensation for each period of training.

independent contractor—A person contractually retained by another (other than as an employer) to perform certain specific tasks. The other person has no control over the independent contractor other than as provided in the contract. In the context of group travel, a tour manager or tour brochure designer/writer might be retained in this capacity.

independent show management—A for-profit exhibit management company.

independent tour—An unescorted tour sold through agents to individuals. For one price the client receives air travel, a hotel room, attraction admissions, and typically a car rental.

induction information—See **joining instructions.**

induction loop—The closed electric circuit within a building that relays sound to a hearing aid; also known as **inductive transmitter for hearing aids.**

inductive transmitter for hearing aids—See induction loop.

industrial show—An exhibit of related or similar products by various companies for the purposes of introducing new products, sales promotion, and increased visibility to the general public; also known as **exhibition, exposition,** or **trade show.**

industrial theater—See **corporate theater.**

informal dress—See **business attire.**

informal meeting—See **get-together.**

information bulletin—An update-information sheet used for promotional purposes; also known as **newsletter.**

information desk—A stand at which an official gives information.

information kit—See **conference pack/kit.**

infringement—1. The use of floor space outside the exclusive booth or stand area. 2. The use of copyright without permission.

inherent flameproof—Material that is permanently flame-resistant without chemical treatment; for theatrical and stage use.

in-house—A term referring to corporate, event, and travel services located within and staffed by a company.

in-house services—Those services (audiovisual, florist, etc.) available within an event facility.

inland bill of lading—A bill of lading (B/L) used in transporting goods overland to the exporter's international carrier.

in-line booth—Exhibit space with exhibit booths or stands on either side and back; also known as **inside booth.**

in-plant—A term referring to corporate travel services located within a company, but staffed by an outside travel agency.

inquiry cards—Requests collected from exhibit attendees or readers of trade magazines for further information about products and services.

insert—1. A matted or framed portion of a picture. 2. An additional shot added to a scene at a later time. 3. Additional promotional material included in a mailing or publication.

inset—A small scene set inside a larger one.

inside booth/stand—An exhibit space surrounded by other booths or stands at both sides and the back; also known as **in-line booth.**

inspection trip—See **familiarization trip (FAM).**

installation—The activity of setting up exhibit booths or stands and related services according to instructions and drawings.

installation and dismantle (I&D)—Installation and dismantle of an exhibit (setup/teardown), generally performed by an exhibitor-appointed contractor.

installation contractor—The firm or individual responsible for supervision and coordination of installation and dismantle labor for an exhibitor. May be either an official firm (as designated by show management) or an independent firm (hired directly by the exhibitor).

institute—An in-depth instructional meeting comprised of attendees from two or more countries and located outside the national borders of attending countries or within the borders of one of the participant nations; see **foreign meeting** or **international meeting.**

instruction booklet—See **packing drawing.**

instructions for poster presenters—The guidelines for presenting a poster.

instructions for speakers—The guidelines for those presenting an oral presentation.

instructions for the preparation of papers—See **guidelines for authors.**

insurance—A contractual relationship that exists when one party, for a consideration, agrees to reimburse another party for loss to property, life, or person caused by specified contingencies such as fire, accident, or death.

Insurance Conference Planners Association (ICPA)—An organization providing information, education, and resources to professional conference planners in the insurance industry and those who supply products and services to insurance conference planners.

in sync—The concurrence of two or more audio and/or visual events.

intangibility—The aspect of a service that cannot be examined physically before purchase.

integrated amplifier—A single unit containing both a preamplifier and a power amplifier.

integrated marketing—The unification and coordination of marketing activities between partners to complete marketing exchanges.

integrated meeting—A meeting that forms part of a larger event.

integrated seminar—A seminar that forms part of a larger event.

Integrated Services Digital Network (ISDN)—A way to move more data over existing telephone lines. ISDN provides speeds of roughly 128,000 bits per second over regular phone lines. In practice, most people are limited to 56,000 or 64,000 bits per second.

intelligent lighting—A remote-controlled theatrical lighting instrument whose beam can spot or go to flood, vary from bright to dim, move horizontally (pan) and vertically (tilt), and change color. All of these operations can be computer programmed to allow for very rapid and precise changes. A series of gobo patterns also are built into the fixture.

interactive exhibit—An exhibit that involves the visitor in a proactive way.

interactive marketing—A form of two-way marketing communication that utilizes the World Wide Web, the Internet, an on-line service, CD-ROMs, or interactive television.

interactive response—A system that enables the audience to respond at their seats to prepared questions by means of a multifunction keypad. Responses are fed to a computer, which tabulates them and displays the results graphically on a projection screen.

intercity transport—The means of traveling between two cities.

intercom—An audio system permitting two-way local communication, with a microphone and a loudspeaker at each end.

intercommunication system—An intercommunication system using headphones and microphones for communication between adjoining or nearby studios or offices; also known as **two-way loudspeaker.**

intercontinental meeting—See **international meeting.**

interest—Any money paid for the use of money that has been borrowed.

interest-free loan—The money received by loan to be refunded not subject to any interest charges.

interline connection—An airline connection that involves transferring from one airline to another and baggage is automatically transferred; also known as **off-line connection.**

interlock—The synchronization of two or more sound and/or picture sources.

intermediate carrier—A carrier that transports a passenger or piece of baggage as part of an interline movement, but on which neither the point of origin nor destination is located.

intermezzo—The break or interval before the entrée during a meal. A sorbet is often served as the intermezzo to cleanse the palate.

intermodal tour—A tour using several forms of transportation such as plane, motor coach, cruise line, and railroad to create a diversified and efficient tour package.

International Alliance of Theatrical Stage Employees (IATSE) (eye-ah-tzee)—A United States trade union representing professional theatrical stagehands.

International Association for Exhibit Management (IAEM)—A trade association that provides information, education, and resources to members representing exposition management and managers worldwide, and those who provide services and products for this industry.

International Association of Assembly Managers (IAAM)—An organization providing information and resources for its members, who represent auditorium managers, arena stadium managers, and managers of other event facilities and those who provide services and products for this industry.

International Association of Conference Centers (IACC)—A trade association whose members are conference centers worldwide.

International Association of Convention and Visitors Bureaus (IACVB)—A trade association providing resources, education, and information to members, who represent convention and visitors bureaus worldwide and those who provide products and services for conference centers.

International Association of Travel Agents (IATA) (eye-ah-ta)—A trade association providing information and resources to travel agents all over the world who deal with international trade and those who provide products and services for this industry.

International Brotherhood of Electrical Workers (IBEW)—A United States–based professional union of electrical workers.

International Congress and Convention Association (ICCA)—An organization providing information and resources to members involved in the coordinating of congresses and in various categories (such as hotels, congress centers, airlines, and professional congress organizers) within the travel and hospitality industry.

International Exhibitors Association (IEA)—An organization providing information, education, and resources to members, who are exhibitors and those who provide products and services for the industry.

International Festival and Events Association (IFEA)—An organization providing information, education, and resources to members, who are festival and event managers and those who provide products and services for this industry.

International Food Service Executives Association (IFSEA)—A trade association providing information, education, and resources to members in the food industry and those who provide products and services for this industry.

International Laser Display Association (ILDA)—An organization providing information, education, and resources to members, who are involved in laser design and production and those who provide products and services to this industry.

international meeting—1. International/intercontinental: A meeting of an organization with multinational membership that is available to meet on more than one continent. 2. International/continental: A meeting of an organization with multinational membership that is available to meet on only one continent. 3. International/regional: A meeting of an organization with multinational membership that is available to meet in only a given region of one continent. 4. See **foreign meeting** or **institute.**

international sales agent—An individual or firm that serves as the foreign representative of a domestic supplier and seeks sales abroad for the supplier.

International Special Events Society (ISES) (eye-sis)—An organization providing education, certification, resources, networking, and information to its members, who are professional event managers and those who provide services and products to this industry.

Internet—An electronic network connecting millions of computers with information technology via a computer network consisting of two or more smaller networks that can communicate with each other.

Internet address—The name or the number of a host machine that identifies it on the Internet. The mailbox is usually one's user name and location.

Internet Architecture Board (IAB)—Formerly the Internet Activities Board, this organization oversees, with the help of the Internet Assigned Numbers Authority, standards and development for the Internet and administrates the Internet subtree in the global tree in which all networking knowledge is stored.

Internet Assigned Numbers Authority (IANA)—An Internet organization responsible for assigning values for networks, attributes, etc. Operated by the University of Southern California Information Sciences Institute, it verifies that the same identifier values are not assigned to two different entities.

Internet Relay Chat (IRC)—A service on the Internet that extends talk capabilities to allow multiparty conversations.

Internet service provider (ISP)—An organization that provides access to the Internet in some form, usually for a fee.

Internet Society (ISOC)—An international organization that promotes the use of the Internet for communication and collaboration.

interpretation/interpreting—An oral translation from one language to another.

interpretation in relay—An oral translation utilizing two interpreters because the first is not a master of the language and requires another to make the final interpretation; also known as **relay interpreting.**

interpreter's booth/stand—A soundproof cabin in which an interpreter works.

interruption of the meeting—A temporary break in a meeting for a specific and unprogrammed reason.

interval—See **recess.**

in-the-clay decoration—Designs that are cut or printed on moist clay.

in-the-glaze decoration—Decorating done by coloring the glaze itself.

in the round—A stage technique where the stage is placed in the center with the audience on all four sides.

intranet—An Internet system used within a single organization.

introductory offer—A special price offered to stimulate interest in a new or improved product or for first-time buyers.

inventory—1. The total amount of furniture and equipment available for a show. 2. A detailed list of supplies owned by an organization.

inventory loss—Any waste, including theft (both internal and external), damaged product, lost product, slippage, spoilage, or other cause, that prevents the sale or use of an item.

inventory restrictions—The fact that services cannot be inventoried and can be used at only one specific time.

investment spending—Increased advertising or promotion expenditures for a product or service, typically funded by temporary reductions in the profit rate in the expectation of future increases in sales and profits.

invitation call—Asking the celebrity or speaker to come onstage from the audience to make a presentation.

invitation program—A provisional program, which sometimes incorporates a call for papers and may include information on location, participants, agenda, and accommodations.

invited paper—See **guest speech.**

invited speaker—1. A person invited to deliver a speech whose fee, travel, and housing expenses are paid. 2. A prospective speaker who has not been confirmed.

invocation—A prayer given at the beginning of an event function. The benediction is given at the end.

involuntary upgrade—An airline term used when a passenger is moved to a higher class at no charge.

IRC—See **Internet Relay Chat.**

IRCA—See **Immigration Reform and Control Act.**

iris—1. A circular lens diaphragm found in cameras that regulates the entry of light onto film. 2. A variable aperture (opening of lens).

iris fold napkin—A brightly colored floral napkin fold used for a sophisticated brunch, a special luncheon, or an informal dinner.

Irish stew—Lamb stew with dumplings. Traditionally served on St. Patrick's Day.

iris shutter—A manually operated shutter for varying the size of a light beam emitted from a lighting instrument.

ironstone—A type of earthenware that is thicker and heavier than china, is opaque, and may absorb moisture when chipped.

ISDN—See **Integrated Services Digital Network.**

ISES—See **International Special Events Society.**

island booth/stand—Four or more exhibit spaces with aisles on all four sides; see **freestanding.**

ISOC—See Internet Society.

ISP—See Internet service provider.

itinerary—A detailed schedule of a visit or tour.

J

jacket—A clear plastic covering used to protect slides or badges.

jackknife stage—Two portable stages with narrow ends parallel to foots and on pivots that permit quick changes of scenery.

janitorial service—A service offered to exhibitors for cleaning booths or stands and for general cleaning for event sites.

jardiniere—Diced, mixed vegetables.

Java—A network-oriented programming language designed for writing computer programs that can be safely downloaded to a computer through the Internet.

jigger—A standard measure of liquor equaling 30ml, approximately 1½ ounces.

jigger spout—An adapter for a liquor bottle that delivers a premeasured amount, usually 1½ ounces.

job description—A list of duties that make up a particular job position.

job foreman—A person who is in charge of specific projects, such as loading or unloading equipment.

job specification—A list of qualities, such as work experience and skill.

job tender—See **bid manual/specifications.**

Johnny Carson setup—An arrangement for a panel discussion with the moderator's desk perpendicular to the panelists' chairs; also known as **host interview setup.**

johnson bar—A long-handled wooden pry bar with a metal tip and wheels used in freight handling.

joining instructions—The document or letter sent to all registered delegates confirming that they are fully registered for the event and giving details of where and when they register their attendance, confirmation of accommodation, booking for special events, etc; also known as **confirmation letter** or **induction information.**

joint agreement—Union contract covering more than one employer and a union, more than one union and an employer, or a number of employers and a number of unions.

joint fares—Through-fare for travel on two or more airlines.

Joint Photographic Experts Group (JPEG)—A computer format for image files. JPEG is preferred to the GIF format for photographic images as opposed to simple line art or simple logo art in computers.

joint venture—A partnership in which all the activities involved with a project are shared between two or more organizations.

jones plug—Theatrical term for a multiprong electrical disconnect.

journeyman—A worker who has satisfactorily completed an apprenticeship in a skilled trade.

JPEG—See **Joint Photographic Experts Group.**

Jughead—A service on the Internet that helps make certain Gopher searches easier and more manageable.

julienne—Vegetables cut in long thin slices.

junction box—A distribution point for electrical power.

jurisdiction—1. The jobs that may be performed by a specific labor union. 2. The locality where a contractual dispute is decided.

jurisdictional dispute—A conflict between unions concerning the right to control certain jobs in a particular trade or industry.

jurisdictional strike—A work stoppage as a result of a jurisdictional dispute.

justified margin—See **flush.**

justified type—A style of type set with both margins adjusted with type and spacing to be equal; also known as **flush.**

K

K—See **Kelvin.**
KD—See **knockdown.**
keg—A bulk container for beer or wine, which affords better pricing.
Kelvin (K)—1. A scale used to measure absolute temperature with zero equal to -459.4 degrees Fahrenheit. 2. A scale on which the unit of measure equals the centigrade degree and according to which absolute zero is 0 degrees, the equivalent of -213.16 degrees centigrade.
kelvin box/kelvin light—See **light table/kelvin box/kelvin light.**
keyboard—1. A set or row of keys in a keyed machine or instrument. 2. A computer keyboard.
key light—The principal source of illumination on a subject or area.
keynote speaker—A speaker who sets forth the theme or tone for an event.
keystoning—A distortion of a projected image.
kickback—A less-than-legitimate payment made in return for influencing a buying or hiring decision.
kick base—Base molding or band added to a structure to absorb marring caused by brooms, mops, etc.; also known as a **toe base.**
king pole—The center pole used in a peg-and-pole tent in South Africa.
king room—A room with a king-size bed suitable for one or two persons.
king-size bed—A large bed usually measuring 76" x 80" (190cm x 200cm). A long king-size bed measures 76" x 84".
kiosk—1. A small enclosure for ticket sales, information, etc. 2. A freestanding pavilion or lightweight structure with one or more open sides.
kit—See **service kit.**
klieg light—A slang term taken from the brand name for a variety of outdated spotlights.
knockdown (KD)—An unassembled exhibit requiring on-site assembly.
kosher—Food that is prepared according to Jewish dietary laws.

kreplach—Jewish ravioli.

krypton—The gas placed inside a laser tube that creates a cool red color or a mixture of red, green, blue, and yellow.

L

label—1. A message fixed to a unit container of a product shipping and contact information. 2. A brand name used for conference title, venue name, and logo in South Africa.

labor—A term that refers to contracted workers who perform services.

labor call—A method of securing union employees through the local union.

labor cost percentage—The total payroll and related expenses divided by total revenue.

labor desk—An on-site area from which service personnel are dispatched at an event such as an exposition.

labor policy—The principles established by a company to govern its dealings with its employees.

labor relations—Dealings between an employer and its employees or their representatives concerning matters of mutual interest.

lace line—The joint or seam between roof sections where one is joined to another. Tents are generally made up of several roof sections fastened together with heavy zippers or jackknife-type lacing through grommets.

lagniappe—Creole term for something extra.

laminate—See **credentials.**

lamp—A light source for a projector or lighting instrument.

lamp life—The estimated hours of lamp's life.

LAN—See **local area network.**

lanai—A hotel or resort room with a patio or balcony overlooking a garden or water.

lance—In pyrotechnics, a short paper tube packed with an explosive that displays a 2" flame of color for 30 to 45 seconds.

land arrangements—See **ground arrangements.**

land operator—A company that provides local services, transfers, and sightseeing guides; see **receptive operator/reception agency.**

landscape (horizontal)—A sign whose width is larger than its height.

langostino—Spanish word for prawn (jumbo shrimp).

langouste—French word for spiny lobster (giant crawfish).

langoustine—French word for prawn (jumbo shrimp).

lanyard—A type of string or band worn around the neck that holds the exhibition or conference registrant's badge and/or badge holder.

lapel microphone—See **lavaliere microphone.**

laptop—See **portable computer.**

laser—A device that produces an intense ray of deeply colored, bright light, about ⅛" thick as it emerges from the laser. The tube is filled with a noble gas, which determines its emitted color(s) when excited electrically. The construction of the laser tube causes the light to become parallel, pure, and intense.

laser pointer—See **electric pointer/laser pointer.**

late charge—See **after-departure charge.**

late night—An evening on which the exhibition will remain open later than usual.

late registration—A booking received after a stated deadline and usually imposing a penalty fee.

lavaliere microphone—A portable monodirectional microphone that hooks around the speaker's neck or is attached to the speaker's clothing with a clip. It may be wireless or wired and is usually not visible to the audience. It frees the speaker's hands and allows for movement; also known as **lapel, neck/necklace, pendant,** or **clip microphone.**

layout—An artist's or designer's description of how a printed piece will look.

LC—See **letter of credit.**

LCD projection television—Front-projection television that projects liquid crystal display pixels from a single lens onto a screen.

LCL—Less than carload.

LCM—Least common multiple.

L&D—Loss and damage.

leader—A utility tape added to an audiotape or film to create a visual starting point.

leadman—An employee who sets the pace for a group working on the same job or as a team.

lead time—The time prior to a meeting or other key event during which work is to be completed.

leaflet—See **brochure.**

le café table—See **cabaret table.**

lectern—A stand upon which a speaker may rest notes or books. A lectern may be a piece of furniture that rests on the floor, a standing lectern, or a tabletop model that is one-half the size of a standing lectern and rests on a table.

lectern microphone—An amplifying device that is attached to a lectern; see **cardioid microphone.**

lecture—An informative or instructional speech.

leg—1. A component that holds the roof of a tent to the ground. 2. A curtain along the side of a stage; also known as **tormentor.**

legal connection—A minimum time regulated by the Federal Aviation Administration (FAA) to leave one flight and board another.

leg extension—A component that makes a tent leg longer.

legit—Popular abbreviation for the legitimate stage.

leisure service—Services associated with the organization of activities during free time for relaxation.

Leko—A slang term derived from Lekolite, a lighting instrument manufactured by Strand Lighting, and commonly used for any ellipsoidal reflector spotlight. A Leko contains a movable lens that enables the beam to be focused with either a hard or soft edge. A group of internal shutters allows the beam to be cropped, and many Lekos have an adjustable iris that allows a variation of the beam diameter. Lekos can accommodate a pattern holder containing a gobo for projecting a specific image.

lenticular—A type of screen surface used for front projection, characterized by tiny corrugations or grooves molded or embossed into the screen surface.

lessee—An individual or organization to whom a lease is given.

less than truckload (LTL)—Rates applicable when the quantity of freight is less than the volume of the truckload minimum weight.

letter of agreement—1. A document outlining proposed services, space, or products that becomes binding upon written approval by both parties; see **contract** or **commitment.** 2. A document used in lieu of a formal contract that lists services, foods, beverages, etc.

letter of credit (LC)—A document issued by a bank per instructions from a buyer of goods, authorizing the seller to draw a specified sum of money under specified terms.

letter of intent—A letter confirming intent to use a supplier's service, usually issued before the formal contract.

level—See **gain.**

liability—A legal responsibility to make good a loss or claim.

liability insurance—A type of insurance that provides coverage in the event an organization becomes liable to another.

liability laws—Laws protecting individuals from physical injury or property damage caused by a party behaving in an intentional, negligent, or reckless manner.

liable—Legally responsible.

liaison interpreter—An individual interpreting a conversation between two or more persons from one or more foreign languages into his mother tongue and vice versa.

licensing—A business arrangement in which the manufacturer of a product grants permission to some other group or individual to manufacture that product in return for specified royalties or other payment.

lifetime customer value—The total amount of money that a customer will spend at one company for the entire length of the business exchange.

lift truck—see forklift.

light box—An enclosure with lighting and a translucent face made of plastic or glass.

lightface—A typeface distinguished by light, thin lines.

lighting—A service offered by a production or lighting company for lights or special effects for stage, theater, or venue.

lighting control console—A desktype housing used to contain the controls required for adjusting production lighting; also known as **master control.**

lighting desk—See **console.**

lighting director—An individual who designs the lighting, directs placement of lighting equipment, and calls lighting cues on-site.

lighting grid—A structure used to support lights and electrical outlets.

light organ—An electronic device that allows sound waves to determine the color or intensity of lighting.

light table/kelvin box/kelvin light—An illuminated glass-covered table used for viewing and editing slides, transparencies, and art-layout graphics.

limitation of speaking time—The duration of time accorded to the speakers.

limited distribution—Distribution of a product to one or more specific geographical areas rather than nationwide.

limiter—See **effects device.**

limits of liability—The maximum amount an insurance company agrees to pay in the case of loss and, therefore, the most an insured may collect by the terms of the policy.

line doubler—An electronic device to enhance a video picture by doubling the number of broadcast lines per frame.

line drawings—Blueprints from which sets and set pieces may be constructed without reference to any other drawings or specifications.

linen—A collective term for tablecloths and napkins; also known as **napery.**

line of sight—An unobstructed line of vision from audience to stage; also known as **sight line.**

lines—Speeches in a play.

line stage preamplifier—The stage of a preamplifier that accommodates all sources other than a turntable.

line switch—An electrical on/off switch used directly in wiring to control, by make or break, the flow of current.

linings—Internal decorative cladding in a tent, also known as **draping.**

lining-up—See **cueing.**

Linnebach projector—A large metal box with a concentrated light source for projecting pictures from a gelatine or glass slide.

lip microphone—A microphone designed for use in contact with the lips of the speaker.

liqueur—A spirit- or wine-based liquor highly sweetened and flavored with an aromatic substance; also known as **cordial.**

liqueur cart—A rolling cart that includes a selection of cordials; usually passed around after dinner.

liquidated damages—The amount of money that the parties agree to pay in the event of a breach of contract.

list of exhibitors—A list of exhibiting firms, usually indicating location, and which may be arranged alphabetically, by category, or booth/stand, and listing personnel in attendance.

list of participants—A register of delegates and accompanying persons attending an event.

listserv—A mailing list that automatically forwards messages to one's e-mail address and allows for communication between listserv members.

liter—A metric unit of measurement equal to approximately 33.8 ounces or 1 quart and used to package spirits and wines.

lit rack—A device used to hold literature or brochures.

live operation—The operation of a laser device by a trained operator from a real-time control device.

load factor—1. The maximum weight allowed by a venue for hanging equipment from a ceiling or for supporting floor equipment. 2. An average number of airline or other transportation seats occupied.

load-in—See **move-in**.

load in/load out—The scheduled time for a crew to load or unload equipment.

loading dock—The area on premises where goods are received.

loadlock—A metal brace to secure partial loads within trailers and railcars.

load-out—See **move-out**.

lobby—A public area that serves as an entrance or waiting area.

lobster scope—A spotlight-effect machine producing a flicker of light.

local—The organization of employees in one area or a group of companies, chartered by and affiliated with a national or international union.

local advertising—1. Advertising placed by local businesses. 2. Advertising placed at rates available to local businesses.

local area network (LAN)—A computer network limited to the immediate area, such as the same building or a floor of a building.

local beer/wine—Beer or wine produced and served locally.

local event—A function that draws its audience primarily from the local market.

local host—A group of people who carry out strategies and policies established for the organization of an event; also known as **organizing committee**.

local media—Communications media whose audiences are primarily drawn from the same locality and media.

lockout—1. Refusal by a facility to allow guests access to their rooms. 2. Refusal by owners to allow employees to return to their jobs following a strike.

lockup—1. A storage area that can be secured. 2. A jail or temporary holding area for suspected criminals at a venue.

logo—1. A symbol identifying an organization or event. 2. A trademark used exclusively by one company or association.

logotype—A brand name, publication title, or the like, presented in a special lettering style or typeface and used in the manner of a trademark.

loop—1. A closed electric circuit. 2. A continuous audio or video program.

loose jig—A removable support in a shipping case.

loss leader—An item offered by a retailer at cost or less than cost to attract customers; also known as **price leader.**

lost business—A business or contract not secured.

lost-property office—A stand or office where lost items may be found.

louvers—Concentric rings of thin metal strips fitted to the front of a projector to cut off all but the straight beam of light; also known as **spill rings and baffles.**

lowboy—A type of truck that can be adapted for picking up loads at ground level.

lowercase—Small letters, as distinguished from capital letters.

low-key lighting—Lighting in which picture intensity produces limited bright areas.

low season—The time of year when travel and hotel rates are at their lowest.

low voltage—A term applied to currents of 24 volts or less that must be transformed from normal 110-volt input.

LTL—See **less than truckload.**

lumina—A nebulous effect produced by transmitting laser light through a textured plastic.

luminaire—A theater spotlight.

luncheon—A noonday meal, sometimes accompanied by speeches or presentations.

luncheon plate—A plate used for the main course at a luncheon.

lyonnaise—Cooked with onions.

M

macédoine—A mixture of vegetables or fruits.

macroscale—Duplication larger than life-size.

magnetic planar loudspeaker—A planar loudspeaker employing a large panel transducer onto which a copper wire has been attached, thus acting as a distributed coil across the surface.

magnetic sound—A sound that is recorded on magnetic tape and may be incorporated into a film.

mail and messages—A place where mail and messages are kept or transmitted; also known as **message center.**

mailing list—A list of prospective attendees, prepared for direct mail solicitation.

mail-in premium—A premium obtained by mailing in a suitable response to the manufacturer or distributor, with or without money.

main tent—A room or hall where business sessions and entertainment productions are held.

maître d'—The floor manager or head waiter at a restaurant or catered function; also known as **banquet captain/banquet manager** or **supervisor.**

majolica—A type of earthenware that is tin-glazed.

make ready—To mount and prepare artwork for shooting or reproduction.

make-work practices—Union practices for spreading work by limiting production or by requiring employment of more workers than necessary for a particular job.

management committee—See **executive committee.**

management consultant—An agent retained by an event organization to provide ideas regarding the manner in which the organization's operations, plans, or personnel may be improved.

management prerogatives—Rights and powers essential to the operation of a business, such as hiring, production methods, and the like, that management claims are outside the scope of collective bargaining and over which management maintains authority and responsibility.

manager—See **banquet captain/banquet manager.**

manager on duty (MOD)—The person at a hotel or conference center who is currently in charge; also known as **duty manager.**

managing director—The head executive officer of an event company.

Manhattan clam chowder—Red clam soup made with tomatoes.

manifest—An official listing of all passengers and/or cargo aboard a transportation vehicle or vessel.

manpower agency—A firm specializing in providing day-labor or casual workers; also known as **temporary labor** or **extra-man.**

MAP—See **modified American plan.**

march—A demonstration wherein an organization or group walks a specific route and/or distance to promote a cause and bring attention to specific issues.

margin—1. The difference between the cost and the selling price of a product. 2. The blank space around the text in a document.

marine insurance—Insurance covering the loss or damage of goods at sea that compensates the owner of the goods for losses sustained from fire, shipwreck, piracy, and various other causes, but excludes losses that can be legally recovered from the carrier.

marker board—A white surface on which washable color markers are used.

market—The potential consumer group likely to be interested in or need a service or product.

marketable securities—The securities held as short-term investments that are intended to be converted to cash within 12 months of the balance sheet date.

marketing—The activity of research, planning, and coordinating strategies to sell products or services.

marketing flights—A series of advertising or public relations events all relating to the same marketing effort or theme.

marketing mix—The combination of product, place, price, and promotion that most effectively satisfies customer needs.

marketing public relations—An open two-way communication between a company and its stakeholders that directly promotes marketing efforts and results.

market profile—A summary of the characteristics of a market, including information on typical purchasers and competitors, and often general information on the economy and retailing patterns of the area.

market research—The gathering of marketing information about a target audience's motivations, desires, and needs in order to design an advertising campaign that is appropriate for the audience.

market response—The sales consequences of stimulation provided by marketing spending.

market segment—A categorization of an organization or business by professional discipline or primary area of interest for the purpose of sales analysis or assignment.

market subgroup—A market that piggybacks on another market.

marks—See **spike marks.**

markup—1. The difference between the cost and the selling price of a given product. 2. The difference between the net rate charged by a tour operator, hotel, or other supplier and the retail selling price of the service. Generally markup is a percentage of the net rate rather than a fixed amount, as in a 20 percent markup on the net.

marquee—A long and narrow tent without sides used for sheltering walkways, defining an entry to a tent, or to seat guests. In Australia, Great Britain, and other countries this term means a tent used for parties or exhibitions.

marshalling yard—A holding area where trucks check in and wait for further instructions before delivering freight to the exhibit hall.

mascarpone cheese—A rich Italian cream cheese, often used in tiramisu.

mask—1. A scenic tarp used to obscure undesirable views from the audience. 2. To partially cover the aperture of a laser projector to circumscribe the laser field to conform to a screen area and to trap the laser output if it strays from its intended path, protecting the audience from accidental exposure to direct laser scanning.

masking drapes—Drapes used to cover storage, backstage, and other unsightly areas.

mass marketing—1. The process of using one marketing strategy to market a product to all market segments. 2. Large-scale marketing.

master—The original, best quality, and final edited version of an audiotape, videotape, or fill recording of a production; also known as **master tape.**

master account—An organization's account to which approved facility expenses can be charged during a designated stay.

master bill—All items contracted by the operator and supplier, to be paid by the operator.

master contract—See **blanket contract.**

master control—See **lighting control console.**

master key—A key that will open all function rooms, guest rooms, and facility areas.

master monitor—A video monitor that shows only the picture being presented for broadcast.

master of ceremonies (MC)—An individual who introduces persons or elements of an event; see **compère, moderator,** and **toastmaster.**

master tape—See **master.**

matte—A lusterless surface.

matte white—A type of screen surface used for front projection, characterized by a rough surface free from shine or highlights.

matzo ball soup—A Jewish dish with large dumplings.

MC—See **master of ceremonies.**

measurement ton—A space measurement, usually 40 cubic feet or 1 cubic meter. The cargo is assessed a certain rate for every 40 cubic feet of space it occupies; also known as **cargo ton/freight ton.**

medallion—A small, round piece of meat.

media center—The area where all media communications are located at the event.

media contact person—A person who is responsible for identifying key news media and key personnel within the media, making contact with the key people, and handling all logistical details concerning media inquiries and activities.

mediation—A third-party attempt to reconcile the differences between disputing parties by finding some middle ground on which the controversy may be voluntarily settled.

medical meeting—A meeting focused on health care, medical research industries, or medical professions.

medical service—The first-aid provider at an event.

meet and greet—A prepurchased service for meeting and greeting a client upon arrival in a city, usually at the airport, pier, or rail station, and assisting the client with entrance formalities, collecting baggage, and obtaining transportation.

meeting—An assembly of individuals gathered to discuss items of mutual interest or engage in professional development through learning activities.

meeting announcement—A leaflet or brochure announcing an upcoming event or the preliminary information about a future meeting.

meeting date—The date when a meeting takes place.

meeting duration—The length of time from the opening session to the closing session. Additional days for optional excursions are not included.

meeting frequency—The frequency in which the event takes place, i.e., annually, biannually, biennially.

meeting point—A meeting space in a venue for individual appointments with delegates.

Meeting Professionals International (MPI)—An organization providing education, representation, information, and resources to its members, who plan meetings or provide services and products to meeting planners.

meeting site—The building and environment area where a meeting takes place.

meeting termination—A provision in a contract setting forth events that allow parties to terminate the contract if they occur.

meeting theme—The fundamental theme of a meeting, which is proposed by the organizer with reference to the title of the meeting.

meeting tour/conference tour—A tour designed around a specific meeting or conference for the participants.

meet-the-press setup—A panel setup with the questioners placed opposite the guest panelists and moderator.

mega event—See **hallmark.**

melamine—A hard, durable plastic usually found in bright colors for lightweight, inexpensive dinnerware.

melodrama—An exaggerated, romantic, exciting, and improbable play.

merchandise gift—See **giveaway.**

mercury vapor light—A source of ultraviolet rays.

mesclun—Field greens for salad.

message board—A board on which messages are displayed and often includes communication among attendees of an event.

message center—See **mail and messages.**

message repeater—A device with a recorded tape in cartridge form, used to repeat a recording continuously or on call.

method of payment—The method of settling a bill or account; also known as **mode of payment.**

meunière—Sautéed in butter with lemon and parsley and seasonings.

microphone—1. A basic element of all sound systems. It causes sound waves to be generated or modulated using electrical current and transmits or records sound; also known as a **mike/mic.** 2. An instrument that converts sound into electrical signals and is the primary input for all sound systems.

microscale—Duplication smaller than life-size.

microswitch—A miniature circuit breaker that is opened and closed mechanically.

middle of the road (MOR)—A mixture of contemporary, top 40, and soft music.

midget microphone—A small microphone.

midrange—The drive element in a loudspeaker responsible for reproducing the midband of an audible signal, typically operating anywhere between 350Hz and 3kHz. Also refers to those specific frequencies.

mike/mic—See **microphone.**

military meeting—A meeting attended by members of the armed forces or suppliers to the armed forces.

minestrone—Italian vegetable soup.

mini-Italian lights—See **B lights.**

minimum—The smallest number of food and/or beverages, products, or service to be served at an event. A surcharge may be added to the client's bill if the minimum is not reached.

minimum land package—The minimum tour expressed in terms of cost and ingredients that must be purchased to qualify a passenger for an airline-inclusive tour or contract-bulk-inclusive tour fare. Such packages usually must include lodging for a certain number of nights, car rental, and/or other specified ingredients such as sightseeing or entertainment. The minimum rate for the combined airfares and ground package is often expressed as a percentage (often 100 percent or 110 percent) of the lowest regular fare for the air travel scheduled.

minutes—A formal written record of a meeting; also known as **record.**

mirror ball—A large sphere with small mirrors fixed over its surface and that revolves when electrified. When a spotlight is lit and focused upon the ball, it creates a mass of small light beams that swirl around the room.

mirrors—Reflecting material used for laser lighting. Scanner mirrors are tiny, lightweight, and heat resistant and used to reflect and guide laser light to create a graphic. Beam-sculpture mirrors are larger and mounted at a distance from the laser projector so that beams can be bounced off them to create beam sculptures.

misconnect—A term used to indicate that insufficient time is allowed for connection between planes, as regulated by the FAA.

miter—The joint created when two pieces of material cut at equal angles butt together to form a corner.

mix—1. Visual: a repetitive and alternating projection of two different slides used to add emphasis. 2. Sound: an adjustment of each input for volume and sound quality.

mixer—1. An audio engineer, the technician who operates the console controlling the audio mix and level of a production; also known as **operator sound.** 2. In audiovisual recording, a device from which sound from all microphones feeds into one system and required if three or more microphones are used in one room. 3. The sound recording or the reproducing system or the device, capable of handling two or more inputs in conjunction with a common output, that is used to control the balance of all dialogue, music, and sound effects to be recorded; also known as **console** or **preamp desk.** 4. A split that goes with an alcoholic beverage.

mixing—The technique of combining audio and visual sources.

mixing board/mixing desk—See **sound board.**

mixing of foldback sound—A sound desk used to mix backline equipment for a live band.

mobile—An art form suspended or balance with freedom of movement.

mobile simultaneous interpreting system—A system that can be transported and set up at any venue without the need for built-in stands/booths or electric circuits.

mobility impairment—The inability to ambulate without great difficulty due to a variety of reasons. An individual who is mobility impaired may use a wheelchair, a walker, crutches, leg braces, etc.

mock-up—A full-scale model of a proposed structure.

MOD—See **manager on duty.**

model—1. An object made in miniature representing something to be made. 2. An individual in an exhibition that demonstrates a product, greets guests, etc.

modem (modulator demodulator)—A device that connects to a computer and to a phone line and allows the computer to talk to other computers through the phone system.

mode of payment—See **method of payment.**

moderator—A person who presides over sessions, panels, and forums; also known as **compère, discussion leader, master of ceremonies (MC),** and **toastmaster.**

modified American plan (MAP)—A room rate that includes two meals, usually breakfast and dinner although lunch is sometimes substituted for dinner; also known as **demipension** or **half board.**

modular—Structural elements that are interchangeable with maximum flexibility in arrangement and size.

modular exhibit—An exhibit constructed with interchangeable components.

modular panels—Partition units (walls, doors, frames, etc.) in standard sizes used for building booths or stands in the sizes desired.

module—A repeating element within an exhibit.

mold—A material suitable for shaping anything in a fluid or plastic condition.

mold-blown glass—An expensive molded glass made by glass blown into molds.

mom and pop exhibitor—A small, family-owned exhibitor.

monitor—1. A television set with direct audio and video input. 2. A loudspeaker used by performers to hear music onstage.

monitor mixing console—A sound board used to regulate and mix black-and-white television.

monochrome—A single-color image such as those reproduced on a black-and-white television.

monopitch—A single pitched roof such as an awning-type tent structure in South Africa.

montage—1. A composite image made by combining several separate pictures. 2. A rapid succession of images to illustrate an association of ideas.

MOR—See **middle of the road.**

mornay sauce—A cream sauce thickened with eggs and grated cheese.

motel—An establishment that provides housing with limited services, for persons away from home; also known as **motor inn.**

motion—A formal proposal to be discussed and voted on in a meeting.

motor coach—A large, comfortable, well-powered bus that can transport groups and their luggage over long distances.

motor coach tour operator—A company that creates group tours that travel via motor coach to their destination and include itinerary activities.

motor inn—See **motel.**

moussaka—A Greek layered casserole with chopped meat and vegetables.

mousse—1. A light dessert made with beaten egg whites and whipped cream. 2. Finely ground meat, seafood, or poultry, served in a mold.

mousseline—Hollandaise sauce or mayonnaise with whipped cream, usually added on top as a dollop.

movable wall—See **air walls.**

move-in—The date and time set for installation of exhibits, decorations, and other equipment by exhibitors and decorators; also known as **bump-in, load-in,** or **setup.**

move-out—The date and time set for dismantling of exhibits and other equipment by exhibitors and decorators; also known as **breakdown, bump-out,** or **load-out.**

moving magnet cartridge—A phono cartridge that produces a signal by moving a small permanent magnet.

moving screen—A screen intended to provide information and to notify participants who are called away for urgent reasons during a session, without disturbing the meeting.

Moviola—A portable motor-driven device that is used for viewing film but primarily for editing.

MPI—See **Meeting Professionals International.**

multichannel—A term indicating two or more communications bands (receivers).

multichannel tape—Tape having more than one channel on which to record.

multicraft union—A union that includes membership from more than one skilled craft group.

multi-image—A visual presentation technique using more than one projected image at a time; also known as **multiscreen** or **multivision.**

multimedia—The use of two or more audiovisual media in one presentation. Usually audio material is synchronized with a visual image presentation.

multinational meeting—An international meeting with a minimum of 100 participants from at least four countries.

multiple exposure—See **build.**

multiple-story exhibit—See **double-decker.**

multiplexer—1. A unit designed for selective projection of 16mm film, 2" x 2" slides, or filmstrips into one television program. 2. A device used to transmit several messages or signals simultaneously on the same circuit or channel.

multiscreen—See **multi-image.**

multitrack conference—A conference with parallel program sessions in which participants have the choice to follow one track or to move from one track to another during the duration of the meeting. Tracks are often divided according to experience and skill level.

multivision—See **multi-image.**

Murphy bed—A retractable bed built into a wall.

MUSA—See **Musician Union of South Africa.**

Musician Union of South Africa (MUSA)—The organization that protects and promotes musicians' rights and social security.

music stand—A sheet-music holder of varying sizes and requiring attached lights when used on a darkened stage.

muslin—Wide-loomed fabric used for artwork.

MW—Minimum weight factor.

Mylar—The trade name for a shiny, plastic material used for ballrooms and decorations.

mystery tour—A tour to a surprise destination. The passengers are not told their destination until en route or upon arrival.

N

NACE—See **National Association of Catering Executives.**

NAEM—See **National Association of Exposition Managers.**

Nagra—The standard state-of-the-art portable tape recorder, using ¼" reel-to-reel magnetic tape.

name card—A name on a card that identifies an individual; see **place card.**

name tag—An identification label or badge worn by a delegate indicating name, company, and title.

napery—See **linen.**

napkin—A piece of cloth or paper used for protecting clothing, wiping the lips, etc.; also known as **serviette.**

napkin folds—Napkins folded decoratively.

napoleon/napolean—A French pastry with cream or custard filling, topped with icing.

National Association of Catering Executives (NACE)—An organization of professional on- and off-premise caterers and their suppliers that provides education, resources, and information.

National Coalition of Black Meeting Planners (NCBMP)—An organization providing education, resources, and representation to its membership of black meeting planners and others who provide services and products for their meetings.

national dress—The national costume of a specific country; also known as **traditional dress.**

National Institute for Occupational Safety and Health (NIOSH)—The United States government agency that performs and analyzes measures of workplace safety.

national meeting—A meeting of organizations or individuals from one nation; also known as **domestic meeting.**

National Occupation and Safety Association (NOSA)—An organization in South Africa similar to the **National Institute for Occupational Safety and Health.**

National Restaurant Association (NRA)—A national organization based in Washington, D.C., that provides education, marketing, and lobbying for restaurant professionals and their suppliers.

national tourist office (NTO)—An official government agency that promotes a country's tours and activities and provides information services to visitors.

national union—A union having membership only within the United States.

natural water—Water from protected underground sources. It cannot be processed, but it may be purified or filtered.

Naugahyde—A synthetic, leatherlike material.

NCBMP—See **National Coalition of Black Meeting Planners.**

near-plant—A term that indicates a company's travel reservations may occur at a travel agency or at the company, and actual ticketing occurs at the travel agency branch; also known as **converted in plant.**

neck/necklace microphone—See **lavaliere microphone.**

negative—1. A reversed image of art or type; also known as **reverse.** 2. See **adlux.**

negligence—The failure to use that degree of care that is considered reasonable precaution under given circumstances.

negligence, contributory—The lack of ordinary care on the part of an injured party, which helped to cause the injury.

negligence, gross—Reckless and willful misconduct, where the standard of due care of a reasonably prudent person has been ignored by such a shockingly wide margin that it reflects an indifference to the natural and probable consequences and almost amounts to an intentional act.

neoprene—A rubberlike mold reproduction material.

nerve center—A designated area at an event that serves as a center for emergencies, contact with coordinators, as well as a communications center for messages; also known as the **command center.**

nested—Three or more different sizes of an article are placed within each other so that each article will not project above the next lower article by more than 33⅓ percent of its height.

nested solid—Three or more different sizes of an article are placed within each other so that each article will not project above the next lower article by more than ¼".

net—The profit that remains after all allowable deductions, such as charges, expenses, discounts, commissions, taxes, etc., are made.

net assets—A company's total liabilities subtracted from the total assets.

net balance—The proceeds from a sale, after deducting expenses associated with the sale.

net book value—The current book value of an asset or liability.

net cash flow—The cash inflow minus cash outflow.

net cost—The actual cost of an event found by deducting any income or financial gain from the total cost.

net income—The income subject to taxation after deductions and exemptions have been subtracted from gross income.

net investment—The net cash required at the beginning of an investment event.

netiquette—The etiquette on the Internet; see **flaming.**

net/net—The actual cost of an event excluding mark-ups or commissions.

net operating income—Income generated from the operations of an event reduced by operating expenses.

net operating loss—The excess of operating expenses over revenues.

net per capita—The net profit after operating expenses (both fixed and variable) divided by total attendance.

net square footage—The amount of space occupied by exhibits in a facility, not including aisles, columns, registration areas, etc.

net square feet—The actual amount of salable space available for exhibit booths or stands.

nett—British variation of *net.*

net wholesale rate—A rate usually slightly lower than the wholesale rate, applicable to groups of individuals when a hotel is specifically mentioned in a tour folder. The rate is marked up by the wholesaler of the tour to cover distribution, promotion, etc.

New England clam chowder—White clam soup made with milk and potatoes.

new registration—A registration received at a meeting and generally incurring payment of a penalty fee or differential.

newsletter—See **information bulletin.**

Niagara Falls—In pyrotechnics, a set of gerbs chained together with fuse and rope, set and hung so that a white color is displayed downward, creating an effect of a waterfall at night.

niche market—A small market within a market segment, such as the reunion market.

nineteen hundred box—A metal electrical junction box normally accommodating electrical receptacles.

NIOSH—See **National Institute for Occupational Safety and Health.**

NMFC—National Motor Freight Classifications.

nodes—Individual computers on the Internet that make up a network; also known as **stations.**

NOE—Not otherwise enumerated.

no-fault coverage—In an automobile accident, policyholders must recover from their own insurance companies for injuries and property damage.

NOHP—Not otherwise herein provided.

NOIBN—Not otherwise indicated by number; not otherwise indicated by name.

nomenclature of customs cooperation council—The customs tariff used by many countries worldwide, including most European nations, but not the United States; also known as the **Brussels Tariff Nomenclature.**

noncommissionable—A type of sale in which the agent or purchaser does not receive a percentage of the sale amount.

noncurrent assets—Accounts that are not to be converted to cash or used in operations within 12 months of the balance sheet date.

nonprofit marketing—Communications whose goals may or may not include excess revenue over expense.

nonprofit organization—An organization holding 501(C)(3) status with the Internal Revenue Service and that funds or serves various philanthropic, educational, or other purposes.

nonsked—An airline offering charter service on a nonscheduled basis.

nonstop flight—A flight from one city to another with no stops.

no-op—An airline flight not operating.

nori—Sheets of roasted seaweed used to wrap sushi (sticky rice and fish eaten raw).

NOS—Not otherwise specified.

NOSA—See **National Occupation and Safety Association.**

no-show—1. A hotel, airline, or meeting reservation made but not kept without notice or without canceling according to guidelines. 2. A scheduled exhibitor who does not show up to claim booth or stand space or ordered services.

notes payable—Short-term notes that are due within 12 months of the balance sheet date; also known as **current liabilities**.

notice board—A board displaying one or more notices or warnings.

notice of meeting—A written notice that is given to persons to attend a meeting.

NRA—See **National Restaurant Association.**

NSPF—Not specifically provided for.

NTO—See **national tourist office.**

NTSC—A video standard primarily broadcast in the United States and Japan that produces 525 I.

number stand/booth—A stand or booth used to hold numbers designating specific event activity areas.

O

O/A—Open account.

OAG—See **Official Airline Guide.**

objectives—A statement of expected achievement in a marketing event; see **goals.**

O'Brien—Sautéed with onions and green peppers.

observer—A delegate who observes and reports, but does not officially participate in activities at the event.

obstructed view—A blocked view of the stage as seen from audience seating; also known as **impaired-vision seating.**

occupancy rate—The percentage of the total number of available sleeping rooms actually occupied, derived by dividing the total number of rooms occupied during a given period (night, week, year) by the total number of rooms available for occupancy during that same period.

Occupational Safety and Health Administration (OSHA)—The United States agency that requires employers to provide a safe workplace by saving lives, preventing injuries, and protecting the health of America's workers.

occurrence—An accident, including continuous or repeated exposures to substantially the same general harmful conditions.

ocean bill of lading—A bill of lading (B/L) indicating that the exporter consigns a shipment to an international carrier for transportation to a specified foreign market. Unlike an inland B/L, the ocean B/L also serves as a collection document. If it is a straight B/L, the foreign buyer can obtain the shipment from the carrier by simply showing proof of identity. If a negotiable B/L is used, the buyer must first pay for the goods, post a bond, or meet other conditions agreeable to the seller.

off-camera—A performance or action not seen on camera, such as narration.

Official Airline Guide (OAG)—A geographically categorized publication providing information on airline schedules, airports, connecting times, etc.

official carrier—An airline company designated as the preferred transport for an event in exchange for special rates or services.

official contractor—A general contractor chosen as the main vendor for an event.

official language—An official language to be used for a meeting.

official receipt—An official acknowledgement of money or equipment received.

officials—The appointed personnel with specific tasks.

off-line—1. To talk about a meeting topic outside the meeting. 2. The first step in video editing used to make decisions about all edits in a production. The next process is usually on-line editing, or the final editing stage.

off-line connection—See **interline connection.**

off-line editing—The editing of a film or videotape that involves cuts and splices only and no special effects. An economical process that provides time to plan and organize on-line editing and helps avoid wasting valuable time and effort.

off-peak—A term used in reference to a lower fare other than the period(s) that are usually busiest.

off-premise caterer—A professional caterer who specializes in providing food and beverage services to locations outside a normal facility, such as tents, museums, office buildings, sound stages, open fields, parking garages, or empty warehouses, or at event facilities that allow outside catering.

off-print—The separately issued reprint of a part of a publication or document; also known as **separate reprint.**

off-season/out of season—A term that indicates the facility occupancy is at its lowest level.

offset—1. A photographic printing process. 2. The unwanted transfer of a freshly printed wet image onto the back of another sheet of paper.

off-shore meeting—A meeting occurring in a country outside the originating body.

off-site event—An activity scheduled away from the main event facility.

offstage—A term indicating a stage area that is not in view of the audience.

oilcloth—A material used for signs and banners.

oil cracker—A compressor that forces air into a chamber containing pure oil, breaking down molecules and creating a very fine mist that enhances light beams.

olio curtain—A curtain that rolls up from the bottom; also known as **drop curtain.**

omnidirectional microphone—A microphone that picks up sound from all directions, used in lavalieres and for conferences; not recommended for entertainers.

Omni pole and tubes—The trade name for a system of steel extrusions. Hardware designed for flexible arrangements of vertical and horizontal structures.

O/N—Order notify.

on-center—A term that refers to the measurement of the space from the center of a solid object, such as a column, to another point.

one for fifty or 1/50—A complimentary room policy that offers one complimentary room night for every fifty room nights booked; normally not to exceed four or five rooms.

100 percent star billing—A contractual requirement that an artist's name will appear in a type style and size equal to or greater than other names in advertising and promotional materials; also known as **top of bill.**

one-shot—An exhibit or display fabricated for onetime use only.

one ten/sixty—A common term describing normally available current in the North American continent. The full expression is 110 volt/60 cycle. Many European and South American areas have 220-volt, 50-cycle power only.

on-line—All the preedited tapes tied into the tape mastering units for the full mix.

on-line editing—The editing of film or videotape done at a facility equipped to handle special effects and maximum manipulation of the material. The most expensive form of editing, it ultimately offers greater visual opportunities.

on-premise caterer—A caterer who provides food and beverage service to a specific facility, such as a convention hall, hotel, or banquet facility.

on-site—See **at-site.**

on-site order—1. A labor or service order placed on-site. 2. A floor order placed at a venue.

on-site registration—The process of signing up for an event on the day of or at the location of the event.

OP—See **opposite prompt.**

opaque—An object that blocks all light and cannot be seen through.

open—Rooms that are available for sale or occupancy; also known as **vacant.**

open bar—A private room bar setup where drinks are paid for by a sponsor and usually includes a full range of spirits; also known as **host bar** or **sponsored bar.**

open cold—To give the first public performance for critics without invitational previews.

open discussion period—See **round robin.**

open end—An unlimited number of winners eligible for incentive travel.

open house—An event held at a place of business to provide customers, peers, members, the public, the media, or employees' families a firsthand look at a facility, products, and the way business is conducted.

opening ceremony—The formal opening session of an event; also known as **opening session.**

opening hours—The hours during which an exhibition is open to the public or trade visitor.

opening session—See **opening ceremony.**

open insurance policy—A marine insurance policy that applies to all shipments made by an exporter over a period of time rather than to one shipment only.

open shop—A company in which union membership is not a condition of employment.

open-space event—A meeting organized in an open-space environment; also known as **outdoor event.**

open-space technology (OST)—An approach to event facilitation that enables groups from 5 to 1000 to efficiently deal with complex issues by creating self-managed task groups.

open ticket—A ticket valid for transportation between certain points, indicating no specific reservation date or time.

open union—A union that maintains no prohibitive restrictions for membership. It may be a union that agrees to accept any qualified employee of the employer as a member of the union.

open-U setup—See **horseshoe setup** or **U-shaped setup.**

operating expenses—All of the expenses associated with the operation of a facility, including fixed and variable expenses, depreciation, interest, and income taxes.

operating profit margin—The net result of revenue minus expenses not including interest, depreciation, and income taxes.

operating supplies—The items specifically utilized for retail sale and maintenance supplies.

operations—Performing the practical work of operating a program. Usually involves the in-house control and handling of all phases of the services, both with suppliers and with clients.

operations manager—The individual in charge of performing the practical and detailed work of a program; see **operations.**

operator—A loose term that may mean contractor, tour operator, or wholesaler, or a combination of any or all of those functions.

operator desk—See **central console.**

operator sound—See **mixer.**

opposite prompt (OP)—Known in South Africa as the side of the stage on a performer's right side.

optical effects—The modifications of a photographic image, filmed in a motion picture camera of normal type, produced in an optical printer.

optical printer—An apparatus with an internal camera or projector interlink, designed to make the final optical negative that can also be used for superimpositions, titling, and special effects.

optical sound—A sound that is recorded by photographic means on film.

option(s)—1. Space, products, or services reserved but not yet contracted for, with the right of refusal to confirm a tentative space reservation if there is demand from another group; also known as **first option, provisional reservation,** or **tentative hold.** 2. Activities other than those included in the formal agenda that are not required and often demand the payment of an additional participation fee.

optional items—Additional services or tours that may be booked or not according to the preference of the purchaser.

option date—The date agreed upon when a tentative agreement is to become a definite commitment by the buyer.

OR—Owner's risk.

oration—A formal and dignified public discourse.

order form for facilities—The preprinted document on which facilities can be ordered.

order of preference/preferred order—A system that ranks dignitaries according to international protocol for purposes of seating, honors, or ceremonies.

organizing committee—See **local host.**

organizing secretariat—Providing secretarial services in connection with the organization of a meeting or event.

original language—The initial language in which a document is drafted or a speech is delivered.

OS&D—Over, short, and damaged.

OSHA—See **Occupational Safety and Health Administration.**

OST—See **open-space technology.**

OT—1. On truck. 2. See **overtime.**

OT labor—In the United States, work performed on overtime.

outbound operator—A company that takes groups from a given city or country to another city or country.

outbound tour—Any tour that takes groups outside a given city or country to another city or country. Contrasts with inbound tours.

outdoor event—See **open-space event.**

outlets—Restaurants and lounges within an event facility.

outline decision—See **framework decision.**

outline of services—See **event specification.**

out of order—An event room or facility space or equipment under renovation or requiring maintenance.

outside exhibit/external exhibit—A booth or stand located outdoors.

outside line—A telephone line from in-house to the outside obtained through the in-house operator.

outsourcing—Hiring external companies or individuals that can handle certain functions of an event more efficiently than the event planning organization can.

outtake—A taped or filmed scene deleted from the final production.

ovenware—Dinnerware that is able to withstand the heat of a kitchen oven without damage.

overage—A surplus, excess, or extra.

overbook—The activity of accepting reservations for more guest rooms, aircraft seats, or services than are available, in anticipation of no-shows; see **oversold.**

overdrape—Embellishment on top of draping to contrast color or self-color but adding depth of detail.

overflow—Hotel guest/sleeping rooms booked by the planner for attendees at other locations after headquarters facilities are full.

overhead projector—A piece of audiovisual equipment that produces a magnified image on a vertical screen by passing light through a horizontal transparent slide or other transparency.

overlay—1. A decorative cloth used to dress a banquet table. 2. A decorative cloth to go over a base cloth. 3. A clear acetate film used to separate different components of artwork. 4. A tissue sheet over artwork on which corrections or alterations are indicated. 5. A panel mounted to another surface.

override—A commission over and above the normal base commission percentage.

overset—A number of places set for a food event in addition to the guaranteed amount; also known as **additional seating.**

oversold—The number of confirmed reservations that exceed the number of seats on an aircraft; see **overbook.**

overtime (OT)—Labor work performed in excess of 40 hours per week; also known as **rostered times.**

overview—See **scenario.**

P

PA—1. Particular average. 2. See **public address system.**

pacing—The fullness or emptiness, fastness or slowness of a tour itinerary. The scheduling of activities within an itinerary to make for a realistic operation and to give a certain balance of travel time, sightseeing, social events, free time, and rest.

package—1. A single-fee booth or stand package offered by show management. 2. A conference or tour arrangement combined and sold at a single all-inclusive price. 3. A combination of benefits received by workers, such as insurance, paid holidays, paid vacation, and sick leave.

package insert—A piece of advertising or promotion matter placed in a package.

package plan—A management practice of providing furniture and/or services to exhibitors for a single fee.

package tour—A vacation plan arranged by tour operators (wholesalers) that provides (for a set fee) all or most of the required services, such as transportation, hotel room, sightseeing, attractions, and entertainment.

packing drawing—A visual to supplement written instructions; also known as **instruction booklet.**

packing list—A list showing the number and kinds of items being shipped, as well as other information needed for transportation purposes.

padded van—A type of vehicle used for uncrated shipments.

padding—1. Protection, usually a blanket, for uncrated material. 2. A material put under a tablecloth for added comfort when dining.

paella—A Spanish rice dish.

paid-out—The amount of a cash withdrawal requested by the event organizer and charged to the facility's master account, often used to set up registration cash boxes.

pain grille—Toast.

painter—A laborer who is responsible for painting and graphics. May also have other duties depending upon jurisdiction and agreements.

pallet—A wooden platform used for storing and transporting equipment; also known as **skid.**

pamphlet—See **brochure.**

pan—The sideways movement of a camera to film or videotape a wide scene.

panache—Mixed (usually two vegetables).

panel—A format for discussion by a moderator and two or more panelists.

panorama—The widest view of a scene.

paper contribution—See **contributed paper.**

paper review board—See **paper selection committee.**

paper selection committee—The committee who decides which papers are suitable for presentation and allocates them to appropriate sessions; also known as **paper review board.**

papier-mâché—A tough material made of paper pulp and various glues, used as a sculpting material.

parabolic aluminized reflector light (PAR light)—A lighting instrument available in beam spreads from a very narrow spot to a wide flood. Unlike Fresnels and Lekos, the reflector and the lens are built into the lamp of the PAR light, rather than being part of the instrument's body.

parabolic projection screen—A type of front-projector screen surface that when stretched is very rigid and allows only narrow-angle viewing.

parade—A moving pageant including floats, bands, individual entertainers, and dignitaries.

parallax—The illusion of opacity resulting from the juxtaposition of translucent or polarized surfaces. Also achieved when rows of panels or fins are spaced in such a way as to be seen when viewed directly but that appear to be opaque when viewed from an angle.

parallel—A collapsible frame support for a stage platform.

parallel session—An education or other session that has some correspondence, similarity, and aim that is simultaneous with another session at an event.

paramedic—A person who provides first aid and may transport injured persons to receive medical treatment.

parking attendant—An individual who is employed to park motor vehicles in a designated area.

parliament—Any legal body to which members are elected for the purpose of enacting laws.

PAR light—See **parabolic aluminized reflector light.**

parlor—A room usually equipped with couches that make into beds and connected to a suite bedroom.

parmentier—Served with potatoes.

partial sponsorship—A sponsorship of an event or a television or radio program by several advertisers, each having a separate section of the event or program.

participant—An individual performing an assigned role in a program or event; frequently used incorrectly to mean attendee; also known as a **program participant.**

participant motivation—The absolute reason to turn up for the meeting that is called together by the organizer.

particleboard—A structural panel of compressed, glued wood chips.

partition—See **air walls.**

partner—One who has united with others to form a partnership in business.

partnership—A business owned by two or more persons that is not organized as a corporation.

party—A person concerned or taking part in any affair, matter, transaction, or proceeding, considered individually.

party canopy—A lightweight covering supported by one or more center poles designed to shelter against the sun or light rain, usually supplied as an inexpensive do-it-yourself tent rental.

party planner—An individual who assists private clients with researching, designing, planning, coordinating, and evaluating private parties, such as weddings, bar mitzvahs, bat mitzvahs, and other social life gatherings.

passive language—The language for which interpretation is provided.

passport—A government document issued to a citizen, permitting travel to another country and the right to reenter the country.

password—A code used to gain access to a locked computer system.

paste-up—An arrangement of type and illustrations on an art board, used as camera-ready art.

pastry cart—A serving technique used to select a dessert by displaying them on a rolling tray; also known as a **dessert tray.**

patch—1. To temporarily join wires or slides by overlapping. 2. A plug-in connection between two lines.

patch panel—A plug and jack assembly permitting studio outlets to be temporarily connected to dimmer output circuits.

pâté—A paste of finely ground meats or liver and spices, forming a loaf. Some pâtés are spreadable, some are sliced. Classic meats used include livers from geese, ducks, chicken, and veal.

pâté de foie gras—A paste made from goose liver.

patron—1. A person with a greater level of giving who heads a list of supporters. 2. An individual who lends his or her name as an endorsement or in support of an event.

patronage—1. The trade or business given to a particular business. 2. Leaders (local, state, provincial, federal) who endorse an event.

PAX—Industry abbreviation for passengers.

pay for play—The actual amount recovered for a performance and paid only if the performance is fulfilled.

paying in—The money received on account for payment; also known as **payment on account.**

payment authorization—An officially sanctioned signature that authorizes payment of an invoice.

payment on account—See **paying in.**

payment order—A written authorization for payment to be made; see **purchase order.**

pay own—A term that designates that each guest pays own guest charges; also known as **POA** and **EPO.**

PBX/PABX operator—A telephone switchboard operator.

PCMA—See **Professional Convention Management Association.**

PCO—See **professional congress organizer.**

PC spot—A spotlight filled with a plano-convex lens to project a variable beam spread.

PD—Per diem.

peach melba—A classic dessert of ice cream served on a peach half and topped with raspberry syrup and whipped cream.

peak night—An event management term referring to the night during an event when the most guest/sleeping rooms are used by those in attendance.

peak season—An event industry term that indicates the busiest season when facility occupancy is at its highest level; also known as **high season.**

pedestal—A floor support for an exhibit component.

peek-a-boo cuisine—Menu items where some foods are hidden, such as beans hiding meat; also known as **surprise cuisine.**

peg—A steel bar used for the anchoring of a tent. The size, quality, and length can vary according to soil conditions.

peg-and-pole tent—A PVC structure held up with king poles, queen poles, and side poles; see **polyvinyl chloride (PVC), king pole, queen pole,** and **side poles.**

Peg-Board—The trade name for perforated hardboard; available with holes on various centers.

pegged off—An object mounted away from a supporting surface with spacers.

pendant microphone—See **lavaliere microphone.**

pending registration—An incomplete registration, meaning the fees, full payment, or forms have not been received; also known as **provisional registration.**

penetration—The effectiveness of advertising in reaching and persuading the public.

peninsula booth/stand—A configuration of two or more exhibit spaces back-to-back with an aisle on three sides.

peninsula display—An exhibit exposed to an aisle on three sides.

penthouse suite—A guest room or suite that is the largest and best room, often located on the top floor of the facility.

people magnet—A promotional idea or device that has a compelling ability to draw audiences.

people mover—An individual designated to direct people in a specific direction, with or without signage.

per capita—The total revenue less discounts divided by total attendance including complimentary admissions.

percentage—A payment of a percentage of total billings as a condition of getting a contract for trade show work.

per diem—A fixed amount of funds available each day to a traveler to cover meals and expenses.

perfect binding—A binding process in which pages are glued together at the indicated margin.

perforated metal—Thin sheet metal pierced in a variety of patterns.

performance bond—A legal instrument guaranteeing payment if contractual specifications are not met.

perimeter booth/stand—An exhibit space located on an outside wall; also known as **backwall booth/stand.**

permanent exhibit space—A showroom, mart, or similar space leased on a long-term basis for product displays.

permanent office—Appointment on a permanent basis within an organization.

permit card—A card granting temporary employment rights to a non-union member, issued by a union having a closed contract with an employer.

per person—1. An allowance of food and/or beverages purchased for an expected attendance. 2. Food and beverage priced according to the number of guests expected to attend the catered event.

perquisite—A payment, benefit, or privilege received in addition to regular income or salary; also known as a **bonus** or **gratuity.**

personal manager—An individual who represents an individual artist or group of artists.

personal selling—The process of completing a sale in business-to-business marketing that is one-to-one and requires prospecting, presentation, and follow-up to maintain customer relationships.

PERT—See **program evaluation and review technique.**

PERT chart—An organizational flowchart defining responsibilities, due dates, and other information.

phased budget—See **budget** and **budget chart.**

phosphorescent paint—A type of paint that radiates visibly when activated by ultraviolet light.

photo blowup—A photographic reproduction in a larger size than the original.

photocopier—A machine for photocopying materials or documents.

photographic opportunity—A perfect place or themed area for a photograph to show the style of a venue, event, etc.

photo op—See **photo opportunity.**

photo opportunity—A type of press release tailored to a visual medium, using a brief description of the visual nature of the event; also known as a **request for coverage** when delivered to electronic media; also known as **photo op.**

photo screen—A stencil made photographically for silk-screen reproduction.

photo stats—See stats.

phyllo—Flaky pastry dough.

phytosanitary inspection certificate—A certificate issued by the U.S. Department of Agriculture to satisfy import regulations of foreign countries, indicating that a U.S. shipment has been inspected and is free from harmful pests and plant diseases.

piano hinge—A continuous fixed pin hinge.

piano type—The designation of piano size and quality, such as concert grand, baby grand, spinet, table grand, upright, or electronic keyboard.

pica—A size of type that produces ten typed characters or spaces per inch.

pickup—The number of facility guest rooms actually used out of a room block.

pièce de résistance—A main dish or entrée.

pie plate—A plate used for desserts; also known as **dessert plate.**

pierced—A cut-through surface for rear illumination, identification, or decoration.

pierogi—A thick layer of dough wrapped around a filling, such as cabbage, potato, cheese, prune, etc.

pin beam—A narrow beam of light up to 20', usually produced by a small, 25-watt lamp and used to light banquet table centerpieces, mirror balls, and dance floors; also known as **pin spot.**

pin poles—See **side poles.**

pin spot—See **pin beam.**

pinup—A lighting fixture with a surface-mounting plate or with a clamp base.

pipe and drape—A system of aluminum poles, supported by heavy metal bases, that support lightweight fabric or vinyl where masking is required, as in trade shows or stage productions; also known as **draping.**

piquant—Spicy; highly seasoned.

pit—A sunken area in front of the stage used to accommodate a musical group.

pita—Mediterranean bread.

pitch—1. The slope of the roof of a tent resulting from the difference in height between the center poles and the side poles. 2. The distance between rows of seats of an aircraft. 3. A type size and spacing.

pivot interpreter—The only interpreter in the team assigned to a meeting who is able to translate out of a lesser-used language and who functions as a relay for the rest of the team in relation to that language; also known as **sole relay interpreter.**

pixie tube—A special high-intensity lamp with internal circuits and filaments.

place—1. One of the four elements of the marketing mix; refers to direct and indirect channels that an organization uses to make the customers aware of, reserve, or obtain the product, service, or idea. 2. A particular street address or other designation of a factory, store, warehouse, place of business, private residence, construction camp, or the like, at a point; see **point.**

place card—A small card placed on a banquet table and inscribed with the name of the person designated to sit at the place.

place plate—See **base plate.**

places—A direction given to those involved in an event to be in their places, ready to go.

plan—A diagram showing layout or design.

planting—Floral décor to enhance the appearance of an exhibition.

plants—Fresh, potted plants used as floral décor to enhance the appearance of an event.

plastic laminate—Any one of several of the melamine plastics bonded to paneling for durability and appearance.

plateau—A level, stage, or tier of an incentive travel program at which a sales goal has been reached and a participant can then advance to a higher tier by additionally qualifying or purchasing the difference.

plated—See à la russe.

plated buffet—A selection of prepared foods and entrées set on a buffet table, which are chosen by the guests and served by a waiter.

plated service—A method of service in which foods are arranged on individual plates in the kitchen and then served to guests.

plate microphone—A flat semidirectional condenser microphone, sensitive to input when placed on a floor, wall, or Plexiglas panel. A plate microphone is used for musicals, plays, group choirs, or low-profile situations where the microphone should not appear obvious to the audience; also known as **boundary microphone** or **PZM.**

platform—A raised horizontal surface, stage, or flooring.

plating—A decorative and protective metal finish.

play on/play off—Music that accompanies a performer's or speaker's entrance onto or exit from the stage.

plenary assembly—An assembly that is composed of all the members and is fully attended.

plenary session—A general assembly for all participants; also known as **general session.**

Plexiglas—The trade name for an acrylic plastic material in common use.

plug-in—A (usually small) piece of software that adds features to a larger piece of software.

plumber—A laborer responsible for all plumbing installation.

plus-plus (++)—1. The addition of taxes and gratuities to a price when not included; designated by "++." 2. The additional fees for expenses provided to entertainers or speakers; see **rider.**

plywood—Laminated wood of an odd number of sheets glued together. Often used in exhibit construction.

POA—See **pay own.**

pocket program—A shortened version of the meeting program giving basic information in a way that is easy to refer to and convenient to carry; also known as **at-a-glance program.**

podium—The platform on which a speaker stands; also known as **dais, riser, rostrum,** or **stage.**

point—1. A particular city, town, village, or other community or area that is treated as a unit for the application of rates. 2. A measurement of type size in which 12 points equal 1 pica. A pica is approximately ⅙".

point of presence (POP)—A city or a location where a computer can connect to a network with dial-up telephone lines.

point of purchase—A product display where sales can be made; also known as **point of sales (POS).**

point of sales (POS)—See **point of purchase.**

point source—See **single-source sound.**

pole drapes—Curtains hung from the upper section of the center poles of a tent to hide them and any guy ropes, stakes, or anchors.

pole tent—A heavy-duty tent made of canvas or vinyl and supported by poles at the perimeter and center.

policies—1. Formal rules governing the activities of all members of the organization and, as such, are usually developed and voted on by the board of directors. 2. Unwritten guidelines understood by everyone for actions that are desirable, permissible, or forbidden.

policies, claim-made—A type of insurance policy that requires the policy to be in effect both when a loss occurs and when the claim comes in. Therefore, a claim reported after the policy terminates is not covered.

policies, occurrence—A type of insurance policy that agrees to cover all claims that arise out of incidents that occur during the policy period regardless of whether the insurance policy is still in effect at the time the claim is made.

poll—A method used to determine whether a targeted market has been reached and what their perceptions of a particular event or sponsor are. A poll may be conducted over the telephone, via direct mail, or in person during the event.

polyvinyl chloride (PVC)—A material used for the cladding of tents; see **cladding.**

pony glass—A small stemmed glass used for cordial service.

POP—See **point of presence;** see **post office protocol.**

pop-up canopy—A small, lightweight, collapsible frame canopy with a fabric covering that provides shelter and protection from light rain and is usually provided as a do-it-yourself rental tent that may be erected and removed quickly.

porcelain—A hard, translucent, clayware body that differs very slightly from china in ingredients and manufacturing process.

port—1. A fortified wine developed in Portugal and usually served after dinner. 2. A telephone to be used during a teleconference (one telephone equals one port).

portable camera—See **field camera.**

portable computer—A computer capable of being carried about readily from place to place and used away from a home base; also known as **laptop.**

portable exhibit—A lightweight, crated display unit that does not require a forklift to move it.

portal structure—A tent structure that uses base plates, legs, rafters, apex, and purlins and that eliminates the need for a center pole support and the use of trusses.

porter—1. An individual who carries baggage. 2. In South Africa and some other countries, laborer who performs sweeping, cleaning, and dusting.

porterage—Payment of gratuities for baggage handling at an airport or hotel.

port of call—A destination where air transportation or ground transportation arrives and departs with people and merchandise.

port of entry—A destination providing customs and immigration services.

portrait—A sign with greater height than width.

POS (point of sales)—See **point of purchase.**

poseur table—See **cabaret table.**

positioning—The use of marketing to create a specific image of the product perceived by the target market.

positive—The exact image of a copy as distinguished from reverse image or negative.

positive print—A reproduction similar to the original.

post—1. A metal upright used to support drapes. 2. The process following shooting a film or video where editing takes place.

postcon—See **postevent briefing.**

postconference registration—A registration for an activity or function that follows an event.

postconference reservation—A guest sleeping-room space held following a conference.

postconference tour—An organized outing taking place after the working conference, for participants, attendees, and accompanying persons.

poster—A visual presentation of a specified size, presented on a flat sheet of paper or card with details of a specific topic.

poster board—A soft panel used for displaying copy and/or graphics.

poster exhibition—An area dedicated to the display of posters depicting research findings.

poster presentation—An informal session held near a poster exhibition to present and discuss the content of the posters.

poster session—1. A visual display of reports and papers, usually scientific, accompanied by authors or researchers. 2. A segment of time dedicated to the discussion of the posters shown inside an event area. When this discussion is not held in a special session, it can take place directly between the person presenting the poster and interested delegate(s).

postevent briefing—A meeting between the event manager, key hotel staff, and possibly suppliers after the main event to debrief and critique the planning process and actual implementation; also known as **postcon.**

postgame event—An event designed to attract and entertain spectators and fans immediately following a sport event.

postgraduate course—Continuing education provided for professional accreditation purposes and designed to enhance and reinforce professional knowledge; also known as **professional program.**

posting—1. The physical placement of an outdoor advertisement. 2. Putting an event name on the internal documents and external signs as the end user, not the contracting company.

post office—An official agency handling the transmission of mail.

post office protocol (POP)—The way e-mail software gets mail from a mail server.

posttrip—A tour, optional extension, or side trip package offered after an event, gathering, or convention.

potage—Soup.

potential audience—The number of persons or households capable of exposure to a medium by virtue of ownership, presence, or use of the medium in question.

pottery—A porous and not very durable form of clayware made of crude red or brown clay and fired at comparatively low temperatures.

power—1. The electricity needed to supply an event. 2. In laser technology, the brightness of the laser light, which is measured in watts. A 10-watt laser is enormously powerful compared to a 10-watt lightbulb because the light bulb radiates light in every direction, whereas the laser directs the same amount of light onto a tiny area.

power amplifier—An electrical device used after a console to drive loudspeakers and establish volume. A power amplifier consumes the largest amount of electrical power in the sound system; also known as an **amp.**

power of attorney—A legal document that allows one person to act legally on behalf of another person.

practical demonstration—A special setting for the demonstration of specific methods.

practice room—See projection rehearsal room.

preamp desk—See console or mixer.

preassigned seating—1. The event planning technique of predetermining seat assignments. 2. The procedure for requesting and receiving specific airline seats at the time of reservation.

precon—See preconvention briefing.

preconference—An organized outing taking place before the working conference, for delegates, attendees, and accompanying persons.

preconvention briefing—A meeting with the planner, facility department heads, and key suppliers to review the purpose and details of the upcoming event; also known as **precon.**

preevent meeting—A meeting between a client and a hotel to review an upcoming function and make last-minute adjustments.

prefab—A prebuilt exhibit ready for installation.

prefinished paneling—Factory-finished panels.

preformed group—A tour group in existence prior to the tour, the members of which share a common bond, interest, or organization affiliation. Also referred to as an **affinity group.** Examples of preformed groups include civic clubs, senior citizen groups, special interest groups, and alumni associations.

prefunction space—An area adjacent to the main event location, where receptions, refreshments breaks, displays, and registration often take place.

pregame event—An event designed to attract and entertain spectators and fans prior to the official start of a sport event.

preliminary announcement—See first announcement.

preliminary program—A second mailing introducing a conference and including information on the program structure and key speakers, giving details of the ancillary conference activities, and normally containing the conference registration forms; also known as **provisional program.**

premium—1. Merchandise available for purchase at a discount by an advertiser in order to promote products. 2. The amount paid as the consideration for a contract of insurance.

premium beer—A higher-priced beer that has a higher alcoholic content than light beer and regular beer.

premium brand—A brand of liquor listed by a hotel or an establishment that is among the most expensive brands at that establishment; also known as **call brand.**

premium pay—Extra pay over the regular wage rate for work performed outside or beyond the regular working hours, for work on weekends or holidays, for night-shift work, for hazardous, dirty, or unpleasant work, or for production in excess of established standards.

preopening—A period of time before a business's soft opening.

prepaid ticket advice (PTA)—An airline form stating that payment has been made.

preparation of paper—See **author's guideline/kit.**

preparatory session—A meeting of a specific group in order to finalize preparations before the official assembly.

prep area—A space designated for the preparation of food or displays, not visible to event participants, guests, and/or clients.

prepleated—Fabric that is permanently pleated and ready for installation.

preprint—The printed volume of meeting papers available prior to or at an event.

preproduction—The organizational phase of a film or video project, including preparation of the concept, script, storyboard, and budget, when crew, properties, and location are hired and determined. Traditionally, this is the most important phase of the project.

preregistration list—A document of names of people preregistered for an event versus on-site registration; also known as **printout.**

presentation—A formal face-to-face presentation of factual information, plans, visual material, etc., regarding a subject or proposed course of action.

presenter—An individual discussing and explaining a given topic in an educational session.

preset—The arrangement of food, usually a salad, cold entrée, or dessert, on banquet tables prior to the seating of guests, also known as **preset service.**

president of honor—The senior member of the committee of honor.

press agency—An agency that collects and distributes information to the news media.

press attaché—The title given to the person handling all press and media activities, excluding advertising; also known as **press officer.**

press clipping/cutting—An article cut from a newspaper or magazine.

press conference—An interview granted to the media to announce major information. Since all media will be receiving the same information simultaneously, there will not be a chance for exclusivity, so personalized coverage should be provided for editing, including several spokespeople, visual displays, adequate question-and-answer time, and time for individual interviews.

press day—An invitation to the media to cover an event before it is open to the public, to promote the upcoming event; also known as **press party** or **press tour.**

pressed glass—An inexpensive glass molded by machine.

press gallery—An area set aside for photographers, both still and video, that provides an unobstructed view of an event, as well as an adequate power supply and protection from the elements.

press hot line—A designated direct telephone line reserved exclusively for the media.

press kit—1. A collection of items providing pertinent data on a meeting, such as agenda, historical data, guest speakers, special events, etc., and on the facility, such as photos, descriptions of public areas, local entertainment, etc. 2. A kit that includes information relative to a sponsor's products or services.

press office—An agency that collects and distributes information to news media.

press officer—See **press attaché.**

press party—See **press day.**

press pass—An identification symbol that allows free, unrestricted entry to an event by media personnel and allows staff to provide them with attention and assistance; see **credentials.**

press release—A prepared statement released to targeted news media that succinctly provides information for immediate release or for release at a specified time or date.

pressroom—1. An area reserved for media representatives, with telephones, office machines, or a separate space for radio and television interviews. 2. A room where members of the media may obtain exhibitors' press kits, conduct interviews, or relax.

press tour—See **press day.**

pretrip—A tour, optional extension, or side-trip package conducted before a meeting, gathering, or convention.

previous participation in meetings—The attendance of a participant to previous meetings undertaken by the same organization and by other organizations.

price—One of the four elements of the marketing mix; refers to the unit cost of marketing the product, service, or value to the customers.

price flexibility of demand—A measure of the degree that customers are sensitive to price changes.

price leader—See **loss leader.**

primary audience—The potential audience for a single advertising message.

primary market—Foreign countries where the U.S. Travel and Tourism Administration (USTTA) maintains an office.

print—A copy of the final edited film.

printed design—A design printed on already woven fabric by hand-block printing, roller printing, or screen printing.

printed form—A printed or typed document with blank spaces for completion of specific required or requested information.

printout—1. A documentary copy generated by a computer. 2. See **pre-registration list.**

print production—The process of creating newspaper and magazine ads, brochures, outdoors posters, and all other printed material as a form of advertising.

priority point system—A system of assigning points to exhibiting companies to determine which firms will be allowed to select booth space first.

priority rating system—A method of assigning booth or stand space.

prismatic glass/prismatic plastic—A material that is textured with a multitude of tiny facets that refract and diffuse light.

privatization—Retaining a private company to handle a responsibility, such as operating a convention center, formerly handled by the city or state administration.

proceedings—An official, published volume transcribing full conference sessions, which may or may not include details of any discussion.

procession—A group of individuals moving in an orderly, often ceremonial manner.

producer—An individual responsible for an entire live or electronic stage production.

producer, exhibit—An individual or company that designs and/or builds exhibits and may also provide other services.

producer, show—An individual or an organization that manages trade shows, leases exhibit facilities, hires official contractors, and promotes events.

product—One of the four elements of the marketing mix; refers to the development of a product, service, or idea that can fulfill the needs of customers.

production manager—1. An individual who coordinates the technical production of a live event. 2. An individual responsible for the development of advertising materials for an advertising campaign.

production schedule—A detailed outline of all activities and tasks required to produce an event, the deadlines for each action, and the assignments to the individual, department, or committee responsible for specific acts; also known as **timeline.**

production tape—A direct copy of the master tape used for rehearsal and production so the master will not be damaged; also known as a **show tape.**

production team/production crew—See **event team.**

product launch—An event used to introduce or market a new product.

product life cycle—The process of introduction, growth, maturity, and decline that characterizes a product's typical movement in the market.

product show—The display of products.

professional—1. Of or having to do with a profession. 2. Relating to organizations whose membership holds common professional credentials or interests. 3. Undertaken by professionals rather than amateurs. 4. An individual who makes a business or trade of something that others do for pleasure.

professional association—A group of individuals who practice a particular professional activity.

professional congress organizer (PCO)—1. See **conference officer/ organizer.** 2. The European term for an **event manager.**

Professional Convention Management Association (PCMA)—An organization providing education, information, and resources to members, who are meeting planners or those who provide services and products for meetings.

professional program—See **postgraduate course of study,** such as a certificate program.

professional visitor—A visitor to an exhibition who represents a specific trade or profession; also known as **trade visitor.**

profile spot—A spotlight that projects a hard focused beam.

profit—The excess of income over expenditure.

profit margin—The net income divided by total revenue.

pro forma invoice—An invoice provided by a supplier prior to the shipment of merchandise, informing the buyer of the kinds and quantities of goods to be sent, their value, and important specifications (weight, size, etc.).

program—A schedule of events, giving details of times and places.

program book—A printed schedule of meeting events, location of function rooms, and other pertinent information, which is usually the official program for the event.

program design—The structuring of event program elements, including the presentation method (format), topics, special events, free time, and breaks, to achieve specific goals and objectives.

program evaluation and review technique (PERT)—A graphic tool providing organizational and personnel effectiveness using specific time segments as benchmarks.

program participant—See **participant.**

projected business—See **forward business.**

projection rehearsal room—The room where speakers can check their slides, overhead sheets, and videotapes; also known as **tryout room** or **practice room.**

projection room—The area at the back or above an auditorium used for showing film and storing equipment.

projection screen—A front or rear surface on which images are displayed.

promoter—An individual or organization whose role is to market an event by maximizing media coverage and income.

promotion—1. One of the four elements of the marketing mix; refers to the techniques used to drive interest and sales promotion, merchandising, public relations, and publicity. 2. The publicizing of an event.

promotional fare—An airline fare offered below regular rates, usually with specific travel-time limitations.

prompt book—A book of the play including all business, action, plans, and plots needed for the production; also known as **prompt script.**

prompter—An individual who stands in the wings or out of sight of the audience and assists actors with their lines and cues.

prompt script—See **prompt book.**

prompt side (PS)—1. The side of the stage from which the stage manager runs the show. 2. In South Africa, the side of the stage on a performer's left side.

pro number—A shipment number designated by the common carrier to a single shipment and used in all cases where the shipment must be referred to. Usually assigned at once.

proof—1. A final copy for approval before printing; also known as **blueline** or **blueprint.** 2. To correct before final printing. 3. A standard measure of alcoholic strength, for example 100 proof equals 50 percent alcohol content.

proof of citizenship—A document, necessary for obtaining a passport, that establishes one's nationality to the satisfaction of a foreign government.

propaganda—Information or communications intended to influence belief and action, whether true or false information is contained in such communication.

prop box—A box kept offstage in which props are stored.

property—A lodging establishment such as a hotel, motel, inn, resort, conference center, or event facility.

proposal—1. A plan put forth for consideration or acceptance. 2. A communication sent by a hotel to a potential client detailing the offerings and the asking prices.

props—1. Stage furniture, set dressing, and all articles used by actors or entertainers. 2. When used as room decorations, known as décor.

prop table—A table offstage where props are set prior to the curtain.

proscenium—An arch that separates the stage from the auditorium.

proscenium arch—The edge of the opening in the proscenium.

proscenium opening—The opening in the proscenium through which the audience views the play.

prospecting—The identification of customers who may be interested in purchasing a certain product.

prospectus—Site selection data and event specifications submitted to prospective facilities; also known as **exhibition prospectus.**

protagonist—The hero of a play or the character who carries its principal idea.

protected—As in "commissions protected," "agents protected," or "all departures protected." A guarantee by a supplier or wholesaler to pay commissions, plus full refunds to clients, on prepaid, confirmed bookings regardless of subsequent cancellation of a tour or cruise; see **guaranteed tour.**

protection—A reservation made on an alternate flight to ensure travel on a specific date.

protocol—Customs and regulations dealing with diplomatic formality, precedence, and etiquette.

provisional program—See preliminary program.

provisional registration—See pending registration.

provisional reservation—See option(s).

provolone cheese—Light golden yellow to light golden brown cheese with a shiny surface and mild, sharp, and piquant flavors.

PS—See **prompt side.**

PSA—See **public service announcement.**

PTA—See **prepaid ticket advice.**

public address system (PA)—1. A hotel's in-house public address system. 2. A system used to amplify sound into one or more rooms.

publication—A printed item, such as a book, magazine, newspaper, or conference documentation.

public event—See **civic celebration.**

publicity—The activity of generating interest and attendance at an upcoming event by providing information with news value to the media. This process is controlled by the medium reporting the information, not the sponsor.

publicity person—A person who is responsible for all public appearances and speaking engagements.

public liability—See **comprehensive general (public) liability insurance.**

public relation—1. The presentation of an event via the media or other outlets, stressing the benefits and desirability of such an event. 2. A management function that evaluates public attitudes, identifies the policies and procedures of an individual or an organization with public interest, and plans and executes a program of action to earn public understanding and acceptance.

public service advertising—Advertisements placed by a medium such as television or radio without charge in the interest of promoting the general welfare, awareness, and goodwill of its audience.

public service announcement (PSA)—Free commercial space given, as available, by the media to nonprofit organizations.

public show—An exhibition open to the public, usually requiring an entrance fee; also known as **consumer/trade show** or **gate show.**

public space—Space in a facility that is available for public use.

pull strategy—Marketing communications aimed to end customers who demand the product from channel partners.

purchase order—The written authority to proceed with an item of expenditure; also known as **commitment authorization.**

purchasing agent—An individual who purchases goods in his or her own country on behalf of foreign importers such as government agencies and large concerns; also known as **buying agent** or **commission agent.**

purlin—A horizontal beam in a tent roof at right angles to the rafters or trusses and carried on them.

push-pole tent—A tent supported by a series of center, quarter, and side poles requiring guy ropes that must be secured to anchors or stakes in the ground.

PVC—See **polyvinyl chloride.**

PW—Packed weight.

pylon—A tall exhibit structure normally used for identification.

pyro musical display—A fireworks display staged to music.

pyrotechnics—The art and science of designing, manufacturing, and displaying fireworks.

PZM—See **plate or perimeter-zone microphone.**

Q

Q&A — A question-and-answer period.

quad (quadruple) — 1. A room with two or more beds for four persons. 2. A four-channel audiotape recording system.

quad box — A set of four electrical outlets located in one box.

qualifying — The act of determining an exhibit visitor's authority to purchase a product or service.

quality control — An organizational process and the personnel responsible for maintaining production or service quality at a designated standard level.

quality management — A business practice encompassing eight principles: leadership, policy and planning, information analysis, people, customer service, quality process, product and service, and organizational performance.

quart — A unit measure equal to ¼ gallon, 32 ounces, or 4 cups.

quarter poles — Tent poles positioned between the center and side poles, shorter than center poles but taller than the side poles, that provide additional support, especially for tents 60' or wider.

quartz lamp — A kind of high-intensity projection light.

queen pole — An off-center pole used in a peg-and-pole tent in South Africa.

queen room — A room with one queen-size bed suitable for one or two persons.

queen-size bed — A large bed usually measuring 60" x 80" (150cm x 200cm).

quiche — A savory custard pie.

quiche lorraine — A custard pie of onion, bacon, and mushroom.

quick-change booth/stand — An enclosed or draped area, close to the stage.

quorum — The minimum number of members present to allow voting and official business to be conducted.

quota — The quantity of goods of a specific kind that a country will permit to be imported without restriction or imposition of additional duties.

quotation — The price of an event expenditure specified in a request.

R

rabbet—A saw cut used in the fabrication of wood parts.

raceway—A metal container for electrical wires or a wood channel for rubber.

rack rate—A facility's standard, preestablished guest room rate.

radio—See **walkie-talkie.**

radio mic—See **close-talking microphone/transmitter.**

radio microphone—See **cordless microphone.**

radius mark—An internal or external mark left on acrylic after improper or inadequate bending.

rafter—A sloping member extending from the ridge to the eaves of a tent.

ragout—A stew with rich gravy.

rail—A low drape divider between exhibit booths or stands.

rain check—1. The practice of setting another event date should the original be cancelled. 2. A ticket good for a rescheduled event should the original be cancelled.

rain date—A contractual agreement that sets another event date if the original is cancelled due to poor weather.

rain insurance—An insurance coverage that protects the financial interest of the sponsor or organizer in the event of a predetermined amount of rainfall.

raised letters—Lettering cut out of any material and applied or mounted to a surface or background for dimensional effects.

raked seating—An auditorium where each subsequent row of seats is higher than the previous one.

rally—A gathering to promote enthusiasm and excitement.

ramekin—An earthenware dish, used for baking and serving.

ramp—1. A long, narrow stage reaching into the audience, as for fashion shows. 2. A modeling ramp.

ramset—A device to shoot a bolt into dense material to anchor plates, etc., to the floor, wall, or ceiling.

random access—The ability to retrieve, in any sequence, visual and taped elements regardless of the original placement order.

range rate—The price of a guest sleeping room based on a combination of minimum, middle, and maximum room rates. The number of rooms in each type varies.

rank and file—The membership of a union other than officers and officials.

rapporteur—1. A monitor who evaluates conference sessions. 2. A person appointed to record the proceedings of a session and to write a summary of the paper presented for a final summation session; also known as **reporter.**

rap session—An informal session without a specific agenda at a meeting or conference.

ravioli—Italian pasta pillows stuffed with meat, cheese, and/or vegetables.

raw film—The condition of motion picture film after the printing process but before the surface has been treated.

raw footage—The total collection of all film or videotape shot by a production crew from which the final product is generated.

raw tape—A blank recording medium, ¼" to ½" in width, on reel, cartridge, or cassette, upon which material can be recorded.

R&B—See **rhythm and blues.**

RCMA—See **Religious Conference Management Association.**

reach—A measure of how many people receive a marketing message within a given time period.

reader board—See **directory/directory board** or **function board.**

readily achievable accessibility—Functions, events, and activities that are directly or indirectly related to the primary focus of an event and intended to be available to anyone attending, participating in, or accompanying others to the event.

readout unit—A common expression for an odometer or other calibrated device.

ready for press—The words usually printed on the back of the title page and bearing a signature and the date on which the publication was approved as ready for press; also known as **imprimatur.**

readymen—Temporary labor hired from a personnel agency.

rear-illuminated/rear-lit—The technique of lighting a color transparency or adlux from behind.

rear-screen projection—A process by which an image is projected on the back surface of a screen that is placed between the viewer and the projector; also known as **back projection.**

recall—To require an employee to return to work after leaving for the day.

receding colors—The colors on the right side of the color wheel, such as blues and violets.

receivables—1. That which is due or collectible for work or service performed. 2. The total amounts that are due for products sold, services rendered, or money loaned.

receiving agent—See **receptive operator/reception agency** and **inbound tour operator.**

receiving line—The dignitaries, host, sponsor, and guests of honor lined up to greet guests.

receiving line reception—A stand-up social function with food and beverages.

reception—A typically short social function with beverages, usually also with food displayed on tables for self-service or passed on trays.

reception desk/registration desk—The area to which guests report upon arrival at an event or facility.

receptive operator/reception agency—A tour operator or travel agent who specializes in services for incoming visitors; see **inbound tour operator.**

recess—A break time in an event; also known as **interval.**

recession—A withdrawing procession.

recommendation—A strongly suggested course of action that has binding force.

record—See **minutes.**

reel-to-reel—See **tape recorder.**

reflector—A shiny metal surface used in spotlights and projectors in back of the light source to intensify the light and give it direction.

refresh—The general housekeeping activity of cleaning a room between sessions and after an event.

refreshment break—The time between sessions when coffee and/or other refreshments are served; also known as **coffee break** or **break.**

refreshments—Items of food and drink consumed between main meals and at breaks between meetings.

refund—A reimbursement of money in the form of cash or credit voucher.

refund policy—A policy that determines the allowable reasons and timelines for the return of event fees in whole or part.

refurbish—To repair damage, renew surfaces, and replace graphics, as necessary, to recondition an exhibit and extend its life span.

regional security officer (RSO)—A consular official charged with the security of a country's nationals while they are traveling in that region; also known as **consular security manager.**

regional show—A show targeted to attendees from a specific geographical area.

registrant—An individual who submits a registration form and attends an event.

registration—1. The process by which an individual indicates the intent to attend a conference or stay at a property. 2. The inclusion of a participant in an event. 3. A method of booking and payment.

registration area—A designated area where registration takes place, usually outside the exhibit hall or meeting room.

registration card—A signature form used by a facility when registering a guest.

registration card key—A plastic card used in place of a room key; also known as **computer card.**

registration fee—The amount payable for attendance at a conference that may vary according to the level of participation or type of membership.

registration kit—A packet of event materials, such as a program book, tickets, or maps, that may be given in advance or on-site at the event; also known as **registration packet.**

registration packet—See **conference pack/kit** or **registration kit.**

rehearsal—Practicing a presentation or performance.

reinforced vinyl—Covered cord, wall coverings, or upholstery material; vinyl laminated with fabric.

reinsurance—The transference of many of an insurance company's insurance obligations to another company. It is an insurance company's insurance.

relationship marketing—The process of establishing and maintaining a mutually beneficial exchange relationship between an organization and its customers, partners, and other stakeholders.

relay—An electrical device used to interrupt or sustain the flow of current. Commonly used in low-voltage systems for programmed effects.

relay interpreting—A method of oral translation wherein the interpreter does not translate directly, but interprets the translations of a colleague; also known as **interpretation in relay.**

released value—A carrier's liability is limited to 30 cents per pound of weight of a lost or damaged article.

release form—1. A form provided by management to permit the removal of goods from an exhibition. 2. A form signed by a presenter allowing recording of the presentation.

Religious Conference Management Association (RCMA)—An organization providing information and resources to its members, who are meeting planners for religious conventions, meetings, and assemblies and those who provide products and services for this industry.

religious meeting—A group gathering to discuss religious subjects.

remote ballast—The removal of ballast from fluorescent fixtures to a separate or remote location, to allow for extremely limited space.

remote control—The control of an apparatus, such as audiovisual equipment, from a distance.

remote scanner—A scanning device placed at some distance from a laser and to which laser light is fed by transmission fiber optics or a direct beam-shot, permitting more points of origin for laser effects without reusing additional lasers. Trade-offs are a loss of intensity and a flattening of the beam.

rendering—See **setup drawing.**

rental booth/stand—A complete booth or stand package offered to exhibitors on a rental basis.

rental charge—The cost of hiring a piece of equipment or an exhibit space, which may or may not include ancillary services such as security, connections to water, electricity, gas, etc.

rental specialist—A professional who specializes in providing equipment for events, including tables, chairs, tents, tableware, linen, stanchions, generators, and dance floors.

rep company—A company playing repertory.

repertory—A collection of plays, operas, or parts that may be readily performed because of familiarity with them on the part of a cast or actor.

repetition—The repeat of an advertisement, slogan, or theme to strengthen its impression.

report—An informed, written record of a meeting.

reporter—See **rapporteur.**

reporting pay—A guaranteed payment to employees who report or show up ready for work at their usual time and find no work to do; also known as **show-up time.**

representation—A statement made in an application for insurance that the prospective insured represents as being correct to the best of their knowledge.

reprise—A repetition of a musical number or musical theme.

request for coverage—See **photo opportunity.**

request for proposal (RFP)—A request from the buyer of a service or a product to the potential supplier, outlining all the requirements and necessary information for the supplier to prepare a bid; also known as **bid manual/specifications.**

reservation—1. See **book.** 2. The process by which an individual or group secures space at a facility or books transportation.

reservation center—The reservation sales office.

resolution—1. The ability of a television system to distinguish and reproduce fine detail picked up by the camera. 2. A motion put forward for a joint decision.

resort—An event venue with accommodations associated with recreation and leisure, often located near mountains, oceans, lakes, rivers, or natural or man-made attractions.

resort hotel/motel—A hotel or motel that offers or is located near facilities for sports and recreational activities such as tennis, swimming, sailing, etc.

responsibility clause—That section of a brochure that spells out the condition under which a tour is sold. It should include the name(s) of the company(ies) that is (are) financially responsible.

restricted area—See **sanctioned area.**

résumé—See **banquet event order** or **function sheet.**

retailer—An individual who sells directly to the consumer.

retail event—An event whose purpose is to introduce or sell merchandise to prospective customers.

retour interpreting—Interpreting from and into a foreign language.

retrace—The return line from the end to the beginning of a graphic when a laser refreshes a drawing, visible if not blanked. Imagine that the laser is displaying a word; when the beam finishes the work, it jumps back to the beginning of the word to redraw it. This playback, if not blanked, is seen as a retrace line.

return—1. A panel joined to a back wall at right angles. 2. A reservation for a return journey.

return on investment (ROI)—A measurement of how much benefit an exhibiting company receives from participation in an exhibit event.

reunion—An event held for the purpose of bringing together a group for reminiscence who have past common interests and experiences. The most common of these are school and military reunions, which bring together graduates of schools or military personnel who once served together. Family reunions focus on bringing together family members living distances apart.

reverb—See effects device.

reverse—See negative.

revocable letter of credit—A document that can be cancelled or altered by the drawee (buyer) after it has been issued by the drawee's bank.

RFP—See request for proposal.

rheostat—A device for regulating the strength of an electric current by varying the resistance.

rhythm and blues (R&B)—A style of music.

rib—A framing member, usually termed in circular forms.

ribbon mike—A directional microphone of high intensity; sometimes called an omnidirectional microphone.

rider—1. A clause in an artist's contract stipulating special requirements for travel, dressing rooms, or technical equipment; also known as plus-plus. 2. An insurance term for policy additions.

ridge—The horizontal line or peak between the tops of the center poles in the roof of a tent.

rifle mic—See distant-talking microphone/transmitter.

rigger—A skilled individual used in handling assembly of heavy materials.

right-to-work state—A state where joining a union is not a condition of employment.

rim drive—A turntable operated from its edge rather than the center for heavier or off-center loads.

rimmed soup—A shallow, flat, round bowl without handles, but with a rim or shoulder.

riser—See podium.

risers—1. Platforms of varying heights used together to create a performance stage. 2. Rows of steps used by entertainers during a performance; also known as rostrum steps or treads.

risk—An uncertainty arising from the possible occurrence of given events.

risk assessment—A profile of an overall event that takes into consideration all the threats and risks that may occur during the event.

risk control—Actions and decisions that are made to prevent or reduce losses.

risk financing—Managing and planning for the funds and sources that will pay for the real losses.

risk management—The practice of analyzing all exposures to risk of loss by fortuitous or accidental means and taking steps to minimize those potential or real losses to levels acceptable to the organization.

risk monies—Funds that an agency would not recoup should an event not materialize, such as nonrefundable deposits to suppliers, promotional expenditures, printing expenses, etc.

RIT—Refining in transit.

road show—A theatrical production that tours several cities and towns.

ROI—See **return on investment.**

rollaway—A portable bed that can be provided for an extra person.

roll call—The calling of individuals' names at a meeting to determine who is present.

roller cart—A technique of applying paint with rollers to panel or wall surfaces, usually used with latex or vinyl-based paints.

roll-in—Food and/or beverages preset on rolling tables and then moved into a function room at a determined time.

roll-in meal—A light buffet meal served from a cart rolled directly into the room.

romaine—Lettuce with dark leaves and a nutty flavor, used for Caesar salad.

roman candle—A long paper tube packed with round stars and black powder. When lit, the stars shoot out every four seconds to a height of about 75 feet.

room—1. A chamber used for lodging. 2. A place where an event is held.

rooming list—1. A list of names of the passengers on a tour or other group travel program, submitted to a hotel or motel. Names are not alphabetized as on a flight manifest, but rather listed room by room and indicating who is rooming with whom. Twin-bedded rooms, singles, and doubles are usually listed in separate categories. 2. A roster of individuals requiring guest room accommodations, including type of accommodation, arrival dates, and departure dates.

room nights—The number of rooms blocked or occupied multiplied by the number of nights each room is reserved or occupied.

room only—See **European plan (EP).**

room rate—The amount charged for the occupancy of a room.

room service—A facility department that provides food and beverage service to guest rooms.

room setup—The layout of tables, chairs, other furniture, and equipment for a function.

room, tax, and incidentals (RTI)—The total hotel charge for accommodation, applicable taxes, and miscellaneous charges incurred by a guest.

room turnover/room turnaround—The amount of time needed to tear down and reset a function room.

rope lights—A string of small, low-voltage lights inside a clear or colored transparent plastic tube run by a controller; also known as **tube lights.**

roping—A plush-covered chain that can be attached to stanchions and used to define traffic areas.

rostered times—See overtime.

rostrum—In South Africa, a boxlike unit used to construct a performing stage; see **podium.**

rostrum steps—See risers.

rôti—Roast.

rotisserie—Roasted on a spit.

rough layout—An artist's sketchy rendering of the approximate placement of art and type or an event room layout.

rough sketch—A quick drawing giving indications of a proposed plan.

roulade—Rolled, as in meat.

round—A banquet table, usually 60" in diameter but also available in 66" and 72" diameters.

round robin—1. A contest or tournament in which each participant is matched with every other participant. 2. Open discussion period.

round slide tray—See **carousel tray.**

roundtable—A group of experts who meet on an equal basis to review and discuss specialized, professional matters, either in closed session or, more frequently, before an audience.

round-trip—See **circle trip.**

router—A cutting tool for gouging, scooping, or hollowing out.

roux (roo)—A mixture of butter or other fat and flour used to thicken sauces and soups.

roving microphone/mike—A small microphone, with or without wire, that can be moved easily through an audience for questions or comments.

row booth/stand—A booth or stand within a row of similar booths, with the front opening onto an aisle and with other booths on either side.

RSO—See **regional security officer.**

RS or L—Rates the same or lower.

RTI—See **room, tax, and incidentals.**

rump session—A session added on the end of the day to accommodate an extra plenary lecture, usually after dinner.

run—The number of copies printed.

runner—1. A long, narrow carpet in a hallway or aisle or onstage. 2. A piece of portable or constructed staging that extends a main stage to form a runway. 3. A main cord extending from a microphone to an amplifier. 4. An errand person available for assignment during an event or conference; also known as **gofer.**

running order—1. See **agenda.** 2. See **banquet event order (BEO)** and **event order (EO).**

running schedule—See **banquet event order (BEO).**

running sheet—See **event order (EO).**

runoff—In South Africa, the steps leading up to the stage level.

run-of-the-house rate—A rate for a facility guest room block that does not include suites; also known as **flat rate.**

run-through—A complete rehearsal including all elements of the event production, such as presentations, performances, music or entertainment, lighting, audiovisual, and technical aspects.

runway—A platform that extends from the stage perpendicularly into the audience; also known as **catwalk.**

Russian service—A style of banquet service in which the waiter offers food from a silver platter to guests who help themselves.

S

SA—See **société anonyme.**
SAACI—See **South African Association for the Conference Industry.**
saddle-stitch binding—A binding process using wire staples.
SAG—See **Screen Actors Guild.**
salad plate—A plate used for salads.
sales blitz—An intense selling effort in a particular locality.
sales force/sales team—A group of employees responsible for personally developing prospects and sales.
sales incentive—A reward in excess of salary or commission provided to a salesperson in return for achieving a stated sales goal.
sales manager—An individual who handles specific accounts and reports to the director of sales; see **director of sales.**
sales meeting—A meeting to introduce new products and their applications and to motivate sales staff.
sales portfolio—A manual of information carried by a salesperson for reference or display.
sales promotion—A special event whose objective is to increase sales and customers.
sales team—See **sales force/sales team.**
salute—A fireworks shell filled with an aluminum mixture that produces a loud bang or noise.
sanctioned area—A closed section of a street or area that is accessible only to authorized individuals and not to the open public; also known as **restricted area.**
sandblasting—A technique of etching a smooth surface of glass, plastic, or metal to achieve a matte or textured quality.
sandwiching—A mounting of a transparent subject matter between one translucent and one clear plastic panel.
SARRAL—See **South African Recording Rights Association Limited.**
satellite seminar—A small meeting of experts who have a specific common interest, also known as a **satellite symposium.**
satin finish—A smooth semigloss finish, usually on a metal or lacquered surface.

satire—A form of comedy in which sharp derision is aimed at an idea or individual.

sauerbraten—Beef cooked with vinegar and onions, served with a brown gravy.

sauerkraut—Cooked cabbage, shredded and pickled.

sauté—To fry lightly in a little fat.

scale model—Any model representing all components of the original object, but in a smaller size.

scallion—A young, small green onion.

scanner (laser)—A mirror-bearing device used to guide a laser beam in programmable patterns. Each scanner includes a shaft that rotates within an electromagnetic field like a motor. Unlike a motor, however, the scanner shaft does not rotate a full 360 degrees but only slightly in one direction or the other, that is, about 20 degrees plus and 20 degrees minus electric zero. The shaft of each scanner supports a mirror. The X mirror imparts horizontal positioning to the beam; the Y mirror imparts vertical positioning to the beam. The laser beam travels across both mirrors, allowing the beam to be aimed anywhere within an XY graphic field, thus, to draw pictures. The viewer sees imagery because the scanner repeats, or refreshes, the drawing at least 20 times per second. Analogous to the frame rate of film or video, this rapid repetition creates the phenomenon of persistence; also known as **galvanometer**.

scenario—A list showing all event details with their specific requirements such as date, time, and names of individuals involved and responsible per event; also known as **example** or **overview**.

scene—1. The setting of an action. 2. A division of an act or play.

scene in action—A term for the mechanical animation technique that achieves simulated flow motion by rotating a striped cylindrical acetate drum between a light source and face artwork.

schedule—See **agenda**.

schedule of services—See **event specification**.

schematic model—A diagram of an object in model form.

school desk—A chair with an attached writing surface; also known as **table chair** or **writing chair**.

schoolroom perpendicular setup—A configuration similar to a classroom, with tables set perpendicular to the head table and chairs placed on both sides; also known as **union seating**.

schoolroom seat—Each room of seats provided with a desk space built into the seating unit.

schoolroom setup—A configuration of tables lined in a row, one behind the other, on each side of a center aisle, with chairs facing the head table; also known as **classroom seating**.

scientific committee—The individuals who specifically discuss, supervise, and coordinate the scientific content of a program and select papers and submitted abstracts where appropriate.

scientific marketing—A style of marketing characterized by the use of scientific research, testing, and analytic methods as a means of minimizing risks and maximizing business opportunities.

scientific meeting—A meeting of individuals who are involved in research in the sciences.

scientific program—The content of a meeting described in chronological order and including the full list of speakers and the titles of their papers.

scientific secretariat—Administrative staff appointed to process all aspects of the scientific program of a meeting.

scioptican—A device used to create moving effects such as clouds, flames, waves, etc.

scissor lift—See **high jacker.**

SCMP—See **Society of Corporate Meeting Professionals.**

sconce—An ornamental wall bracket for candles or lights.

scoop—A floodlight.

scooter—See **electric cart.**

score—Sheet music provided to musicians and showing all parts of the instruments or voices.

screen—1. A front or rear projection surface. 2. A self-standing unit used to mask areas in a room.

Screen Actors Guild (SAG)—The professional union representing film actors and actresses.

screen/audience distance—The distance between the projection screen and the front row of the audience.

screen/audience left and right—Stage directions given from the audience's perspective.

screen enamel—A type of enamel ink used for printing on nonporous surfaces.

screening—1. A legal reference check using professional or police security checks to provide background information. 2. Reviewing a film before it is released for the public to experience.

screw post—A recessed, threaded fastening device.

scribe—The technique of fitting a prefabricated unit into an existing site condition by cutting the prefabricated unit slightly to allow a perfect fit.

scribe line—A shallow groove incised into the face of a material.

scrim—1. A translucent material used to diffuse or soften light, usually used onstage. 2. A finely woven material through which light may or may not be seen, depending on how it is lit; also known as **theatrical gauze and bobbinet.**

script—A written text of program presentations.

scroll—A copy of graphics that move slowly up the screen in video or film.

scroller/color changer—A string of gels fitted in front of a lamp that can be programmed to be static in any color chosen or scrolled for an effect and operated from the lighting desk.

SC&S—Strapped, corded, and sealed.

SDD—Store door delivery.

sealing—The technique of applying a sealer coat to porous woods prior to a painting procedure. Sealing prevents the absorption of the final paint finish.

search engine—Software that allows a visitor to search a Web site for Web pages that contain key words of relevant interest.

secateurs—A cutter used by florists.

second option—The organization holding the second option for specific dates at a facility.

second tier—A city where the space limitations of the convention center, the hotels, booths, or stands are more appropriate for smaller meetings and shows.

secretariat—The clerical staff of an organization that sponsors an event.

secretary general—The permanent head of a general organization that sponsors an event.

secret partnership—The existence of certain persons as partners who are not mentioned to the public; also known as **silent partnership.**

security cage—A wire enclosure supplied to an exhibitor to lock up materials for safe storage.

security contractor—A company hired by exhibit or show management to keep individual exhibits and the entire show floor safe using guards, closed-circuit TV, etc.

security deposit—A deposit made to assure credit, usually returned after the event, if there are no damages.

security guard—An individual who is employed to protect a building, people, an event, etc., and who may be hired from a privately operated company.

security lock—See **chain lock.**

security service—A service providing security protection for checking delegates' credentials, searching hand luggage, protecting equipment, and patrolling congress and exhibition areas.

segmentation—Dividing a market into parts by grouping them according to similar geographic, demographic, psychographic, or behavior characteristics.

segue—A transition between two audio passages, video segments, or any event elements.

self-contained—An entertainment act or group that can supply its own sound, music, and lights.

self-contained exhibit—An exhibit where a crate is opened and becomes part of the display.

self-insured—A form of insurance in which an organization assumes responsibility for and pays for all damages as they occur.

self-publishing—The process of privately producing and marketing one's own work.

self-tapping screw—A screw used to attach material to metal in a pre-drilled hole. As the screw is rotated, it threads into the hole and remains secure.

seltzer—Filtered tap water that has been artificially carbonated and flavored with mineral salts.

seminar—A lecture, presentation, and discussion under the guidance of an expert discussion leader allowing participants to share experiences in a particular field.

semiporcelain—A type of relatively high-quality fired earthenware.

semiskilled labor—1. A person whose work is limited to a well-defined work routine. 2. Work in which lapses of performance would not cause excessive damage to the product or equipment.

separate reprint—See **off-print**.

sepia—A printed reproduction of black-and-white art tinted in brown tones, which imparts an antique look.

sequence of events—See **time agenda**.

Serial Line Internet Protocol (SLIP)—A standard for using a regular telephone line (a serial line) and a modem to connect a computer as a real Internet site. SLIP is gradually being replaced by PPP.

series operator—A travel agent, wholesaler, tour operator, broker, etc., who blocks space in advance for a series of movements over a given period of time, not necessarily on a back-to-back basis.

serpent—In pyrotechnics, a short tube packed with a chemical mixture that propels the device with a strong jet flame in a zigzag or circular pattern.

serpentine—A configuration of tables in curving shapes, often S-shaped.

server—A computer, or a software package, that provides a specific kind of service to client software running on other computers.

service—Nonphysical, intangible attributes that management controls (or should), including friendliness, efficiency, attitude, professionalism, responsiveness, etc.

service bar—A bar located outside a function room or outlet, in a service area not visible to guests.

service charge—A fee for the services of waiters, housemen, technicians, and other personnel.

service contractor—The general contractor for an exhibition or convention.

service desk—A central location to order or reconfirm the functions provided by exhibition management.

service kit—A packet for exhibitors containing information and forms relating to the exhibition; also known as **exhibitor's kit** or **exhibitor's manual**.

service level—1. The number of people that one waiter is assigned to serve. 2. The type, coverage, and quality of service offered by a facility or contractor.

service plate—See **base plate.**

service recovery plan—A set of actions that are designed to respond to service failures; see **contingency planning.**

services and facilities—Items provided by or available from an event facility to enable the customer, delegate, or committee to get maximum benefits, such as the provision of secretarial services, cleaning, power, transportation, and catering.

serviette—See **napkin.**

serviette detail—Embellishment on a serviette.

session—A single uninterrupted segment of an event program in a meeting, exhibition, or conference.

set—1. A performance area, including props, equipment, and backdrops. 2. The length of time any musical group plays between breaks. 3. To make preparations for a predetermined number of attendees. 4. To arrange type for printed materials.

set dressing—Props arranged to decorate the set; also known as **trim props.**

set light—A light that illuminates the background or set behind the performers.

set piece—In pyrotechnics, a wooden frame onto which a desired pattern or image is outlined with lances. A traditional Fourth of July set piece is the American flag. Set pieces can be very big and beautiful.

set screw—A threaded machine screw with a flush head, normally used to adjust tension or tighten movable parts on shafts.

setup—1. The configuration of furniture in a function room. 2. The installation of equipment. 3. See **move-in.**

setup drawing—A rendering that shows the installation procedures; also known as **rendering.**

setup personnel/setup crew—Installers who construct exhibits, place furniture, and decorate an exhibition space.

setup plan—See **floor setup diagram.**

setup time—The period of time necessary for the preparation of an event facility before the arrival of participants; also known as commencement time of setup in Australia.

SGMP—See **Society of Government Meeting Planners.**

shadow box—A five-sided enclosure with its face open for the display of art or objects; a niche.

shag—A type of carpet.

shallot—A plant that looks like garlic and tastes like a mild onion.

Sheetrock—Material used in drywall construction and composed of gypsum core and paper veneer. Standard measurements are 4' x 8' and 4' x 10', with thicknesses of $\frac{3}{8}$", $\frac{1}{2}$", and $\frac{5}{8}$".

shelf—A thin wooden or metal board fixed horizontally on a wall for displaying objects or sales materials.

shell—In pyrotechnics, a paper container filled with stars or other fireworks ingredients designed to form a pattern or effect when displayed, such as comets, hummingbirds, lances, serpents, or whistles. A shell is either round or cylindrical, depending on the manufacturer.

shell folder—A brochure with a printed illustration to which varying text can be added.

shell scheme—A European booth or stand system that usually includes a raised floor, back and side walls, and fascia.

sherbet glass—A short glass serving dish with a foot and stem, used for serving ices and desserts.

shiplap—A construction technique of joining two materials by notching both and inserting slots into each other.

shipment—One lot (unit) of freight tendered to a carrier by one consignor at one place at one time for delivery to one consignee at one place on one bill of lading.

shipper—A company or individual to whom exhibit materials are consigned for transportation.

shipper's export declaration—A form required for all export shipments by the U.S. Treasury and prepared by a shipper, indicating the value, weight, destination, and other basic information about an export shipment.

shipping case—A container for exhibit components that is suitable for extended reuse, usually with a hinged lid and felted interior.

shipping crate—A container for exhibit components that is suitable for one use, usually with a screwed or nailed lid.

ship's manifest—An instrument in writing, signed by the captain of a ship, that lists the individual shipments constituting the ship's cargo.

shish kebab—Lamb or other meat pieces and vegetables cooked on a skewer.

shoehorn—1. A term meaning overcrowding of a hotel. 2. People in a congested area where movement stops. 3. Congestion of automobiles; also known as **gridlock.**

S-hook—See **sign hook.**

shop—A service contractor's main office and warehouse.

shore excursion—A land tour, usually available at ports of call, sold by cruise lines or tour operators to cruise passengers.

shot—A 1-ounce measurement of liquor.

shotgun microphone—See **hypercardioid microphone.**

shoulder—The intermediate time in the tourism industry between peak and low season; also known as **low period** in Australia.

show break—The time specified for the close of an exhibition and beginning of dismantling; also known as **strike** or **bump out** in Australia.

show card—A material used for making signs.

showcase—A general term for a glazed or framed enclosure for the display of objects.

showcase theater—A theater whose main purpose is to obtain work in other media for members of the cast.

show curtain—A drop or curtain that is painted and hung behind the front curtain to give atmosphere to the particular play or event being presented.

show daily—A newspaper that is published each day during the run of a show and includes articles about the exhibits and events.

show decorator—The company or individual who is responsible for hall draping, aisle carpeting, and signage and who also performs the same service to individual exhibitors.

show directory—A softcover book containing a listing with booth numbers of all the exhibitors in a show, a map showing booth or stand locations, and advertising.

show management—A company, group, or organization that manages a show or in which the show managers are employed.

show manager—An individual who is responsible for all aspects of an event or trade show; also known as **exhibition manager** or **exposition manager.**

show office—The management office at an event.

show organizer—See **exposition manager.**

show photographer—The official photographer for an event, appointed by the manager.

show plate—A decorative plate preset at each banquet guest place and removed at the start of service; also known as an **underliner.**

show tape—See **production tape.**

show-up time—See **reporting pay.**

show within a show—A show with its own name and own focus that takes place within a larger related event.

shrink-wrap—The process of wrapping loose items on a pallet with heat-sealed, transparent plastic wrapping.

shucker—An individual who opens fresh clams and oysters at a food station in view of guests.

shutter—In laser technology, an attachment that blocks the laser beam, usually from exiting the projector.

shuttle service—Transport facilities for participants, usually by coach or van.

SIC—See **Standard Industrial Classification.**

side chair—An armless chair.

side fills—Loudspeakers located stage right and stage left and used to project amplified sound to the full stage area.

side poles—The support poles placed around the perimeter of a tent; also known as **pin poles.** In South Africa, known as **pole tent.**

side rail—A low divider wall in an exhibit area.

side-stitch binding—A binding process by which folded sections of a book or magazine are placed on top of one another and stitched together from top to bottom.

side trip—See **extension.**

side walls—Detachable canvas or plastic walls used to create the sides of a tent.

sight act—A performer who must be watched to be appreciated, such as a mime, juggler, dancer, or acrobat; also known as **incidental entertainment** and **variety artist.** In the United Kingdom, known as a specialty act that focuses on entertainment.

sight draft—A draft that is payable upon presentation to the drawee.

sight line—See **line of sight.**

sightseeing tour—An excursion to points of interest, often by bus or van.

sign—An informational display used at an event; see **banner.**

signage—All informational and directional signs required for an event.

signaling system—A system of communication between the speaker and the projectionist or the chairman and the speaker.

signal-to-noise ratio—The ratio of the video or audio signal to the noise interference accompanying that signal.

signatory—See **authorized signature.**

signature dish—A food item a facility is known for or specializes in; also known as **house specialty.**

signature item—A product or service for which an event organization is known.

sign cloth—A lightweight material, as opposed to canvas, used for banners, signs, and streamers.

sign hook—An "S" shaped piece of hardware used for holding signs on an exhibit booth or stand.

significant other—An individual who serves an important personal role in another's life; often used to denote the companion of an invited guest at an event when the companion is not a spouse.

sign service—A service that provides signs for exhibitors.

sign standard—A frame on a stand.

silent partnership—See **secret partnership.**

silk screen—A painting stencil used for reproducing one or more times on a variety of materials.

silverprint—See **blueline/blueprint.**

silver service—See **butler service (American)** and **French service.**

Simple Mail Transfer Protocol (SMTP)—The main protocol used to send e-mail on the Internet.

simplex—In communication, allowing users to speak or hear only one at a time, for example, as in a walkie-talkie.

simultaneous interpretation—The process of orally translating one language into another or signing for the deaf while a person is speaking; also known as **consecutive interpretation.**

single—In entertainment, one musician or performer.

single bed—A bed measuring 38" x 75" (95cm x 188cm); also known as **twin bed.**

single room—A guest room occupied by one person.

single source sound—Sound originating from a single point.

single supplement—An extra charge added to a tour purchased for single accommodations.

single weight/matte—A term describing the character and finish of photo blowups necessary for mounting to or wrapping around a panel.

SISO—See **Society of Independent Show Organizers.**

SIT—Stopping in transit.

SITC—See **Standard Industrial Trade Classification.**

site—An area, property, or specific facility to be used for an event.

SITE—See **Society of Incentive and Travel Executives.**

site inspection—A personal, careful investigation of a property, facility, or area, prior to the event.

sitting on their hands—A phrase used to describe an unresponsive audience.

SJ cord—A rubberized cable commonly used as a flexible lead in, where conduit or greenfield are not practical.

sketch model—A three-dimensional sketch.

skewing—A zigzag pattern on a TV screen due to improper head alignment.

skid—A low, small platform used for storing and transporting merchandise; also known as **pallet.**

skin—A tracing of a sketch with explanatory notes.

skin drawing—A preliminary elevation and plan indicating overall dimensions.

skip—A departing guest who fails to pay for accommodations.

skirting—Pleated or ruffled table draping used on buffet, reception, and head tables.

skycap—An airport porter who handles baggage.

sky drop—A drop painted blue to represent the sky.

SL&C—Shipper's load and count.

sleeper—A leveling strip on which flooring or horizontal panels are fixed.

slide—A photographic transparency mounted on a small plastic frame or film arranged for projection; also known as **two-by-two.**

slide animation—A technique that creates the illusion of the movement of an image when a series of slides are projected in rapid sequence.

slider—A telescopic pipe enabling one section to slide inside another and used with draping to allow various widths and lengths.

slidetray—See **carousel tray.**

SLIP—See **Serial Line Internet Protocol.**

SMERF—See **Social, Military, Educational, Religious, and Fraternal.**

smoke generation—The creation of fog using chemicals and heat. A dry-ice machine is a 30-gallon to 55-gallon drum containing a heating element and an exhaust fan. When dry ice (frozen carbon dioxide) is submerged in hot water, the machine produces a fog that is forced out of the machine by a fan and directed through a 4"-diameter vent hose. Dry ice produces a low-lying fog. Burn units use a noncarbon liquid chemical and are about the size of a bread box. The liquid is heated in the unit, and the resulting fog is expelled under pressure toward the desired area. Older burn units use petroleum-based fluids, which produce a noxious odor and slippery residue. Burn units are the most practical way to create fog or smoke in mid-air. The fog is often referred to as Rosco fog, named after Rosco Laboratories, the major supplier of the chemical fluid used.

SMPTE timecode—A numeric code developed and approved by the Society of Motion Picture and Television Engineers (SMPTE) to identify individual frames in film and video.

SMTP—See **Simple Mail Transfer Protocol.**

snifter—A large, short-stemmed goblet used for cordials, cognac, and brandy.

snow peak—A South African term for a pointy shape to the roof of a tent.

snug banqueting—A tailored, stretch cover to fit over the standard banquet chair found in many events.

SO—Ship's option; shipping order; seller's option.

social dinner—A nonworking evening function at which a meal is served.

social event—A life-cycle celebration, such as a wedding, bar mitzvah, bas mitzvah, anniversary, birthday, etc.

Social, Military, Educational, Religious, and Fraternal (SMERF)—A catchall category of meeting market segments including social, military, educational, religious, and fraternal groups.

société anonyme (SA)—A French expression meaning a corporation.

society music—Dance or period music of the 1930s, 1940s, and 1950s.

Society of Corporate Meeting Professionals (SCMP)—An organization providing information and resources to its members, who coordinate corporate meetings and those who provide services and products for this industry.

Society of Government Meeting Planners (SGMP)—An organization providing information and resources to its members, who coordinate events for government agencies and those who provide services and products for this industry.

Society of Incentive and Travel Executives (SITE)—An organization providing information and resources to its members, who coordinate corporate incentive programs and those who provide products and services for this industry.

Society of Independent Show Organizers (SISO)—A trade association for independent exposition producers.

soffit—A lowered portion of a ceiling.

soft opening—A period of time when a new facility is open for business prior to the grand opening.

software—A computer program that causes equipment to "think" in a particular format.

solarized—An overexposed photographic print, purposely done for artistic effect.

sole relay interpreter—See **pivot interpreter.**

solvency ratio—The total assets divided by total liabilities.

sommelier—A wine steward.

sorbet—A frozen product having a mushy consistency that is designed to be a palate cleanser and served just prior to the entrée.

Soss hinge—The trade name for a concealed barrel-shaped hinge installed in the recess of cabinet doors and jambs to eliminate a revealed hinge.

soufflé—A baked, fluffy dessert or main dish of milk, egg yolks, stiffly beaten egg whites, and seasonings.

sound bite/video bite—A short sound or visual message that summarizes the major point of a story.

sound board—A console with separate channels to control the volume and sound quality produced by each microphone; also known as **mixing board/mixing desk** and **console.**

sound control stand/sound control booth—An area from which a technician operates the sound system in a room.

sound effect—A recorded or live sound used for special theatrical audio effects.

sound mix—The procedure of combining independently recorded narration, music, and/or sound effects onto a single master tape or film, while at the same time establishing time, volume, and balance between the elements.

soundproof wall—A barrier, usually permanent, that prevents sound from carrying to and from adjacent rooms.

soundscaping—A composition of recorded audio that creates a particular mood.

sound strip/sound track—A band of sound reproduced on motion picture film.

sound system—An electric audio speaker system used to amplify sound.

sound wings—Risers on the stage right and stage left for stacked sound equipment that allow storage space to be hidden from the audience's view; also known as **speaker platforms.**

source language—See **floor language.**

South African Association for the Conference Industry (SAACI)—A professional association whose members are active in the conference industry in South Africa.

South African Recording Rights Association Limited (SARRAL)—A not-for-profit organization that looks after the rights of composers of musical works wherever such musical works are recorded.

spa—A facility that provides baths, hot springs, health facilities, and other services.

space—An exhibitor location in a hall.

space assignment—The booth or stand assigned to an exhibiting company.

space rate—The cost per square foot for space rental.

space requirements—An amount of stand or booth space required by exhibitors.

space reservation form—A form to officially request to utilize a particular space.

space stage—The method of staging plays with lights focused on the actors so that no setting is necessary.

spade connectors—Fork-shaped metal connectors soldered to wire ends for connection to terminals having machine screw or knurled nut contacts.

spaetzle—Tiny dumplings.

span—The width of a structure, such as a tent.

spanakopita—A phyllo pie triangle stuffed with spinach.

spark pot—A pyrotechnic device that emits a burst of sparks, usually silver, when ignited.

speaker—1. An individual who presents an address on a specific topic or topics, including keynote. 2. A general session or seminar leader who is a topic specialist. 3. A trainer or workshop leader who allows for group participation and interaction. 4. A "change of pace" speaker, such as a humorist or entertainer. 5. A mechanical transducer that converts electrical impulses back into sound waves. 6. The output source of all sound systems. 7. A device for talent to hear music onstage.

speaker platforms—Risers on the right and left stage used to elevate sound equipment; see **sound wings.**

speaker's guidelines—Instructions regarding the required format to be used for the written preparation of a speech.

speaker's room/lounge—An area with audiovisual equipment for speakers to prepare prior to or between speeches.

spec book—Written specifications, requirements, and instructions for all functions, room setups, services, and purveyors, which includes names of key personnel, their areas of responsibility, special events, and any other related information; see **staging guide.**

special—A light focused on a particular area of a room or stage.

special committee—See **ad hoc committee.**

special-effects editing—The electronic assembly of film or videotape using dissolves, fades, wipes, or other unusual visual manipulation of an image. It can be used to create or sustain a mood or to join segments of a presentation that would not ordinarily match and can be accomplished only in an on-line edit suite.

special event—A unique moment in time celebrated with ceremony and ritual to satisfy specific needs.

special events market—The market for functions that are planned in advance, arouse expectation, and have celebration as the motivating force.

special event tour—A tour designed around a particular event such as the Kentucky Derby, Mardi Gras, or Rose Bowl Parade.

special event tourism—A planned activity such as a fair or festival or parade that promotes tourism in a destination.

special general meeting—A meeting other than an annual general meeting, which all members are entitled to attend.

special handling—Requiring extra labor, equipment, or time in delivery to the booth area.

special interest group—See **conclave.**

special interest tour—A tour designed to appeal to clients with a curiosity or a concern about a specific subject. Most such tours provide an expert tour leader and usually visit places and/or events of specific interest to the participants.

special lighting—In film and video production, lighting equipment that exceeds what a typical two-person video crew would carry and is used to create special effects, moods, or alter existing lighting. Examples include spotlights and strobes.

special rate—An amount charged for the occupancy of a room, usually at a reduced rate and negotiated as a group rate by the conference organizers.

special-rate package—A lowered, all-inclusive rate, frequently including one or more meals for two or three nights, that is offered to the general public; often used to generate off-season or weekend business.

specialty contractor—A supplier of a specific show service, such as photography, rental of furniture, audiovisual equipment, or floral decoration.

specifications—A complete written description of event requirements; see **request for proposal (RFP).**

Speedball—The trade name for a type of pen used in calligraphy and sign writing.

spike marks—Tape or chalk marks on studio or stage floors designating the exact placement of props and actors; also known as **marks.**

spill rings and baffles—See **louvers.**

spinning—A technique for working sheet metal into concave or convex shapes.

splice—The twisting together of two or more electrical wires to provide continuous power.

spline—A thin metal or wood strip glued into a groove cut in panel edges to reinforce the joint between panels.

split—A small bottle containing about one-quarter (6–6.5 ounces) of the usual quantity of liquor.

split charter—Two or more groups sharing the same flight.

split screen—A horizontal or vertical separation of video images shown simultaneously.

splitter—In laser technology, an attachment that divides the beam into two parts according to power, not color.

spokesperson—A designated representative who has the authority, knowledge, and credibility to speak to and be interviewed by the media.

sponsor—1. An individual who assumes all or part of the financial responsibility for an event. 2. A commercial sponsor that provides financial backing for an aspect of an event and who in return receives visibility, advertising, or other remuneration in lieu of cash.

sponsored bar—See **open bar.**

sponsoring body—An organization or institution that endorses an event, often by financially underwriting all or a portion of the event.

sponsorship plan—A plan that is reviewed with management, sponsors, and/or venue officials to assemble the details and policies on sponsorship elements in relation to overall event and legal agreements.

sport event—An event where athletes compete and spectators view the athletic activities and ceremonies.

sporting service—A service concerned with arranging sports activities or activities involving physical exertion and skill.

spot exchange—The purpose of sale of foreign exchange for immediate delivery.

spotlight—A movable lighting instrument designed to produce a concentrated beam of light focusing upon a particular individual or object.

spot line—A single rope specifically rigged from the gridiron to fly a piece of scenery that cannot be handled by the regular lines.

spot rehearsal—A practiced run-through of any segment of a production.

spot time—Time that staff or equipment is to be "seen" on-site.

spouse—A husband or wife of an event attendee; also known as **accompanying person.**

spouse program—An educational and/or social event planned for spouses and guests of event participants.

spring water—Water that flows naturally to the surface from a deep underground source.

sprinkler system—A fire protection system consisting of multiple overhead water outlets set to respond automatically in the case of fire.

spumoni—Ice cream with fruits and nuts and molded into sections.

SQL—See **Structured Query Language.**

squeeze connector—A fitting used to secure SJ cords to plugs and splice boxes.

squib head—An electrical igniter used to initiate a pyrotechnic effect; also known as **fuse head.**

squirrel cage/barrel—A spinning drum used for selecting winning raffle tickets for a drawing.

SS—Shipside.

S/S—Steamship.

stable—A group of speakers or entertainers usually under agreement with a particular bureau or agency.

stacking chairs—Chairs that save space by stacking on top of each other.

stadium seating—Seating where each row is set a few inches higher than the one in front of it.

stage—1. The entire floor space behind the proscenium arch. 2. See **catwalk**. 3. See **podium.**

stage call—1. A notice to performers to gather at a certain time and place for a review of responsibilities. 2. A meeting of the cast and director onstage to discuss problems before a performance or rehearsal. 3. To ask a celebrity or speaker to return to the stage after completing a presentation.

stage directions—Instructions in the script concerning movements and arrangements on the stage.

stagehand—A union laborer who handles spotlights, rigging, and scenery for theatrical productions. In some cities, stagehands may also handle decorating tasks, such as hanging draperies at convention facilities.

stage left, stage right—A description of directions from the perspective of an individual who faces the audience from the stage.

stage lighting—Lighting designated for the stage area only.

stage manager—An individual responsible for supervising the stage area including speakers, entertainers, technicians, and others; also known as **stage master.**

stage maroon—A pyrotechnic device that produces a very loud bang when ignited.

stage master—An employee of a venue who is in charge of stage facilities; also known as **stage manager.**

stage plot—A diagram, drawn to scale, indicating placement onstage of artists' equipment, props, and microphones.

stage wait—A period of time when there is no dialogue or action onstage.

staging—1. The design and placement of elements for an event. 2. The implementation of an event.

staging area—1. A place for a demonstration. 2. A platform for a performance. 3. An area adjacent to the main event area, for setup, dismantling, and temporary storage.

staging guide—A compilation of function sheets, scripts, instructions, room setup diagrams, directory of key personnel, forms, and other material relating to an event.

stakeholders—All individuals who are invested in an event, such as the organizations, guests, vendors, media, and others.

stakes—Pointed pegs used to secure the guy ropes of a tent in the ground. Wooden stakes are used for grass-covered earth. Steel stakes are required when the ground is extremely hard, rocky, or paved; also known as **anchors.**

stanchions—Decorative upright bars, or posts, that hold markers, flags, or ropes to define traffic areas at gatherings.

stand—A European term for booth; see **booth.**

standard agreement—The contract suggested by a national or international union as a guide for adoption or use by its locals.

Standard Industrial Classification (SIC)—A standard numerical code system used by the United States government to classify products and services.

Standard Industrial Trade Classification (SITC)—A standard numerical code system developed by the United Nations to classify commodities used in international trade.

standby—An attempt to travel on a flight without a confirmed reservation.

stand contract—A contract stating the terms and conditions for the rental of an exhibition venue or for an individual stand or booth within a venue.

stand equipment—The items that can be supplied on hire to stands, such as lighting, shelves, carpet, etc.

stand-in—An individual substituting for a performer, speaker, or VIP.

standing committee—A permanent committee, defined by organizational by-laws, that meets to conduct its specific responsibilities.

standing microphone—A microphone attached to an adjustable vertical stand.

star—The leading actor or actress.

star billing—See **100 percent star billing.**

stars—In pyrotechnics, the colored fire produced by a mixture of fine-grade chemicals that appears when a fireworks shell displays in the night sky; may be round (the size of a dime) or square (the size of a sugar cube) depending on the manufacturer.

state-controlled trading company—In a country with a state trading monopoly, a trading entity empowered by the country's government to conduct export business.

statement of account—A financial report of income and expenses.

statement of income and expenditure—An accurate account of the financial position at any given date showing all credits and debits within categories of income and expenditure.

state-of-the-art—The newest technology available.

state term contract—A contract negotiated by the state to assure the best price for certain services and goods.

state travel office—An official government agency or privately run nonprofit organization responsible for travel development and promotion of a state (or territory). Often, an office responsible for travel development is part of another department or agency of a state government, such as commerce and economic development. State travel offices vary in sizes of staffs and budgets.

station—1. A location or area where a server is assigned. 2. Individual food or beverage stations may be located throughout a reception area, with each table offering one food or beverage item or representing one theme.

stations—See **nodes.**

stats—The photographic material used in preparing camera-ready art; also known as **photo stats** or **Velox.**

stay-over—A guest who stays at a facility beyond the stated departure date.

steak tartare—Raw, ground filet mignon; highly seasoned.

steamship conference—A group of steamship operators that operate under mutually agreed-upon freight rates.

steering committee—A group of individuals created by an organization who set policies and make basic decisions relative to a group or an event.

step-on guide—A freelance guide who comes aboard a motor coach to give an informed overview of the city or attraction to be toured; also known as **tour guide.**

stepper switch—An electrical relay that is timed to activate further mechanisms after it has been itself activated.

stet—A proofreading term noted when copy marked for change is to be put back in its original form.

steward—See **business agent.**

ST labor—Work performed on straight time.

stock—The resident company of players performing one play nightly for a week and rehearsing another play for the following week.

stock bill—A list of specific materials and sizes.

stock exhibit—A predesigned unit adapted to a particular use by identification, color graphics, and minor structural modifications.

stock requisition—A document used to obtain merchandise from the storeroom.

stoneware—A hard clayware made of light-colored clay and fired at high temperatures.

stop motion—See **freeze-frame.**

storyboard—A series of rough sketches that depict the scene and action in a planned film or program; see **field production.**

story pole—A fixed pole with predetermined layout markings.

str.—Steamer.

straight brace—A tent component that is designed to prevent a tent from collapsing.

straight time—Labor performed and paid at the standard rate for work during normal business hours as established by unions.

street beat—A drumbeat accompanying a band that is marching but not playing.

stretcher—1. A general term for a cross member mounted between the sides or legs of a cabinet to insure rigidity. 2. A device used to transport the injured at an event.

strike—1. A collective refusal to work by union workers; also known as **walkout.** 2. To remove all scenery and props from a stage. 3. To dismantle and remove an exhibit.

strip—To put a negative into place as part of a larger or composite negative in preparing to make an offset printing plate.

striplight—A long, narrow fixture with a row of lamps, often with reflectors and color gels, used in color lighting.

stripped package—1. A package that includes the bare minimum of ingredients necessary to qualify it for an Inclusive Tour number. 2. Any package or tour offering inferior accommodations and/or omitting some of the many features usually included in an inclusive tour.

strobe light—An electronic lighting instrument that emits extremely rapid but brief flashes of brilliant light; with better models, the range and intensity of these flashes can be adjusted. When the flat rate is properly adjusted, it is possible to create the illusion of slow motion. Requires posting of caution signs to alert event participants of usage.

stroboscope—An instrument for producing the illusion of motion by a series of pictures viewed in rapid succession.

strong back—A framing member using the triangular system to support a cantilevered load.

Structured Query Language (SQL)—A specialized programming language for sending queries to databases.

stub space—See **feeder space.**

stud—A vertical structural wall support of wood or metal.

studio—A guest room with couches that convert to beds.

study mission—An educational visit to a workplace or manufacturing plant of interest to meeting participants; also known as **educational visit** or **technical tour** that is usually combined with business travel.

stuffing—The repetitive act of placing assembled written materials in an envelope, folder, or other presentation packet.

Styrofoam—The trade name for a lightweight rigid form of compressed polystyrene crystals.

SU—Setup.

subcommittee—A group of individuals, frequently including one or more members of the main committee, meeting outside of the main committee, with responsibilities for specific items.

subcontractor—A company retained by a general contractor or event manager to provide services or products.

submersible pump—A pump that operates underwater.

subsidies—See **grants.**

SUCL—Setup carload.

suite—A parlor with one or more guest rooms.

SULCL—Setup in less than carload.

summary/brief—A written short version of a speech or paper; also known as an **abstract.**

summary of discussions—A short report of discussions that have taken place in the event hall.

summary record/report—A short account of a speech, debate, or discussion.

super-APEX fare—An airline APEX fare at a lower rate but with more restrictions than a regular APEX fare.

superimposition—The projection of two images on a screen at the same time.

supernumerary (super)—An extra or walk-on in a production who has no individual lines of his own to speak.

supervising committee—A committee to watch over, direct, and check.

supervisor—See **banquet captain/banquet manager** and **maître d'.**

supper—The evening meal; also known as **dinner.**

supplemental airline—A nonscheduled airline.

supplier—A facility, company, agency, or individual offering space, goods, or services.

surcharge—A charge over and above established rates.

surety—A corporation or individual who guarantees the performance or faithfulness of another.

surprise cuisine—See **peek-a-boo cuisine.**

survey—1. An evaluation tool used to collect exhibitors' opinions regarding services or attendees' reactions to an event. 2. See **poll.**

sushi—A raw fish dish.

suspended element—An attachment of devices to the framework of an exhibition hall.

suspension of the meeting—A definite break in a meeting for a specific and unprogrammed reason.

suspension paint—A general term for paint that has one or more additional pigments floated in the base color. When sprayed onto the surface of a material, it achieves a multicolored splatter pattern.

sweep—A method used for setting up and cutting circles or arches.

Swiss cheese—White or pale yellow cheese with many large holes.

switchboard—A combination of switches, dimmer plates, and fuses for controlling light; also known as **dimmerboard.**

switcher—1. The engineer, or technical director, who changes from video camera to video camera. 2. In TV, the control room technician in charge of electronically switching from one camera to another. 3. A panel with rows of buttons and levers that allows shifting from one camera or sound source to another.

SWOT analysis (strengths, weaknesses, opportunities, and threats)—An analytical tool used to forecast the potential benefits and deficits of a future event based on the strengths, weaknesses, opportunities, and threats of past or comparable events.

symposium—1. A meeting or conference at which experts discuss a particular subject and express opinions. 2. A meeting of a number of experts in a particular field, at which papers are presented and discussed by specialists, with a view to making recommendations.

synchronization—The recording of sound and image at the same time.

synch sound—The sound that matches frame-to-frame with the picture, which is critical in close shots.

system—A stock set of components that can be put together to make an exhibit.

T

tabbouleh—A Middle Eastern relish.

tableau curtain—A curtain that is gathered up in an ornamental arch.

table center—See **centerpiece**.

table chair—See **school desk**.

table d'hôte—A full-course, fixed-price meal; in some areas may be served by a waiter.

table microphone—A microphone on a short stand placed on a table for seated speakers.

table service—A style of banquet service at which guests are served, at each course, a full plate with every item already on it.

table tent—A small sign used to identify the speaker or speakers.

tabletop display—A portable display that can be set up on top of a table.

tabletop presentation—A small exhibit on tables, often used in combination with posters.

table wine—A class of wine fermented to about 12 to 14 percent alcohol.

tabs—The main front curtain of a stage.

taffeta—A stiff, lustrous fabric used for skirting or special draping.

tag—The final speech of a scene, act, or play, serving as a cue for the curtain.

take down—See **dim**.

take stage—To move into an area of greater prominence on the stage with other actors yielding focus.

talent agent/booking agent—A representative for talent who locates and contracts for booking events.

talk—An electronic service that allows two users logged onto the Internet to communicate with each other in real time.

talkback—A loudspeaker system that connects the director's control room with the studio.

tallow carving—A display piece carved from a combination of hardened lamb's fat and wax.

tally sheet—A form used to keep track of rooms sold and/or those still available; also used to account for event attendees, equipment, etc.

tap—A device used for starting or stopping the flow of a beverage from a container.

tape blip—An audible impulse that activates an electric mechanism.

tape deck—See **tape recorder.**

tape player—A machine that is designed for the playback of recorded magnetic tapes only.

tape recorder—A device for recording and playing back audio signals from a tape medium; the most cost effective means of providing pre-recorded material for events; also known as **tape deck.** Audiotapes can be of three types. A cartridge is a ¼" closed-loop tape with one or two tracks, which automatically recycles and is of broadcast standard. It is used for special effects such as prerecorded announcements and is semiautomated. A cassette is a ¼" tape in a closed case with one to four tracks, which can be continuous loop, autorepeating, and automated. It is the standard product for broadcast music and prerecorded shows. A reel-to-reel tape is an open-reel tape, ¼" to 2" in width, with 1 to 32 tracks for recording.

tapered edge—Any material that is reduced in thickness at its outer edge.

tapping—The technique of threading a hole in metal to receive a machine screw.

tare weight—The weight of a container and/or packing materials deducted from the total weight to determine the weight of the contents or load.

target audience—1. The audience intended to be reached by an advertiser in using a given communications medium or set of media. 2. The group of people that a marketing message is intended to reach.

target language—The language into which a speech or document is translated.

target market—The precise group of people who need, want, and desire an event, product, or service.

target price—A product price established by a seller who derives it by specifying a desired rate of return on costs or investment at the anticipated sales volume.

tariff—1. A fare or rate from a supplier. 2. A class or type of fare or rate. 3. A published list of fares or rates from a supplier. 4. An official publication compiling fares or rates and conditions of services. 5. A tax that is imposed on imported or exported products.

tax withholding—A certain amount of money that must be withheld from a payment as an income tax.

TCP/IP—See **Transmission Control Protocol/Internet Protocol.**

TDBA—Trading and doing business as.

teach-in—A session specially held for the application of modifications and additions necessary to keep a particular subject up-to-date.

teacup and saucer—A traditional-sized cup and saucer used for either tea or coffee.

team of interpreters—A group of people responsible for interpreting simultaneously by utilizing simultaneous interpretation equipment.

teardown—The dismantling of equipment at the conclusion of an event.

teaser—1. The horizontal curtain that runs from stage right to left connecting the vertical tormentor curtains; also known as **valance** or **border**. 2. A printed promotional piece designed to build interest in an event.

tech check—A confirmation that all the technical aspects of a production or event are in working condition.

technical director—A trained individual who calls for cues for a performance.

technical meeting—1. A meeting of a group whose members and suppliers work in technical, engineering, research, or applied sciences. 2. In the United States and Canada, a nonmedical meeting of professional organizations.

technical rehearsal—A run-through of the technical aspects of a show, including lighting, sound, and special effects.

technical tour—See **study mission.**

technical visit—A tour by conference participants to a workplace related to their particular interests.

technician—An individual who runs lights, sound, or special effect equipment.

Teflon—The trade name for a self-lubricating plastic material with an opalescent appearance; used as glides, bearings, and linings to reduce friction.

Telecine—A device used originally to send out motion pictures over a TV channel. Now it is used to convert original film to video prints.

teleconference—A type of event that brings together three or more people in two or more locations through telecommunications. Audioconference refers to audio only, such as a telephone. Videoconferencing refers to a combined audio and visual link through a satellite or other type of network.

telefax/telecopier—A type of equipment for sending and receiving facsimiles of printed or pictorial matter by analog or digital transmission either over a telephone line or via a telecommunications network; also known as **facsimile machine** or **fax.**

teleinterpreting—Simultaneous interpreting using telecommunications facilities; also known as **distance interpreting.**

telemarketing—The sale of a product that takes place over the telephone.

telephone connection—The socket into which a telephone can be plugged for external communication.

teleprojector—See **video projector.**

TelePrompTer—The trade name for an electronic device that allows a display of script to aid a speaker or performer.

telescopic pipe—A drape support where one section slides inside another for use at various lengths; see **slider.**

Telnet—A program on the Internet that provides support for a variety of terminals to allow for logging into a network from a remote location.

tempered pressed wood—A hardwood product generally used in backwall paneling.

template—An accurate pattern or guide for various repetitive shop functions.

temporary labor—See **manpower agency.**

tension structure—A tent designed to have all perimeter loading equally distributed over a series of catenary arches, which provides greater stability.

tent—A portable canvas or vinyl shelter for an outside function.

tentative agenda—A proposed agenda as circulated prior to its approval at the meeting.

tentative hold—A space temporarily held by a facility pending a definite booking; also known as **option.**

tent specialist—A rental specialist who rents and installs tents for events.

terfer—The equipment used in South Africa to lift up a tent during the erection process.

terminal—1. The central location for departures and arrivals for airplanes, buses, ships, and trains. 2. A freight-handling location at a dock area or at an airport.

terrine—Any food baked in an earthenware dish from which it is served.

theater booking—Reservation of seats at a theater.

theater setup—A configuration of chairs, set up in rows facing the head table, stage, or speaker. Variations are semicircular and V-shaped; also known as **auditorium setup.**

theatrical case—A telescoping fiber case with canvas straps.

theatrical gauze and bobbinet—See **scrim.**

theme break—A break during a formal program session, with special food and beverages pertaining to a theme and often including decorations, costumes, and entertainment.

themed/special interest tour—A tour designed around a specific theme with special interest to the participants, such as fall foliage.

theme party—A type of party in which the invitation, food, decorations, entertainment, and other elements all relate to a central concept.

think tank—A group of specialists organized by a business enterprise or governmental body and commissioned to undertake intensive study and research into specified problems.

thin wall—A lightweight electrical conduit.

third party—Any individual who is not party to a contract, agreement, or instrument of writing but whose interest in the thing conveyed is thought to be affected.

third-party policy—See **automobile liability insurance.**

three-dimensional (3-D)—A flat image having the effect of three dimensions.

three wire—A term describing an electrical cable with one continuous ground wire in addition to positive and negative wires.

through bill of lading—A single bill of lading covering both the domestic and international carriage of an export shipment. An air waybill is essentially a through bill of lading used for air shipments. Ocean shipments usually require two separate documents—an inland bill of lading for domestic carriage and an ocean bill of lading for international carriage.

throw—A projection distance for lighting, video, or film.

TIA—See **Travel Industry Association of America.**

ticket—See **congress card.**

ticket exchange—A banquet control procedure whereby guests exchange an event coupon from their registration packet for an actual event ticket and seat assignment.

ticket revalidation—A technique of amending an airline ticket to reflect new flights booked.

tie beam/tie rod—The lowest horizontal member in a truss holding the rafters together in a tent; used in portal tent structures, too.

tie-off—A method of securing a shipment by the use of nylon belts and block latches.

tiered—An arrangement of rows of chairs one row above the other.

timber batten—See **batten (bat).**

time agenda—An outline containing a program of events and the time of commencement that is tailored to the needs of the event; also known as **sequence of events.**

time and materials (T&M)—A method of charging for services and materials used on a cost-plus basis.

timecode—The sequential numbers assigned to each frame of video or film, representing the passage of time in hours, minutes, seconds, and even tenths of seconds, for example, 01:20:35:10, which indicates that this frame can be found in the first hour, twentieth minute, thirty-fifth second, and first tenth of a second of the videotape or film. Timecodes are used for catalog purposes when identifying scenes and are most important during editing, saving valuable time in locating scenes needed for a particular edit.

timecoding—The numerical synchronization of sound and film elements, encoded with matching numbers (frame to frame) to ensure synchronicity.

time delay—The length of time between the production of live sound and when it is actually heard.

time draft—A draft that matures a specified number of days after acceptance or after the date of the draft.

timeline—See **production schedule.**

tip—An amount of money given to service workers to show appreciation; also known as **gratuity.**

tiramisu—An Italian dessert including mascarpone cheese and flavored with coffee.

title role—A character whose name appears in the title of the play.

titles—Written or graphic materials shown on camera, such as credits.

TL—Truckload.

TLO—Total loss only.

T&M—See **time and materials.**

toastmaster—See **master of ceremonies (MC).**

toe base—See **kick base.**

toggle switch—A lever that moves back and forth to open or close an electric circuit.

ton—A unit of measurement based on either volume or weight; see **measurement ton** and **weight ton.** Freight rates for liner cargo generally are quoted on the basis of a certain rate per ton, depending on the nature of the commodity. This ton, however, may be a weight ton or a measurement ton.

T-1 line—A leased line connection capable of carrying data at 1,554,000 bits per second.

tongue and groove—A construction technique of assembling two wood elements, one having a protrusion, the other having a recess.

top of bill—See **100 percent star billing.**

tormentor—One of a pair of vertical side curtains that, when combined with a horizontal teaser curtain, frame a stage; also known as **leg.**

tortoni—Vanilla ice cream blended with crushed macaroons and frozen in little frilled paper cups.

total admission per capita—The total admission revenue less discounts divided by total attendance including complimentary admissions.

total attendance—The total number of guests entering a facility, including complimentary admissions.

total net revenue—The sales revenue less discounts, returns, and allowances.

total revenue—The sales revenue from all revenue-generating departments at gross, before discounts, returns, and allowances.

touch-up paint—A paint accompanying an exhibit, in the necessary color, for the purpose of painting nicks and scratches.

tour—See **excursion.**

tour-based fare—A reduced-rate excursion fare available to those who buy a prepaid tour or package.

tour conductor—See **escort.**

tour consultant—An individual within a travel agency who sells to and advises clients regarding a tour; sometimes a travel consultant or salesperson with particular experience in escorted tour sales.

tour departure—Related to the operation of any published tour: the date of the start of a particular travel program by any individual or group; by extension, the entire operation of that single tour.

tour escort—A professional travel escort. Often called tour leader or tour manager; see **escort.**

tour guide—See **step-on guide.**

tour guide/travel guide—An individual who takes people on sightseeing excursions of limited duration; see **courier.**

tourism—The industry providing services and facilities for business and leisure travelers. The concept of tourism is of direct concern to governments, carriers, lodging, restaurant, entertainment industries, and event management and indirect concern to virtually every industry and business in the world. Tourism is believed to be the world's largest industry.

tourist card/tourist visa—A kind of visa issued to a tourist prior to entering a country and required in addition to a passport or other proof of citizenship.

tourist information board—See **convention and visitors bureau (CVB).**

tourist office—An organization that exists to promote a town or country to groups or individuals as a tourist destination.

tourist service—A service concerned with the organization of excursions that are purely for pleasure.

tour leader—See **escort.**

tour manual—1. A summary of facts about a tour company's rules, regulations, and official procedures. 2. A compendium of facts about a destination, including its attractions, accommodations, geography, special events, etc., used by a destination marketing organization to attract tour operators and visitors to their area.

tour menu—A menu that limits group clients to two or three choices.

tour operator—A person or company that creates and/or markets inclusive tours and/or subcontracts their performance. Most tour operators sell through travel agents and/or directly to clients. See **contractor, operator,** and **wholesaler, tour.**

tour option—Any component of a package tour that is not included in the package price, but may be purchased as an added feature or to extend the length of the package. Tour options are purchased at additional cost; also known as **add-on** or **enhancement.**

tour order—A coupon given to the purchaser of a tour package, identifying the tour and the seller and indicating that the tour is prepaid. The purchaser then uses this form as proof of payment and receives vouchers for meals, baggage handling, transfers, entrance fees, etc.

tour organizer—A person who locates and creates groups for a prepaid tour. May be an outside sales representative of a travel agency. Often compensated with a free trip and/or commission.

tour package—See **package.**

tour series—A prearranged link of stopovers for customers traveling by motor coach, usually carrying a theme.

tour voucher—A document issued by a tour operator to be exchanged for accommodations, meals, sightseeing, or other services; sometimes called **coupon.**

tower—A vertical, metal structure used to hold lighting equipment above a performance area.

tow motor—See **forklift.**

tracking—A method for monitoring, such as tracking the number of guests that come into a specific event, hotel, restaurant, or area.

track lighting—Lighting attached to a rodlike metal track mounted on a ceiling or wall, which allows for flexible spotlighting and other lighting effects.

tractor trailer—The tractor is the driving unit of a large truck; the trailer is the container unit.

trade—A line of work or occupation pursued as a business, such as event management.

trade association—A group of individuals employed in a particular trade.

trade day—A day that attendance to an exhibition is restricted to professional or trade visitors.

trade fair—An international term for an exposition.

trade mission—A group tour with a business rather than a vacation purpose. Usually planned for business or government representatives traveling overseas to secure new business in foreign markets for their product, city, or other entity.

trade-out—A type of barter. For example, a show manager might do a trade-out with a publishing company, giving the publisher a free booth or stand in exchange for free advertising.

trade show—See **exhibition.**

Trade Show Exhibitors Association (TSEA)—A trade association for organizations that use exhibits as a marketing, promotional, or communications medium. Formerly known as the International Exhibitors Association (IEA).

trade show organizer—An individual who plans a trade show, reserves the space, markets to exhibitors, and promotes attendance by buyers.

trade show producer—An individual who plans the logistical arrangements in connection with an exhibition.

trade visitor—See **professional visitor.**

traditional dress—See **national dress.**

traffic flow—1. The movement of people through an event area. 2. The movement of vehicles in and around a venue.

tragedy—A drama in which the protagonist fights a losing battle.

trainer—An instructor of techniques and skills on a specific subject.

training meeting—A structured learning session in which a teacher presents specific information and techniques.

tramp steamer—A ship not operating on regular routes or schedules; calls at any point where cargo is available.

transfer—1. The process of moving equipment and/or guests from one point to another. 2. To copy picture or sound that is transmitted by one recorder to another, or to make a tape copy from film.

transient space—A short-term rental space.

transit—A passenger changing planes without going through security or customs.

transit and exhibition insurance—A type of insurance that covers loss or damage caused deliberately or accidentally by third parties during loading, unloading, transshipment, transport, and exhibition.

transit visa—A government-issued permit allowing its holder to stop over in a country to make a travel connection or for a brief visit.

translation—A conversion of one language to another, orally or in writing.

translation service—An individual or business that translates written material or conversation from one language to another.

translucence—The ability to view light through a solid object such as a china plate. A silhouette of the hand will be visible through the fine china that makes it semitransparent.

translucency—A sheet of treated thin material that may be used to produce silhouette effects.

Transmission Control Protocol/Internet Protocol (TCP/IP)—The system that networks use to communicate with each other. Software packages for hooking up to the Internet are based on TCP/IP.

transmission fibers—Fiber optics used for light or information transmission; also known as **fiber optics.**

transmitter unit—An apparatus for transmitting radio waves through space.

transparency—An image on a plastic sheet or roll, clear or colored, viewed by projecting from an overhead projector to a screen.

transport—See **cartage.**

transport coordinator/officer—An individual in charge of planning and managing transportation arrangements for participants.

travel agent/agency—An individual or firm qualified to arrange for hotel rooms, meals, transportation, cruises, tours, and other travel requirements.

traveler/traveler curtain—A large curtain that opens horizontally from the middle or from one side of a stage; see **draw curtain.**

travel guide—See **tour guide/travel guide.**

Travel Industry Association of America (TIA)—An organization comprised of individuals and organizations in the United States travel industry whose purpose is to conduct research and promote travel products and services.

travel insurance—A type of insurance against accidents that occur in the course of travel to or from a meeting, traveling abroad on business or pleasure.

travel mission—See **trade mission.**

traverse—A curtain across a stage, usually toward the back of the stage.

tray service—See **butler service (American).**

treadmill stage—A machine device consisting of belts running on a stage floor, where actors may give the illusion of traveling over a distance.

treads—See **risers.**

treasurer—An individual appointed to control the finances of an event or organization.

trestle table—A rectangular table ranging from 4' to 12' in length and 2½' in width.

trim props—See **set dressing.**

trip director—An escort of an incentive company. Larger companies reserve this title for the person who directs all personnel and activities for a particular incentive trip.

triple sheet—A bed made with a third sheet on top of the blanket.

trip tray—A box rigged to empty its contents, such as snow or confetti, onto a stage.

trolley—See **wheeler.**

trouble box/tool box—A nickname for an equipment box most exhibitors carry that contains tools and supplies to repair an exhibit or product in case of trouble; also known as **gang box.**

troubleshoot—The activity of identifying potential or existing problems and repairing malfunctions.

truckload—Truckload rates apply if the tariff meets a truckload minimum weight. Charges will be at the truckload minimum weight unless weight is higher.

truck loader—Union labor specifically responsible for loading and unloading equipment.

truffle—1. A fungus that grows underground in France; highly prized and very expensive. 2. A chocolate candy.

truss—1. A frame to carry the roof of a tent. 2. A structure of steel bars used to suspend lighting or other technical equipment over a stage.

trust receipt—The release of merchandise by a bank to a buyer in which the bank retains title to the merchandise. The buyer, who obtains the goods for manufacturing or sales purposes, is obligated to maintain the goods(or the proceeds from their sale) distinct from the remainder of his assets and to hold them ready for repossession by the bank.

tryout room—See **projection rehearsal room.**

TSEA—See **Trade Show Exhibitors Association.**

T-shaped setup—A configuration of tables arranged in the shape of a block T, with chairs set around all but the head table.

T-3 line—A leased line connection capable of carrying data at 44,736,000 bits per second.

tube lights—A string of small, low-voltage lights contained in a clear or transparent colored plastic tube, generally wired to be run by a three- or four-circuit sequencer (controller); used as a highlighter around signs, stages, or entrances. They can be bent and mounted on Peg-Board or other surfaces to form lighted words; also known as **rope lights.**

tunnel—A horizontal cone of light produced by lasers and fog.

turnaround—An action required to break down and reset a room.

turnbuckle—Hardware installed between stretched cable to adjust tension.

turndown service—A service in which beds are prepared for sleeping and usually includes the replacement of bathroom linens.

turnkey exhibit—A system whereby the exhibit manager turns responsibility of the display over to an exhibit house. In essence, the exhibitor simply "turns the key" upon arrival at the show and opens the booth.

turnover—The time required to break down and reset an event.

turntable—A motorized rotating platform.

turret projector—A general term for a slide projector that stores slides in a rotating cylinder, dropping or passing slides one at a time between the light source and lens.

TV monitor—A type of screen used to show a video image.

twenty-footer—A 20' by (usually) 10' exhibit space. Similar terminology (a thirty-footer, etc.) may be used.

twin bed—A bed measuring 38" x 75" (95cm x 188cm); also known as **single bed.**

twin double room—A twin room occupied by two people.

twinkle lights—Flickering or intermittent lights; also known as **fairy lights** in Australia.

twin room—A room with two twin beds, suitable for two persons.

twist lock—A type of electrical plugs that are connected by twisting them together, as opposed to the standard male and female plugs.

two-by-two—A piece of 35mm photographic film usually in a 2" x 2" cardboard, glass, or plastic mount; also known as **slide.**

two-way loudspeaker—See **intercommunication system.**

typecasting—Selecting actors for roles because they resemble in real life the characters.

typeface—The name of a type design, such as Helvetica, Schoolbook, Times Roman, etc.

typeset copy—Text whose type has been mechanically set prior to reproduction.

typesetting—See **copyfitting.**

Tyrex cord—A type of cord that, within proper specifications, makes an acceptable electrical cord for exhibits.

U

UCT—See **Universal Coordinated Time.**

UL—Underwriters Laboratories.

ultraviolet lamp—A source of ultraviolet light used with phosphorescent and fluorescent paints.

unanimous—All who voted are in agreement.

underliner—See **show plate.**

underpayment—An insufficient payment of funds for items ordered.

underscore—To play music during a video or film scene.

under the auspices of—A measure of responsibility for, or guidance in, the organization of an event.

under-the-glaze decoration—A type of decoration in which the glaze goes over the pattern.

under the patronage of—A phrase used to indicate the endorsement of an event by an eminent individual.

undifferentiated—A single marketing strategy to reach an entire market.

unexpected departure—A guest who leaves a facility before the stated departure date.

unidirectional microphone—A microphone that is sensitive to sound coming from the direction in which it is pointed.

union—An organization of workers formed for their mutual benefit and for the purpose of dealing collectively with their employer in wages, hours, working conditions, and other matters pertaining to their employment.

union call—1. The number of union members hired to work for an event. 2. Additional servers obtained from a labor source shared by several hotels.

union contract—A written agreement between an employer and a union specifying the terms and conditions of employment for workers, the status of the union, and the procedure of settling disputes arising during the contract term; also known as **collective agreement.**

union jurisdiction—1. The group of employees that a union seeks to represent. 2. The jobs that a union claims should be filled by its members. 3. The crafts covered by a specified national or international union.

union official—A representative of a union either selected or elected by the membership to conduct the affairs of the union.

union seating—See **schoolroom perpendicular setup.**

union shop—An establishment in which newly hired employees are required to join the union within a specified time after employment, and in which all employees must maintain good standing in the union as a condition of employment.

union steward—An on-site union official.

Universal Coordinated Time (UCT)—A standard for time whose master clock is maintained by the United States Naval Observatory in Washington, DC; see **Greenwich Mean Time (GMT)** or **Zulu Time.**

unsettled account—An invoice not yet paid.

upgrade—To change to a superior standard.

uplinking—The sending of video signals via microwave to an existing satellite for transmission to selected sites or anyone capable of satellite reception for that signal; used for teleconferencing or broad distribution of a message on a national or international basis.

uppercase—A capital letter.

Upson board—Fiberboard of varying thicknesses, used as the surface for visual enhancement such as paint or decoration.

upstage—The part of the stage farthest from the audience or camera.

usability—A lesser standard of accessibility that does not meet ADAAG minimum requirements, but that may be functionally usable by some people with disabilities.

Usenet—A very large electronic bulletin board system of thousands of discussion groups and forums about a broad range of topics.

U-shaped setup—A configuration of chairs arranged in a U shape that faces the head table or speaker; also known as **horseshoe setup** or **open-U setup.**

USSG—U.S. Standard Gauge.

utility box—An area in a floor, wall, or column that houses electric outlets and other utility sources.

U/W—Underwriter.

V

vacant—See **open**.

vacuum forming—A technique for molding plastic sheets by heating and drawing sheets in a vacuum press.

valance—1. A trim or finish curtain, usually 12" deep with a scalloped edge, used to give a tent a finished appearance. 2. An overhead border used as a light baffle. 3. See **teaser**.

validated export license (VEL)—A document issued by the United States government, authorizing the export of commodities for which written export authorization is required by law.

valley—The South African term for the point at which the two different planes of a tent roof meet.

value-added tax (VAT)—A tax system that adds a fixed percentage of taxation on products and services at each step of production or service delivery.

value season—Some suppliers use this term to describe the times of the year when prices are lower (not peak season); see **low season**.

van shipment—A shipment within a moving van of large pieces of furniture or display material, which may be crated or uncrated.

vapor lights—Special effects lighting of high intensity.

variable costs—The expenditures that change depending on how many units of a product are sold, such as food and beverage and registration materials; see **fixed costs**.

variable expenses—All expenses that an event's management has control over, such as salaries, utilities, supplies, etc., not including depreciation, interest, and income taxes; see **fixed expenses**.

variety artist—See **sight act**.

variety entertainment—Singers, dancers, comics, or other performers with unique skills such as jugglers, magicians, clowns, or acrobats.

VAT—See **value-added tax**.

VCR—See **videocassette recorder**.

Vega—See **cordless microphone**.

vegetarian—An individual who eats no meat.

VEL—See **validated export license**.

Velcro—The trade name for a multipurpose hook-and-loop material used for fastening.

velour—A velvety fabric with a nap.

velouté—A white sauce used as a base for other sauces.

Velox—See **stats.**

vendor—An individual who sells and provides services or products.

ventilation—The process of supplying or removing air by natural or mechanical means to or from any space.

venue—An event's physical site.

verbatim report—The full and exact transcript in writing of all speeches, debates, and discussions.

Veronica—A service on the Internet that helps make Gopher information searches easier and more manageable.

veronique—Prepared with a creamy white sauce and green grapes.

vertical cuisine—See **architectural cuisine.**

vertical show—A show in which the products or services being displayed represent one element of an industry or profession.

vertical union—A union with jurisdiction over all occupations, skilled and unskilled, in an entire industry.

VHS—A videotape recorder and player utilizing the ½" VHS format; not compatible with Beta format.

vibrancy—See **brilliance.**

vichyssoise—A chilled potato and chicken broth soup.

videocassette recorder (VCR)—A device used for audio and video recording; see **videotape recorder.**

video character generator—A computer-assisted device used to generate and create letters, numbers, and symbols electronically. In simple terms, it creates a video image. It can also be used to recap key points made by a speaker or to supply basic information such as final credits.

videoconferencing—See **teleconference.**

videodisc/videodisk—A recorded disc containing images and sound.

video enhancement—The enlargement of a video image from the size of a typical consumer television screen to dimensions for large projection screens, used when attempting to present a larger-than-life image to an audience; also known as **video magnification.**

video formats—Standard sizes of videotape, including ¾" and ½" (VHS and Beta).

video magnification—See **video enhancement.**

video projector—A piece of equipment used to project a video image on a large screen; also known as **teleprojector.**

videotape recorder (VTR)—An electronic device used for audio and video recording; see **videocassette recorder (VCR).**

vinaigrette—Served with an oil and vinegar dressing.

vinyl—A plastic material used for drapes, skirting, banners, paneling, flooring, or covering tabletops.

vinyl top—A plastic tabletop cover.

VIP (very important person)—An organization's officers, celebrity speakers, panel moderators, industry experts, or others who are distinguished from the majority in attendance.

VIP identification—A means for identifying the very important people at an event, using badges, flowers, or special seating.

visa—A government endorsement stamped inside a passport by an official of the country a traveler wishes to visit and allowing entrance for a specified period of time.

visitor—An attendee at an exhibition or conference.

visqueen—A type of clear plastic sheeting used to protect carpeting from the time it is laid to the time the show opens.

vitrified—Material that is changed into a glasslike substance by fusion due to heat.

vol (volume)—Volume rates or classes are those for which a volume minimum weight (vol. min. wt.) is provided. Charges will be assessed at the volume minimum weight shown in the tariff, except that actual weight will apply when in excess of the volume minimum weight.

vol-au-vent—Puff pastry shell or cup, usually filled with a creamed meat entrée or a fruit/custard dessert.

voltage—The measurement of the force needed for the flow of electricity.

voluntary upgrade—1. An act in which a passenger moves to a higher-priced class for additional fare vouchers.

voucher—A ticket that a traveler exchanges for prepaid services such as accommodations, meals, and tours.

V-shaped setup—A configuration of chairs arranged in rows, separated by a center aisle, and slanted in a V shape facing the head table or speaker; also known as a **chevron** or **herringbone setup**.

VTR—See **videotape recorder**.

W

WA—See **with average.**

wage rate—The rate of pay per period of time or per unit of production for an employee on a given job.

wages—The total of all salaries, wages paid, contract labor payments, worker's compensation, consultant fees, benefit costs, and payroll taxes that are made to employees for work carried out.

WAIS—A service on the Internet that can be used to gather information about a topic from various locations and provide easier access to the information.

waiting time—See **dead time.**

waiver—A written statement waiving a right, claim, or privilege against an individual.

waiver of indemnity—The intentional or voluntary relinquishment of responsibility for payment for a damage, loss, or expense incurred by another party.

waiver settlement—A type of settlement in which a claimant is offered a lump sum in return for a waiver and a release from the claimant stating the amount paid is in full satisfaction of the claim and releasing the organizer from any future liability.

wake-up call—An operator or automated call to wake up a guest in a hotel.

Waldorf salad—A dish of diced apples, celery, chopped walnuts, mayonnaise, and whipped cream.

walk—A term indicating a guest holding a confirmed reservation but sent to another facility because of overbooking.

walk-away clause—See **cancellation clause.**

walk clause—See **double-booking clause.**

walkie-talkie—A mobile, wireless radio that transmits and receives oral communications; also known as a **radio.**

walk-in—A term indicating a guest requesting accommodations without a reservation.

walk-in/walk-out music—1. Music accompanying arriving and exiting guests at an event; also known as **cocktail music.** 2. Music accompanying guests receiving awards; also known as **chaser music.**

walkout—See **strike.**

walk-through—A physical venue inspection.

wallboard—A soft wood product used in onetime paneling or where whiteness and softness are desired.

Walsh-Healy Act—A federal law establishing wage, hour, and working conditions for government contractors.

wardrobe—1. Costumes and all articles of dress for a play or production. 2. A room in which costumes are stored or fitted.

wardrobe mistress, master, or supervisor—An individual in charge of costumes and their upkeep.

warehouse—See **boneyard.**

warehouse receipt—A receipt issued by a warehouse, listing goods received for storage.

warm-up—An activity used to liven up the audience prior to show time.

warranty—A statement made on an application for insurance that the applicant warrants to be true. If untrue, in any respect, any insurance relating to that warranty can be voided.

wash light—Broad, even light that softly illuminates all or part of a room or stage, created by a group of floodlights (usually PARs or Fresnels) and used to provide general illumination of one or several colors. More than one wash can be set up to cover an area, allowing not only for a choice of colors by changing washes, but also for the creation of a wide range of colors by blending the washes.

wash-up—See **closing ceremony.**

waste removal—The disposal of trash, often accomplished by a contracted environmental specialist.

water closet (WC)—A bathroom with toilets.

water connection—The temporary supply of water to a booth or stand.

water cooling—A method used to cool high-power lasers; requires a standard water supply (such as a janitor's sink drain). In some circumstances the water is maintained in a closed system, and the heat is extracted by a heat exchanger.

water lily fold napkin—A napkin fold that is used as a service napkin.

water station—A table with pitchers of water and glasses for self-service.

water weights—Large barrels filled with water and used for anchoring a tent.

watt—A unit of electric power equal to a current of one ampere under one volt of pressure.

waybill—A list of enclosed goods and shipping instructions, sent with material in transit.

WC—See **water closet.**

wedding—A religious or legal ceremony of marriage, often accompanied by social celebrations.

wedges—See **cleats.**

weight ton—A unit of measurement equal to 2000 pounds.

welcome cocktail—1. A drink served as an introductory gesture of welcome. 2. A reception where such drinks are served.

welcome reception—An opening event at which drinks and food are served.

well brand—See **house brand.**

wet lease—The rental of an airplane with crew, supplies, fuel, and maintenance service.

wet mount—The process of wetting a photo blowup prior to wrapping it around a panel.

wharfage—A charge assessed by a pier or dock owner for handling incoming or outgoing cargo.

wheeler—An upright, manually propelled, two-wheeled cart used to move objects such as boxes; also known as **trolley.**

whispered interpretation/interpreting—An interpretation in a low voice to participants, usually sitting next to the interpreter.

whistles—In pyrotechnics, serpents with loud, multitone whistles.

white page directory—A resource providing electronic address listings for users on the Internet.

white tie—Formal dress requiring white tie and tails for men and formal evening dress for women.

wholesaler, tour—A company that packages various components of tours and travel programs for sale through travel agencies.

W&I—Weighing and inspection.

wide-angle lens—A special lens on a projector for wider-than-normal image projection.

windscreen—A porous foam cover for microphones to block unwanted sound.

wing nut—A commonly used threaded nut with flanges for easy adjustment by hand; also known as **butterfly nut.**

wings—1. The space outside the acting area, at the right and left of the stage. 2. Draperies that hang at the sides of the stage to mask the offstage areas.

wipe—A scene in a motion picture that appears to be pushed off the screen by a new scene.

wired system interpreting—See **cabled interpreting system.**

wireless infrared interpreting system—An interpreting system operated by radio waves and hence without wire or cable connections to the headsets.

wireless microphone—See **cordless microphone.**

wire nut—A plastic thimble with a recessed spring that closes spliced wires so that electrical contact is maintained.

wishbone leg—A fold-up leg on a table.

with average (WA)—A marine insurance term meaning that a shipment is protected from partial damage whenever the damage exceeds some percentage.

without reserve—A term indicating that a shipper's agent or representative is empowered to make definitive decisions and adjustments abroad, without the approval of the group or individual represented.

wonton—Chinese ravioli.

word processor—A computer-based system for writing, editing, and formatting letters, reports, and books.

working drawing—A detail drawing.

working foreman—An employee who functions both as a workman and a foreman at the same time.

working language—The language in which the various aspects of a meeting are conducted in practice.

work lights—Lighting used for rehearsal or technical work onstage.

work rules—Regulations that govern union craftspersons' working conditions; includes what type of work an exhibitor may perform, when overtime begins, etc.

workshop—1. A training session in which participants develop skills and knowledge in a given field. 2. An event designed to stimulate intensive discussion and compensate for diverging views in a particular discipline or subject. 3. An informal public session of free discussion organized to take place between formal plenary sessions on a subject chosen by the participants or on a special problem suggested by the organizers.

work time—Paid time that begins as soon as a worker commences work for an exhibitor and finishes when the exhibitor releases the worker.

world meeting—Event participation of organizations or individuals open to all nations and countries.

world's fair—An infrequently occurring celebration that typically showcases the latest or future advances in the arts, culture, and technology.

World Wide Web (WWW)—A compendium of information sources and libraries available through the Internet; a tool for providing access to hypertext-based information.

woven design—A design or print made up of fibers woven into a fabric.

WPA—With particular average.

wrap up—1. To conclude an event. 2. To prepare the final report on an event.

writing chair—A chair with an attached writing surface; also known as **school desk** or **table chair.**

WWW—See **World Wide Web.**

X

xenon lamp—An extremely high-intensity light source for projection.

Y

yield—1. The desired return from an event investment. 2. The number of pieces kept from any given unit. 3. The number of usable servings per raw unit.

yoke—A metal U-shaped support that holds a lighting instrument.

Z

zone—The rightmost part of an Internet address is called its zone. Name zones are divided into two categories: the three-letter kind and the two-letter kind. Three-letter zones are categorized by type of organization: edu stands for educational institutions, gov represents government bodies and departments. Two-letter zones are categorized by geographic name, country, or other recognized political entity: uk stands for the United Kingdom, ca stands for Canada. Within the United States, most Internet sites have names in one of the three-letter zones; elsewhere, it is more common to use the two-letter kind.

zoom lens—A projector or camera lens of variable magnification that permits a smooth change of subject coverage between distance and close-up without changing the projector or the camera position.

Zulu Time—Greenwich Mean Time, the world time standard; see **Universal Coordinated Time (UCT).**

PART TWO

Categorical Listing by Knowledge Domain for Certified Special Envents Professional (CSEP) Study

Administration

Coordination

Marketing

Risk Management

Administration

abstract

acceptance

accompanying person

account code

account executive

accreditation

accreditation form

accreditation rules

accreditation supervising
    committee

accrued expenses

actual cash value

AD (after date)

add-on

administration

admission

admission card

advance order

advance purchase excursion fare
    (APEX fare)

advance registration

advisory capacity

affiliation

affreightment (contract of)

after date (AD)

after-departure charge

after sight

agenda

aggregate limit

air waybill

allowances

alteration

amortize

angel

A1

APEX fare (advance purchase
    excursion fare)

application to present a
    demonstration

application to present a film

application to present a paper

application to present a poster

approximate calculation

arbitrage

AS&D

associate director

association

at liberty

at sight

attendance

audience count

audit

authorized signature

average room rate

badge

badge holder

badge stock

balance sheet

bank draft
bank guarantee
bank remittance
bank transfer
banquet check
banquet event order (BEO)
bar reading
B/E (bill of exchange)
BEO (banquet event order)
best price available
bid document
bid manual/specifications
billed on consumption (BOC)
billing cycle
bill of exchange (B/E)
bill of lading (B/L)
bill of sight
B/L (bill of lading)
blackout
black out
block
block booking
blocked space
blueline/blueprint
boarding pass
board of trustees
BOC (billed on consumption)
body type
boldface
bonded warehouse
bonding
bonus
book
booking form
book of abstracts
book on payment (BOP)
bootleg wages
BOP (book on payment)
B/P
break-even analysis

breakpoint
brief
brilliance
brownline
browser
Brussels Tariff Nomenclature
budget
budget chart
buffer zone (Canadian)
business class
business occurring
CAD (cash against documents)
call for papers
canapé
capital
capital expenditure
capital letter
carpet tape
carrying capacity
cash
cash against documents (CAD)
cash bar
cash flow
cash flow chart
cash in advance (CIA)
cash registration
cash reservation
cash with order (CWO)
CC
cel animation
center sections
CEO (chief executive officer)
certificate of manufacture
certificate of origin
CEUs (continuing education
     credits)
C&F (cost and freight)
CFO (chief financial officer)
change order
charge per square meter

charitable contribution
charitable corporation
charitable deduction
charitable foundation
charity
charter
charter flight
charts
check-in
check-in time
checkout
checkout time
chief executive officer (CEO)
chief financial officer (CFO)
chief information officer (CIO)
chrome finish
C&I (cost and insurance)
CIA (cash in advance)
CIF (cost, insurance, freight)
CIF&C (cost, insurance, freight, and commission)
CIF&E (cost, insurance, freight, and [currency] exchange)
CIO (chief information officer)
city tour
clean bill of lading
clean draft
clearance
closed/fully booked
closed-end
closeout
closing date
coach fare
coated stock
COBRA (Consolidated Omnibus Budget Reconciliation Act)
COD
code of accounts
cold call
commercial invoice

commercial rate
commissionable
commitment
commitment authorization
comp
complimentary
complimentary registration
complimentary room
comp rooms
computer card (registration)
computerized registration
concessionaire
conditions
conferee
conference administrator
conference handbook
conference pack/kit
conference papers
conference report
conference secretariat
confidential tariff
confirmation
confirmation of order
confirmed letter of credit
conflict of interest
conformation letter
conform date
congress auxiliaries
congress card
connecting canopy
consignee
consignment
Consolidated Omnibus Budget Reconciliation Act (COBRA)
consular declaration
consular invoice
consumer profile
continuing education credits (CEUs)
contract

contracting
contributed paper
contribution margin percentage
controllable net per capita
convention center
convention résumé
convertibility
cookie
copyfitting
corporate public relation
corporate rate
COS
cost and freight (C&F)
cost and insurance (C&I)
cost box
cost charge per square meter/foot
costing
cost, insurance, freight (CIF)
cost, insurance, freight, and
    commission (CIF&C)
cost, insurance, freight, and
    (currency) exchange (CIF&E)
cost of products sold/cost of sale
counselor
count
cover charge
CR
crating list
credentials
credit line
credit memorandum
creditor
credit rating
credit report
credit risk insurance
credits
credit sale
crime reports
CTLO
current assets

customer service
customs
customs duties
cutoff date
cutoff time
cutout
cut rate
cut-rate
CWO (cash with order)
CWT
dark day/period
dark night
database
data selection
date draft
date protection
day rate
dead time
debit
debt
debt adjustment
debt capacity
debtor
declared value
deductible
deferred charge
definite booking
delegate card
delegate profile
delft
deluxe
demipension
demographics
denied-boarding compensation
departure date
departure tax
deposit
deposit policy
depreciation
destination controls

destination marketing
 organization (DMO)
devaluation
direct billing
discount
discussion form
dismantling deadline
display rules and regulations
DMO (destination marketing
 organization)
DNS (domain name system)
dock receipt
document distribution
document duplication
document for acceptance
domain name system (DNS)
donation
double booking
double-occupancy rate
double room for single
 occupancy
downgrade
downline space
draft
drawback
dry lease
dual capacity
duty-free imports
EAP (employment assistance
 program)
early arrival
early-bird rate
EBDIT
EBIT
EBITDA
economic strike
ECU (European currency unit)
editorial alteration
educational credit
educational program
electronic mail (e-mail)

electronic payment
elite
e-mail (electronic mail)
employers' association
employment assistance program
 (EAP)
endorsement
entrance card
EO (event order)
EP (European plan)
equal opportunities
equity
escrow account
estimate
ETA
E-ticket
Eurodollars
European currency unit (ECU)
European plan (EP)
evaluation
event order (EO)
event specification
example
excess baggage
exchange rate
exclusive
executive secretary
exhibit directory
exhibitor's pass/badge
export
export license
extended type
extra overnight stays
Fair Labor Standards Act (FLSA)
family name
family plan
fare
fee
feeder space
FI (free in)

film report
final account
final program/blueprint
final report
final statement of account
finance committee
financial procedures
financial report
fine china
FIO (free in and out)
first announcement
fixed assets turnover
fixed costs
fixed expenses
flaming
flat rate
floor order
FLSA (Fair Labor Standards Act)
flush
FOB (free on board)
folio
font
food cost percentage
food inventory turnover
forecast
foreign flag
foreman
for-profit show management
    company
forward business
foul bill of lading
four-hour call
free in (FI)
free in and out (FIO)
free on board (FOB)
free paper
free-rider
full board
full house

function bill (account)
function book
function sheet
future bookings
galley proof
gauge
general export license
given name
goals
gobo
good standing
government event
grants
graphics
gratuity
gross per capita
gross profit
gross revenue
gross square feet
gross weight
group booking
group rate
GT
guarantee
guaranteed late arrival/
    guaranteed arrival
guaranteed number
guaranteed payment
guaranteed reservation
guaranteed tour
guest account
guest list
handbill
handout
head count
header
head tax
hidden charge
high season

hiring cost

historical report/guest history report

history

hit

honorarium

honorary

honorary secretary

hotel accommodation form

hotel classifications

hotel reservation form

house account

house count

housekeeping announcement

housing bureau

HTML (hypertext markup language)

HTTP (hypertext transport protocol)

hypertext

hypertext markup language (HTML)

hypertext transport protocol (HTTP)

ICC (Interstate Commerce Commission)

idiot card

ID sign

immigration

import license

imprimatur

incentive

incidental entertainment

inclusive

inclusive cost

inclusive rate

indentured apprenticeship

information bulletin

information desk

inland bill of lading

inquiry cards

integrated services digital network (ISDN)

interest

interest-free loan

Internet address

Internet service provider (ISP)

Interstate Commerce Commission (ICC)

inventory

inventory restrictions

involuntary upgrade

ISDN (integrated services digital network)

ISP (Internet service provider)

itinerary

Java

job tender

joint agreement

joint fares

Joint Photographic Experts Group (JPEG)

JPEG (Joint Photographic Experts Group)

julienne

justified margin

justified type

K (Kelvin)

Kelvin (K)

keyboard

kickback

label

labor cost percentage

labor policy

laminate

LAN (local area network)

laptop

late registration

LC (letter of credit)

lead time

legal connection
lessee
less than truckload (LTL)
letter of agreement
letter of credit (LC)
letter of intent
licensing
list of exhibitors
list of participants
Listserv
liter
local
local area network (LAN)
loss leader
lowercase
low season
LTL (less than truckload)
mailing list
mail-in premium
manifest
MAP (modified American plan)
margin
marketable securities
markup
master account
master bill
master contract
meeting announcement
meeting date
method of payment
minimum
minutes
modem (modulator demodulator)
mode of payment
modified American plan (MAP)
mom and pop exhibitors
multicraft union
MW
name card
name tag

National Occupation and Safety
    Association (NOSA)
national union
net
net assets
net balance
net book value
net cash flow
net cost
net income
net investment
netiquette
net/net
net operating income
net operating loss
net per capita
net square feet
net square footage
nett
net wholesale rate
new registration
newsletter
Niagara Falls
NMFC
NOE
NOHP
NOIBN
nomenclature of customs
    cooperation council
noncommissionable
noncurrent assets
nonprofit organization
NOS
NOSA (National Occupation and
    Safety Association)
notes payable
notice board
notice of meeting
NSPF
O/A

objectives

observer

occupancy rate

Occupational Safety and Health Act (OSHA)

ocean bill of lading

official receipt

off-peak

O/N

one for fifty or 1/50

on-site order

on-site registration

open

open end

opening hours

open shop

open ticket

open union

operating expenses

operating profit margin

operating supplies

option date

optional items

oration

order form for facilities

order of preference/preferred order

OS&D

OSHA (Occupational Safety and Health Act)

OT (overtime)

OT labor

outline decision

outline of services

overbook

overflow

override

oversold

overtime (OT)

PA

pacing

package

packing list

paid-out

parliament

passport

password

PAX

pay for play

paying in

payment authorization

payment on account

payment order

pay own

PD

peak night

peak season

pending registration

per capita

percentage

per diem

perfect binding

permit card

per person

perquisite

PERT chart

phased budget

photo opportunity

phytosanitary inspection certificate

pickup

place

plateau

plus-plus (++)

point

point of purchase

point of sales (POS)

policies

poll

POP

porterage
port of call
port of entry
POS (point of sales)
postconference registration
postconference reservation
postgraduate course
post office
preassigned seating
preliminary announcement
preliminary program
premium pay
prepaid ticket advice (PTA)
preparation of paper
preprint
preregistration list
press kit
press pass
press release
printed form
printout
priority point system
proceedings
production schedule
professional program
professional visitor
profit margin
pro forma invoice
projected business
prompt book
prompt script
pro number
proof
proof of citizenship
propaganda
proposal
protected
protection
provisional registration
provisional reservation

PTA (prepaid ticket advice)
publication
purchase order
pylon
qualifying
quality management
quorum
quota
rack rate
rain check
rain date
random access
range rate
rank and file
raw film
readymen
recall
receivables
recommendation
record
refund
refund policy
registrant
registration
registration card
registration card key
registration fee
registration kit
registration packet
relay
released value
release form
rental booth/stand
rental charge
report
reporting pay
representation
request for proposal (RFP)
reservation
reservation center

responsibility clause
résumé
return on investment (ROI)
revocable letter of credit
RFP (request for proposal)
right-to-work state
ROI (return on investment)
roll call
roller cart
roll-in
rooming list
room nights
room only
room rate
room, tax, and incidentals (RTI)
rostered times
RS or L
RTI (room, tax, and incidentals)
run
running order
running schedule
running sheet
run-of-the-house rate
SA (société anonyme)
sales incentive
sales portfolio
scenario
schedule
schedule of services
scientific secretariat
search engine
second option
secretariat
secretary general
security deposit
sequence of events
Serial Line Internet Protocol
    (SLIP)
server
service charge

service kit
setup time
shipper's export declaration
ship's manifest
shoulder
show break
show directory
show-up time
SIC (Standard Industrial
    Classification)
sight draft
signatory
Simple Mail Transport Protocol
    (SMTP)
single supplement
skip
SLIP (Serial Line Internet
    Protocol)
SMTP (Simple Mail Transport
    Protocol)
SO
société anonyme (SA)
solvency ratio
space rate
space requirements
space reservation form
special rate
special-rate package
specifications
sponsorship plan
spot exchange
SQL (Structured Query
    Language)
ST labor
stakeholders
standard agreement
Standard Industrial Classification
    (SIC)
standby
stand contract
state-controlled trading company

statement of account
statement of income and
    expenditure
state term contract
stay-over
stet
stock requisition
straight time
Structured Query Language
    (SQL)
subsidies
summary/brief
summary of discussions
summary record/report
super-APEX fare
supplemental airline
surcharge
surety
survey
suspended elements
SWOT analysis
talkback
tariff
tax withholding
T/D/B/A
teacup and saucer
tentative agenda
tentative hold
theater booking
ticket
ticket exchange
ticket revalidation
time agenda
time and materials (T&M)
timecode
time draft
timeline
tip
titles
TLO

T&M (time and materials)
ton
T-1 line
total admission per capita
total attendance
total net revenue
total revenue
tour-based fare
tourist card
tourist information board
tour manual
tour menu
tour order
tour voucher
tracking
transient space
transit visa
treasurer
trouble box
truckload
trust receipt
T-3 line
typeface
typesetting
UCT (Universal Coordinated
    Time)
UL
unanimous
underpayment
unexpected departure
union official
union referral
union shop
Universal Coordinated Time
    (UCT)
unsettled account
upgrade
uppercase
Usenet
USSG

U/W

vacant

validated export license (VEL)

value-added tax (VAT)

value season

variable (controllable) expenses

variable costs

VAT (value-added tax)

VEL (validated export license)

verbatim report

Veronica

videoconferencing

vol (volume)

voluntary upgrade

wage rate

wages

WAIS

waiver settlement

walk

walk-in

warehouse receipt

warranty

white page directory

wholesaler, tour

work rules

workshop

work time

World Wide Web (WWW)

WPA

wrap up

WWW (World Wide Web)

yield

zone

Zulu Time

Coordination

AAF (American Academy of Florists)

A and B roll printing

ABC (Alcohol Beverage Commission)

academic conference/seminar

access panel

accreditation badge

ACEDI (Association of Conference and Event Directors International)

acetate

acetone

acousto-optic modulation

acrylic

acrylic emulsion

action station

active language

Actors' Equity (AE)

ACTRA (Association of Cable Television and Radio Artists)

actuator

AD (assistant director/associate director)

additional seating

ad hoc committee

ad hoc group

adjoining room

adjournment of the meeting

adjustable standard

adlux

ad valorem

advancing colors

adventure tour

adviser

advisory committee

AE (Actors' Equity)

aerial beams

affinity group

affixed merchandise

A-440

AFTA (Australian Federation of Travel Agents)

afterimage

AFTRA (American Federation of Television and Radio Artists)

agent

AGVA (American Guild of Variety Artists)

AH&MA (American Hotel and Motel Association)

AIA (Australian Incentive Association)

AIFD (American Institute of Floral Designers)

air-conditioning

air-cooled laser

airfreight

air space
Air Traffic Conference of
America (ATC)
Air Transport Association of
America (ATAA)
air walls
aisle
aisle carpet
aisle sign
à la broche
à la carte
à la grecque
à la king
à la maître d'hôtel
à la mode
à l'anglaise
à la Provençale
à la russe
à la vapeur
Alcohol Beverage Commission
(ABC)
A-list
all-expense tour
all-inclusive tour
allocation of speaking time
all-space hold
alongside
amandine
amateur
ambient light
American Academy of Florists
(AAF)
American Association of Travel
Agents (ASTA)
American breakfast
American Federation of
Television and Radio Artists
(AFTRA)
American Guild of Variety Artists
(AGVA)

American Hotel and Motel
Association (AH&MA)
American Institute of Floral
Designers (AIFD)
American plan
American Society for Training
and Development (ASTD)
American Society of Association
Executives (ASAE)
American Society of Composers,
Arrangers, and Performers
(ASCAP)
American Standard Code for
Information Interchange
(ASCII)
amorphic lens
amp
amperage
amphitheater
amplifier
analog
anamorphic lens
anchor
angels on horseback
animation (slides)
animation camera
animation stand
animation table
anodizing
answer print
antipasto
anti prost
antistat for carpets
antistat wax
APCOSA (Association for
Professional Conference
Organisers in South Africa)
aperture width/height
appetizer
appliqué

apprentice
apron
arc light
arch
Archie
architectural cuisine
argon
Armorply
arrangement background
arrangement focal point
Arri
arrival pattern
arrival time
art
art principles
ASAE (American Society of Association Executives)
ASCAP (American Society of Composers, Arrangers, and Performers)
ASCII (American Standard Code for Information Interchange)
ash can
ash stand
aside
ASM (assistant stage manager)
aspect ratio
assembly
assistant director/associate director (AD)
assistant stage manager (ASM)
association booth/stand
Association for Professional Conference Organisers in South Africa (APCOSA)
Association of Cable Television and Radio Artists (ACTRA)
Association of Conference and Event Directors International (ACEDI)

Association of Theatrical Press Agents and Managers (ATPAM)
ASTA (American Association of Travel Agents)
ASTD (American Society for Training and Development)
ATAA (Air Transport Association of America)
at a glance program
ATC (Air Traffic Conference of America)
athletic event
atmospheric
ATPAM (Association of Theatrical Press Agents and Managers)
at-site
attendee
attender
attraction
audience left or right
audioconference
audio monitor
audiovisual (AV)
audiovisual aids
audition
auditorium lens
auditorium lights
auditorium setup
au gratin
au jus
au lait
Australian Federation of Travel Agents (AFTA)
Australian Incentive Association (AIA)
author's guideline/kit
automated lighting
automatic advance

auxiliary services
AV (audiovisual)
AV contractor
awards banquet/celebration
awning
baby spot
backbone
back curtain
backdrop
backing light
backing unit
backlight
backline equipment
backloader
back of house
back projection
backstage
back-to-back
back-to-base
backup facilities
backwall
backwall booth/stand
backwall exhibit
baffle
baguette
baked Alaska
baklava
balcony front spotlights
bale ring
ball
bandwidth
banjo (fabric)
banner
banquet
banquet captain/banquet
    manager
banquet round
banquet services manager
barbeque
bargaining agent

bargaining unit
bar mitzvah
barn doors
base
base plate
basic elements
bas mitzvah/bat mitzvah
batten (bat)
bay
B&B (bed-and-breakfast)
BBB (Better Business Bureau)
BBS (bulletin board system)
BDI
bead
beaded screen
beam, ceiling
beam front spots
beams, or beam sculptures
béarnaise sauce
Beaulieu
bed-and-breakfast (B&B)
bed hook
beef Wellington
beep
beignet
Bell and Howell
bell captain
bell end
bell staff/bell stand
Ben Day
Bermuda plan
Beta
Better Business Bureau (BBB)
B/G
binding
bipole
bisque
bit part
Bitnet
blackboard

black light
blackout
black powder
black tie
black tie optional/black tie
    preferred/black tie invited/
    black tie requested
blanket wrap
blanking
bleachers
bleed
blending color
B lights
blintzes
block and tackle
blocking
blocking notation
bloom
blower
blow up
blue sky
BMI
BO
boarding card
board meeting
board of directors' setup
boardroom
boardroom setup
bobbinet
boeuf à la bourguignonne
bombe
bonbon
bone china
boneyard
boom arm
boom microphone
booth
booth/stand area
booth/stand contractor
booth/stand number

booth/stand personnel
booth/stand representative
booth/stand sign
booth/stand size
bordelaise
border
border chaser
borscht
bouillabaisse
bouillon cup and saucer
boundary microphone
bourgeois
boxed
box framing
box lunch
brainstorming
brain trust
bread-and-butter plate
break
break a leg
breakaway
break character
breakdown
breakfast plate
breakout session
break terminal
breakup
bridge lights
bridgeway
briefing
bring a bottle
bring up
bring your own (BYO)
broadcast equipment
broadcast production
brunch
brut
buffer zone (PRS)
buffet
buffet service

build
buildup
bulk carrier
bulkhead
bulk mailing
bullet catch
bullet hit
bulletin board system (BBS)
bullnose
bump-in
bumping
bump-out
bums in bed
bunting
burned-in copy
burn units
bus
business agent
business attire
business center
business manager
business market
busy
butler service (American)
butler service (Australian)
butterfly nut
butt joint
buying agent
buzz session
BX cable
BYO (bring your own)
by the bottle
by the drink
by the person
by the price
cabana
cabaret table
cable ramps
cabled interpreting system

CAC (Canadian Association of Caterers)
cacciatore
CAD/CAM
CAEM (Canadian Association of Exposition Managers)
cafeteria service
calamari
calico
call board
call boy
call brand
calligraphy
call-out
cam
camera chain
camera left and right
camera-ready art
Canadian Association of Caterers (CAC)
Canadian Association of Exposition Managers (CAEM)
Canadian Centre for Philanthropy (CCP)
Canadian Council for the Advancement of Education (CASE)
Canadian Hotel and Motel Association
Canadian Society of Association Executives (CSAE)
Canadian Tourism Human Resource Council (CTHRC)
candelabra
canopy
cantilever
canvas
capacity
capacity control
caper
cap nut

cappuccino

cap strip

captain

car hire

carbonated (sparkling water)

cardioid microphone

cargo ton/freight ton

Carnet

carousel projector

carousel tray

carpenter

carriage bolt

carrier

cartage

cart service

carver

cascade fold napkin

CASE (Canadian Council for the Advancement of Education)

CASE (Council for the Advancement and Support of Education)

cassette

cast

casual attire

CAT (computer-assisted translation)

catenary arch

Caterers Guild of South Africa (CGSA)

catering manager

catering sales manager

catwalk

caviar

CCP (Canadian Centre for Philanthropy)

CD (compact disc)

CDRG (Center for Devices and Radiological Health)

ceiling décor

ceiling height

CEIR (Center for Exhibition Industry Research)

cel

celastic

celebrate

Celotex

CEM (Certified Exposition Manager)

center channel loudspeaker

Center for Devices and Radiological Health (CDRG)

Center for Exhibition Industry Research (CEIR)

centerpiece

center poles

center stage

central console

central staging

ceramics

certificate of inspection

Certified Exposition Manager (CEM)

Certified Manager of Exhibits (CME)

Certified Meeting Professional (CMP)

Certified Special Events Professional (CSEP)

Certified Tour Professional (CTP)

CESSE (Council of Engineering and Scientific Society Executives)

CGSA (Caterers Guild of South Africa)

chai

chain drive

chain lock

chair cover

chairperson

chalkboard

chamfer

channel

character generator

charger

charter operations

charter party

chaser

chaser flasher

chaser lights

chaser music

chateaubriand

cheat

cheddar cheese

chef's choice

chemise

cherry picker

chevron

chief operating officer (COO)

chiffonade

china

chinagraph pen/pencil

chopping

cinema style

Cinemoid

cioppino

circle trip

circline

city central

cladding

clamp-on fixture

claque

classroom seating

classroom setup

CLC (Convention Liaison Council)

clear span

clear-span tents

cleats

climax

clinic

cloakroom/coatroom/coat check

cloakroom attendant/coatroom attendant/checkroom attendant

clogged head

close-talking microphone/transmitter

close-up

closing address

closing ceremony

closing session

closing speech

clothes rail

club manager

club table

cluster

clutch mechanism

CME (Certified Manager of Exhibits)

CMP (Certified Meeting Professional)

CNYT (Current New York Time)

coach

coaxial cable

cochairperson

cockscomb fold napkin

cocktail table/cocktail round

coexhibitor

coffee break

coherent light

collection of ideas

collective ring

collimator

colloquium

colocate

color frame

color key proof

column

combo

comet

command center

commencement/graduation

commission agent

commissionable tour

commitment ritual

committee

committee of honor

committee on the verification of credentials

committee room

common carrier

communication center

community of interest

commuter airline

compact disc (CD)

compact disc player

compact disc transport

compère

complete meeting package

component

composite

comprehensive layout

computer animation

computer-assisted drawing

computer-assisted translation (CAT)

computer-composed script

computer-controlled stereophonic conference system

computer-generated animation

computer graphic

con carne

concept

conceptual art

concierge

conclave

concrete weights

concurrent sessions

condensed type

condenser microphone

conducted tour

cone

conference

conference call

conference interpreter

conference officer/organizer

conference-style setup

conference terminologist

conference translator

configuration

confirmed reservation

congress

congress travel agent

connecting rooms

consecutive interpretation

consensus

console

consolidate

consommé

consular security manager

consultant

consultative committee

consumer affairs

consumer-quality equipment

contact cement

continental breakfast

continental buffet

continental plan (CP)

contingency planning

continuity

contractor

contrast

contributor

control room

control track

convener

convention

convention and visitors bureau (CVB)

convention bureau
Convention Liaison Council (CLC)
convention services manager
conversation piece
COO (chief operating officer)
coordinating committee
copresident
copy
copy negative
cordial
cordless microphone
corkage
corner booth/stand
cornucopia
corporate meeting
corporate picnic
corporate planner
corporate special event manager
corporate theater
couchette
council
Council for the Advancement and Support of Education (CASE)
Council of Engineering and Scientific Society Executives (CESSE)
counter
countermount
countersink
countervailing duty
country-style table service
coupe soup
courier
cover
cover footage
cover plate
covers
cover shot

cover stock
CP (continental plan)
C-print
craft person
craft union
crane
crash box
crash cloth
crate
crawl
crazing
cream cheese
cream-soup bowl and saucer
credentials committee
crème brûlée
crepe
crew
crisis management
croissant
crop
crop mark
cross aisle
crossbar
cross brace
cross-fade
cross-fading
crossover
cross parallel session
crossroads cuisine
crosstalk
crumbdown
CSAE (Canadian Society of Association Executives)
CSEP (Certified Special Events Professional)
CTHRC (Canadian Tourism Human Resource Council)
CTP (Certified Tour Professional)
cubic content
cue

cue card
cueing
cultural services
currants
Current New York Time
(CNYT)
curtain
curtain line
custom exhibit
customhouse
customhouse broker
customized marketing
customized tour
customs
customs broker
cut
cut and lay
cutline
cutoff date
cutout
cuts-only editing
cutting sheet
CVB (convention and visitors
bureau)
cyberspace
cyc, or cyclorama
cycles
cyclorama
DA converter (digital-to-analog
converter)
daily newsletter
dais
damask
dance floor
Danish candle fold napkin
DAT (digital audiotape)
data-mining
dead area
debate
deboarding

debriefing
decorating
decorator
delegate
delegation
demitasse
demonstration
demonstrator
demux (demultiplexer)
Department of Transportation
(DOT)
deputy stage manager
design
designer
dessert plate
dessert tray
destination management
company (DMC)
destination manager
DET (domestic escorted tour)
detail drawing
deviation
diabetic
dialogue
die cutting
differential amplification
diffraction grating
digital audiotape (DAT)
digital recording
digital video effects
dim
dim in/dim up
dimmer
dimmerboard
dine around
dinner
dinner plate
dipole
direct flight
direct mail advertising

Direct Mail Advertising Association (DMAA)
director of catering
director of sales (DOS)
directory
directory board
direct-view television
dirty rice
disclaimer
disco effects
disconnect
discovered at rise
discussant
discussion group
discussion leader
dismantle
dispatcher
display builder
display case
display fibers
display material
display place
display screen
display type
dissolve
dissolve unit
distance interpreting
distant-talking microphone/ transmitter
distributed sound
district sales manager
divergence
diving walls
DMAA (Direct Mail Advertising Association)
DMC (destination management company)
docent
dock
Dolby AC-3

Dolby Pro Logic
dolly
domestic beer/wine
domestic escorted tour (DET)
domestic meeting
Donahue
DOS (director of sales)
DOT (Department of Transportation)
double bed
double cloth
double-decker
double-double room
double-faced/double-sided
double lock
double room
double room rate
doubling
down-linking
download
downstage
draper
drapery
drapes/theatrical curtains
draping
draw curtain
drayage
drayage contractor
drayer
dress
dress code
dressing the exhibit
drinking water
drop
drop curtain
dropout
dry run
dry snack/nibbles
dual setup
dub

dub (dubbing)
duchess potatoes
du jour
dummy
duo
duotone
dupe (duplicate)
duplex outlet
duplicate
dutchman
duty
duty manager
duvetyne
dynamic loudspeaker
earthenware
EASA (Exhibition Association of South Africa)
easel
eaves
eaves troughing
éclair
ecotour
EDAC (Exhibit and Display Association of Canada)
edit
EDPC (Exhibit Designers and Producers of Canada)
educational
educational session
educational tour
educational visit
effect
effects device
efficiency
EFP (electronic field production)
eggs Benedict
electret
electrical contractor
electric cart
electrician

electricity connection
electric pointer/laser pointer
electronic blackboard
electronic editing
electronic field production (EFP)
electronic news gathering (ENG)
electronic pour
electronic whiteboard
electrostatic loudspeaker
element
elevated table
elevation
elevator stage
ellipsoidal spotlight
embossing
E-MEAT (event management entrepreneur assessment tool)
emergency exit
end sections
energy break
ENG (electronic news gathering)
engineering
English breakfast
English service
engraved glass
enhancement
entertainment
entertainment provider
entrance canopy
entrée
Environmental Protection Agency (EPA)
EPA (Environmental Protection Agency)
epergne
epilogue
equalizer
erase
erection

ESCA (Exposition Service Contractors Association)
escargots
escort
escorted tour
E-shaped setup
est. wt.
etched glass
ETD
Ethernet
ethical conduct
ethnic tour
event management
event management entrepreneur assessment tool (E-MEAT)
event manager
event team
exciter lamp
exclusive contractor
exclusive use
excursion
executive board
executive coach
executive committee
exhibit
Exhibit and Display Association of Canada (EDAC)
exhibit booth/stand
exhibit designer/producer
Exhibit Designers and Producers of Canada (EDPC)
exhibit hall
exhibition
exhibition area
Exhibition Association of South Africa (EASA)
exhibition catalog
exhibition contractor
exhibition cooking
exhibition manager

exhibition plan
exhibit manager
exhibitor
exhibitor advisory committee
exhibitor appointed
exhibitor lounge
exhibitor retention
exhibitors newsletter
expedited service
exploder
export broker
export management
export merchant
export trading company
exposition
exposition manager
exposition service contractor
Exposition Service Contractors Association (ESCA)
extension
exterior
extinction
extra-man
extranet
extraordinary session
extra section
FAA (Federal Aviation Administration)
fabrication
FAC (Federal Airports Corporation)
facilitator
facility
facility manager
facsimile machine/fax
fade in
fade out
fader
fair
false bow

FAM (familiarization trip)
family-style buffet
family-style service
family table service
fan
FAP (full American plan)
FAS (free alongside)
fascia
fascia board
fashion show
FDIC (Federal Deposit Insurance Corporation)
feature
Federal Airports Corporation (FAC)
Federal Aviation Administration (FAA)
Federal Deposit Insurance Corporation (FDIC)
feedback
festival
festoon
feta cheese
fete
fete stall
FHC (fire hose cabinet)
fiber optics/fibre optics
FidoNet
field camera
field production
filet mignon
file transfer protocol (FTP)
fill light
film chain
film clip
film projector
filmstrip
filter
Finger
finger bowl

fire exit
fire retardant/fireproofing
fire wall
first aid
first option
fishpole
FIT (foreign independent tour/ free or fully independent traveler)
fixed seating arrangement
fixed theater
flag carrier
flambé
flameproof
flash
flash box
flasher
flash pot
flatbed editing
flat
flip chart
floater/casual
floodlight
floor language
floor load/loading
floor manager
floor marking
floor plan
floor port
floor setup diagram
floor speaker
flop
floppy disk
floral designer
Florentine
fly curtain
foam core
focal length
focus
FOH (front of house)

foil-stamping
follow spotlight
food and beverage director
food cover
food station
foreign independent tour/free or
    fully independent traveler
    (FIT)
foreign meeting
foreign/national
forklift
formal dining service
formal dress
forum
four-color separation
foyer
fraises
framboises
frame
frame tent
framework decision
franchise
fraternal
free alongside (FAS)
free-form
freelance
free paper session
free port
free pour
freestanding
free trade zone
freeze-frame
freight
freight desk
freight forwarder
French action
French service
French (silver) service
frequency
frequency response

Fresnel
frit
froid
fromage
frontages, front
front booth/stand
front desk
front of house (FOH)
front-projection television
front-screen projection
frosted glass
FTP (file transfer protocol)
full American plan (FAP)
full booth/stand coverage
full breakfast
full-service restaurants
full stage
full text
fully equipped booth/stand
fumé
function
function board
function room
function space
fund-raising
fund-raising event
funnel flight
fusion cuisine
gable end
gaffer's tape
gagging
gain
gala dinner
galantine
galvo/galvanometer
gang box
gangway
gap analysis
garment rack
garni

garni, hotel
garnish
gate show
gateway
gateway city
GATT (General Agreement on Tariffs and Trade)
gear drive
gel
gelatine (gel)
gel frame
general agreement
General Agreement on Tariffs and Trade (GATT)
general assembly
general contractor
general session
general strike
gerb/fountain
get-together
GIT (group inclusive tour)
glacé
glass, plate
glass, single thick
glass, solar
glass, tempered
glass, wire
glass-beaded screen
glass-ceramic
glaze
glide
glossy
GMT (Greenwich Mean Time)
gnocchi
goblet
gofer
goodie bag
good one side/surface quality
good theater
Gopher

gopher/gofer
gorgonzola cheese
go to black
gouda cheese
governing board
government meeting
grain of wheat
grand opening
grandstand
gras
greenfield
green room
Greenwich Mean Time (GMT)
gridlock
grid system
grievance
grille
grip
grits
grommet
ground arrangements
ground breaking
ground operator
ground plans
groundrow
ground transportation firm
group inclusive tour (GIT)
group leader
group of experts
group tour
Gruyère cheese
guest room/sleeping room
guest speech
guide
guided tour
guidelines for authors
gusset
guy ropes
half board
half-moon table

half-round step
halftime spectacle
halftone
hall
hallmark
handblown glass
hand service
hand truck
happenings
hard disk
hardwall booth/stand
hardware
HCEA (Health Care Exhibitors Association)
HDCD (high-definition compact disc)
HDTV (high-definition television)
head
headquarters hotel
headset
heads in beds
head table
Health Care Exhibitors Association (HCEA)
HeNe (helium-neon)
herringbone setup
highball glasses
high-definition compact disc (HDCD)
high-definition television (HDTV)
high jacker
high-key lighting
hip
hipped end
holding-down bolts
holiday event
hollandaise sauce
hollow circular setup
hollow square setup

hollowware
hologram
homard
home page
horizontal bar
horn loading
hors d'oeuvres
horseshoe setup
hospitality desk/hospitality room
hospitality suite
host
host bar
host country
hostess
host interview setup
hot microphone/camera
hot spot
hot-tag VIP
house board
house brand
housekeeping
house lights
houseman
house manager
house plan
house specialty
house wines
housing
hub and spoke tour
hue
human resources event
hummingbird
hush puppies
HVAC
hybrid loudspeaker
hypercardioid microphone
Hz (hertz)
IAAM (International Association of Auditorium Managers)
IAB (Internet Architecture Board)

IACC (International Association of Conference Centers)

IACVB (International Association of Convention and Visitor Bureaus)

IAEM (International Association for Exposition Management)

IAMC (Institute of Association Management Companies)

IANA (Internet Assigned Numbers Authority)

IATA (International Association of Travel Agents)

IATSE (International Association of Theatrical Stage Employees)

IBEW (International Brotherhood of Electrical Workers)

ICCA (International Congress and Convention Association)

ice carving

ICPA (Insurance Conference Planners Association)

I&D (installation and dismantle)

IEA (International Exhibitors Association)

IFEA (International Festival and Events Association)

IFSEA (International Food Service Executives Association)

ILDA (International Laser Display Association)

illumination

impaired-vision seating

imported liquor

Impressionism

inauguration ceremony

inbound tour

inbound tour operator

incentive event

incentive meeting/trip

incentive travel

incentive travel company

in-city transport

inclusive tour

independent contractor

independent show management

independent tour

induction information

induction loop

inductive transmitter for hearing aids

informal dress

informal meeting

infringement

inherent flameproof

in-house

in-house services

in-line booth

in-plant

insert

inset

inside booth/stand

inspection trip

installation

installation and dismantle (I&D)

installation contractor

institute

Institute of Association Management Companies (IAMC)

instruction booklet

instructions for poster presenters

instructions for speakers

instructions for the preparation of papers

in sync

integrated amplifier

integrated marketing

integrated meeting

integrated seminar

intelligent lighting
interactive exhibit
interactive response
intercity transport
intercom
intercommunication system
intercontinental meeting
interline connection
interlock
intermediate carrier
intermezzo
intermodal tour
International Association for
 Exposition Management
 (IAEM)
International Association of
 Auditorium Managers
 (IAAM)
International Association of
 Conference Centers (IACC)
International Association of
 Convention and Visitor
 Bureaus (IACVB)
International Association of
 Theatrical Stage Employees
 (IATSE)
International Association of
 Travel Agents (IATA)
International Brotherhood of
 Electrical Workers (IBEW)
International Congress and
 Convention Association
 (ICCA)
International Exhibitors
 Association (IEA)
International Festival and Events
 Association (IFEA)
International Food Service
 Executives Association
 (IFSEA)
International Laser Display
 Association (ILDA)

international meeting
International Special Events
 Society (ISES)
Internet
Internet Architecture Board (IAB)
Internet Assigned Numbers
 Authority (IANA)
Internet Relay Chat (IRC)
Internet Society (ISOC)
interpretation/interpreting
interpretation in relay
interpreter's booth/stand
interruption of the meeting
interval
in-the-clay decoration
in-the-glaze decoration
in the round
intranet
invitation call
invitation program
invited paper
invited speaker
invocation
involuntary upgrade
IRC (Internet Relay Chat)
iris
iris fold napkin
Irish stew
iris shutter
ironstone
ISES (International Special
 Events Society)
island booth/stand
ISOC (Internet Society)
jacket
jackknife stage
janitorial service
jardiniere
jigger
jigger spout

job description
job foreman
job specification
Johnny Carson setup
johnson bar
joining instructions
joint venture
jones plug
journeyman
jughead
junction box
KD (knockdown)
keg
key light
keynote speaker
keystoning
kick base
king pole
king room
king-size bed
kiosk
kit
klieg light
knockdown (KD)
kosher
kreplach
krypton
labor
labor call
labor desk
labor relations
lace line
lagniappe
lamp
lamp life
lanai
lance
land arrangements
land operator
landscape (horizontal)

langostino
langouste
langoustine
lanyard
lapel microphone
laser
late night
lavaliere microphone
layout
LCD projection television
LCL
LCM
L&D
leader
leadman
leaflet
le café table
lectern
lectern microphone
lecture
leg
leg extension
legit
leisure service
Leko
lenticular
level
liaison interpreter
lift truck
light box
lightface
lighting
lighting control console
lighting desk
lighting director
lighting grid
light organ
light table/kelvin box/kelvin
    light
limitation of speaking time

limiter
line doubler
line drawings
linen
line of sight
line stage preamplifier
line switch
lines
linings
lining-up
Linnebach projector
lip microphone
liqueur
liqueur cart
lit rack
live operation
load factor
load-in
load in/load out
loading dock
loadlock
lobby
lobster scope
local beer/wine
local event
local host
lockup
loop
loose jig
lost property office
louvers
lowboy
low-key lighting
low voltage
lumina
luminaire
luncheon
luncheon plate
lyonnaise
macédoine

macroscale
magnetic planar loudspeaker
magnetic sound
mail and messages
main tent
maître d'
majolica
make ready
make-work practices
management committee
management consultant
manager on duty (MOD)
managing director
Manhattan clam chowder
manpower agency
march
marker board
marks
marquee
marshalling yard
mascarpone cheese
mask
masking drapes
master
master control
master key
master monitor
master of ceremonies (MC)
master tape
matte
matte white
matzo ball soup
MC (master of ceremonies)
measurement ton
medallion
media center
media contact person
medical meeting
medical service
meet and greet

meeting
meeting duration
meeting frequency
meeting point
Meeting Professionals
    International (MPI)
meeting site
meeting termination
meeting theme
meeting tour/conference tour
meet-the-press setup
mega event
melamine
melodrama
mercury vapor light
mesclun
message board
message center
message repeater
meunière
microphone
microscale
microswitch
middle of the road (MOR)
midget microphone
midrange
mike/mic
military meeting
minestrone
minimum land package
mirror ball
mirrors
misconnect
miter
mix
mixer
mixing
mixing board/mixing desk
mixing of foldback sound
mobile

mobile simultaneous interpreting
    system
mock-up
MOD (manager on duty)
model
moderator
modular
modular exhibit
modular panels
module
mold
mold-blown glass
monitor
monitor mixing console
monochrome
monopitch
montage
MOR (middle of the road)
mornay sauce
motel
motion
motor coach
motor coach tour operator
motor inn
moussaka
mousse
mousseline
movable wall
move-in
move-out
moving magnet cartridge
moving screen
Moviola
MPI (Meeting Professionals
    International)
multichannel
multichannel tape
multi-image
multimedia
multinational meeting

multiple-story exhibit
multiplexer
multiscreen
multitrack conference
multivision
Murphy bed
MUSA (Musician Union of South Africa)
Musician Union of South Africa (MUSA)
music stand
muslin
Mylar
mystery tour
NACD (National Association for Catering Directors)
NACE (National Association of Catering Executives)
NAEM (National Association of Exposition Managers)
Nagra
napery
napkin
napkin folds
napoleon/napolean
National Association for Catering Directors (NACD)
National Association of Catering Executives (NACE)
National Association of Exposition Managers (NAEM)
National Coalition of Black Meeting Planners (NCBMP)
national dress
National Institute for Occupational Safety and Health (NIOSH)
national meeting
National Restaurant Association (NRA)
national tourist office (NTO)

natural water
Naugahyde
NCBMP (National Coalition of Black Meeting Planners)
near-plant
neck/necklace microphone
negative
neoprene
nested
nested solid
New England clam chowder
Niagara Falls
nineteen hundred box
NIOSH (National Institute for Occupational Safety and Health)
nodes
nonsked
nonstop flight
no-op
nori
no-show
NRA (National Restaurant Association)
NTO (national tourist office)
NTSC
number stand/booth
OAG (Official Airline Guide)
O'Brien
obstructed view
off-camera
Official Airline Guide (OAG)
official carrier
official contractor
official language
officials
off-line
off-line connection
off-line editing
off-premise caterer
off-print

off-season/out of season

offset

off-shore meeting

off-site event

offstage

oilcloth

oil cracker

olio curtain

Omni pole and tubes

omnidirectional microphone

on-center

one shot

one ten/sixty

on-line

on-line editing

on-premise caterer

on-site

OP (opposite prompt)

opaque

open bar

open cold

open discussion period

open house

opening ceremony

opening session

open space event

open-space technology (OST)

open U-setup

operations

operations manager

operator

operator desk

operator sound

opposite prompt (OP)

optical effects

optical printer

optical sound

option(s)

organizing committee

organizing secretariat

original language

OST (open-space technology)

OT

outbound operator

outbound tour

outdoor event

outlets

out of order

outside exhibit/external exhibit

outside line

outsourcing

outtake

ovenware

overage

overdrape

overhead projector

overlay

overset

overview

PA (public address system)

package plan

package tour

packing drawing

padded van

padding

paella

pain grille

painter

pallet

pamphlet

pan

panache

panel

panorama

paper contribution

paper review board

paper selection committee

papier-mâché

parabolic aluminized reflector
    light (PAR light)

parabolic projection screen
parade
parallax
parallel
parallel session
parking attendant
PAR light (parabolic aluminized
    reflector light)
parlor
parmentier
participant
participant motivation
particleboard
partition
partner
partnership
party canopy
party planner
passive language
paste-up
pastry cart
patch
patch panel
pâté
pâté de foie gras
patron
patronage
PBX/PABX operator
PCMA (Professional Convention
    Management Association)
PCO (professional congress
    organizer)
PC spot
peach melba
pedestal
peek-a-boo cuisine
peg
peg-and-pole tent
Peg-Board
pegged off

pendant microphone
peninsula booth/stand
peninsula display
penthouse suite
people mover
perfect binding
perforated metal
perimeter booth/stand
permanent exhibit space
permanent office
personal manager
PERT (program evaluation and
    review techniques)
phosphorescent paint
photo blowup
photocopier
photographic opportunity
photo screen
photo stats
phyllo
piano hinge
piano types
pica
pièce de résistance
pie plate
pierced
pierogi
pin beam
pin poles
pin spot
pinup
pipe and drape
piquant
pit
pita
pitch
pivot interpreter
pixie tube
place card
place plate

places
plan
planting
plants
plastic laminate
plated
plated buffet
plated service
plate microphone
platform
plating
play on/play off
plenary assembly
plenary session
Plexiglas
plug-in
plumber
plywood
pocket program
podium
point source
pole drapes
pole tent
polyvinyl chloride (PVC)
pony glass
pop-up canopy
porcelain
port
portable camera
portable computer
portable exhibit
portal structure
porter
portrait
positive
positive print
post
postcon
postconference tour
poster

poster board
poster exhibition
poster presentation
poster session
postevent briefing
postgame event
posttrip
potage
pottery
power
power amplifier
practical demonstration
practice room
preamp desk
precon
preconference
preconvention briefing
preevent meeting
prefab
prefinished paneling
preformed group
prefunction space
pregame event
premium beer
premium brand
preopening
preparatory session
prep area
prepleated
preproduction
presentation
presenter
preset
preset service
president of honor
press attaché
press clipping/cutting
press conference
press day
pressed glass

press gallery
press hot line
press office
press officer
pressroom
press tour
pretrip
previous participation in
    meetings
print
printed design
priority rating system
prismatic glass/prismatic plastic
privatization
procession
producer
producer, exhibit
producer, show
production tape
production team/production
    crew
professional
professional association
professional congress organizer
    (PCO)
Professional Convention
    Management Association
    (PCMA)
profile spot
program
program book
program design
program evaluation and review
    technique (PERT)
program participant
projection rehearsal room
projection room
projection screen
promoter
prompter
prompt side (PS)

prop box
property
props
prop table
proscenium
proscenium arch
proscenium opening
protagonist
protocol
provisional program
provolone cheese
PS (prompt side)
public address system (PA)
publicity person
public space
purchasing agent
purlin
push-pole tent
PVC (polyvinyl chloride)
PW
pyro musical display
pyrotechnics
PZM
Q&A
quad (quadruple)
quad box
quality control
quart
quarter poles
quartz lamp
queen pole
queen room
queen-size bed
quiche
quiche lorraine
quick-change booth/stand
quotation
rabbet
raceway
radio

radio mic
radio microphone
radius mark
rafter
ragout
rail
raised letters
raked seating
rally
ramekin
ramp
ramset
rap session
rapporteur
ravioli
raw footage
raw tape
R&B (rhythm and blues)
RCMA (Religious Conference Management Association)
reader board
readout unit
rear-illuminated
rear-lit
rear-screen projection
receding colors
receiving agent
receiving line
receiving line reception
reception
reception desk/registration desk
receptive operator/reception agency
recess
recession
reel-to-reel
reflector
refresh
refreshment break
refreshments

refurbish
regional security officer (RSO)
registration area
rehearsal
reinforced vinyl
relay interpreting
Religious Conference Management Association (RCMA)
religious meeting
remote ballast
remote control
remote scanner
rendering
rental specialist
rep company
repertory
reporter
reprise
request for coverage
resolution
resort
restricted area
retailer
retour interpreting
retrace
return
reunion
reverb
reverse
rheostat
rhythm and blues (R&B)
rib
ribbon mike
ridge
rigger
rim drive
rimmed soup
risers
RIT

rollaway
roll-in meal
romaine
roman candle
room
room service
room setup
room turnover/room turnaround
rope lights
roping
rostrum
rostrum steps
rôti
rotisserie
rough layout
rough sketch
roulade
round
round robin
round slide tray
roundtable
round trip
router
roux
roving microphone/mike
row booth/stand
RSO (regional security officer)
rump session
runner
runoff
run-through
runway
Russian service
SAACI (South African Association for the Conference Industry)
saddle-stitch binding
SAG (Screen Actors Guild)
salad plate
sales manager

salute
sanctioned area
sandblasting
sandwiching
SARRAL (South African Recording Rights Association Limited)
satellite seminar
satellite symposium
satin finish
satire
sauerbraten
sauerkraut
sauté
scale model
scallions
scanner (laser)
scene
scene in action
schematic model
school desk
schoolroom perpendicular setup
schoolroom seat
schoolroom setup
scientific committee
scientific program
scioptican
scissor lift
SCMP (Society of Corporate Meeting Planners)
sconce
scoop
scooter
score
screen
Screen Actors Guild (SAG)
screen/audience distance
screen/audience left and right
screen enamel
screening

screw post
scribe
scribe line
scrim
script
scroll
scroller/color changer
SDD
sealing
secateurs
second tier
secret partnership
security cage
security lock
segue
self-contained
self-contained exhibit
self-publishing
self-tapping screw
seltzer
seminar
semiporcelain
semiskilled labor
sepia
series operator
serpent
serpentine
service bar
service contractor
service desk
service level
service plate
services and facilities
serviette
serviette detail
session
set
set dressing
set light
set piece

set screw
setup
setup drawing
setup personnel
setup plan
SGMP (Society of Government
    Meeting Planners)
shadow box
shag
shallot
Sheetrock
shelf
shell
shell folder
shell scheme
sherbet glasses
ship lap
shipment
shipper
shipping case
shipping crate
shish kebab
shoehorn
S-hook
shop
shore excursion
shot
shotgun microphone
show break
show card
showcase
showcase theater
show curtain
show decorator
show management
show manager
show office
show photographer
show plate
show tape

show within a show

shrink-wrap

shucker

shutter

shuttle service

side chair

side fills

side poles

side rail

side-stitch binding

side trip

side walls

sight line

sightseeing tour

sign

signage

signaling system

signal-to-noise ratio

signature dish

sign cloth

significant other

sign service

sign standard

silent partnership

silk screen

silverprint

silver service

simplex

simultaneous interpreter

single

single bed

single room

single weight/matte

SISO (Society of Independent Show Organizers)

SIT

SITC (Standard Industrial Trade Classification)

site

SITE (Society of Incentive and Travel Executives)

site inspection

sitting on their hands

SJ cord

sketch model

skewing

skid

skin

skin drawing

skirting

skycap

sky drop

SL&C

sleeper

slide

slide animation

slider

smoke generation

SMPTE timecode

snifter

snow peak

snug banqueting

social dinner

social event

society music

Society of Corporate Meeting Planners (SCMP)

Society of Government Meeting Planners (SGMP)

Society of Incentive and Travel Executives (SITE)

Society of Independent Show Organizers (SISO)

soffit

soft opening

software

solarized

sole relay interpreter

sommelier

sorbet

Soss hinge

soufflé

sound bite/video bite

sound board

sound control stand/sound
    control booth

sound effect

sound mix

soundproof wall

soundscaping

sound strip/sound track

sound system

sound wings

source language

South African Association for the
    Conference Industry (SAACI)

South African Recording Rights
    Association Limited
    (SARRAL)

spa

space

space assignment

space stage

spade connectors

spaetzle

span

spanakopita

spark pot

speaker

speaker platforms

speaker's guidelines

speaker's room/lounge

spec book

special

special committee

special-effects editing

special event tour

special general meeting

special handling

special interest tour

special lighting

specialty contractor

Speedball

spike marks

spill rings and baffles

spinning

splice

spline

split

split charter

split screen

splitter

spokesperson

sponsored bar

sponsoring body

sport event

spot item

spotlight

spot line

spot rehearsal

spouse

spouse programs

spring water

sprinkler system

spumoni

squeeze connector

squib head

squirrel cage/barrel

S/S

SS

stable

stacking chairs

stage

stage call

stage directions

stagehand

stage left, stage right

stage lighting

stage manager

stage maroon
stage master
stage plot
stage wait
staging
staging area
staging guide
stakes
stanchions
stand
Standard Industrial Trade
    Classification (SITC)
stand equipment
stand-in
standing committee
standing microphone
star
stars
state-controlled trading company
state-of-the-art
state travel office
station
stats
steak tartare
steamship conference
steering committee
step-on guide
stepper switch
steward
stock
stock bill
stock exhibit
stoneware
stop motion
storyboard
story pole
str.
straight brace
street beat
stretcher

strike
strip
striplight
stripped package
strobe lights
stroboscope
strong back
stub space
stud
studio
study mission
stuffing
Styrofoam
SU
subcommittee
subcontractor
submersible pump
SUCL
suite
SULCL
superimposition
supernumerary (super)
supervising committee
supervisor
supper
supplier
surprise cuisine
sushi
suspension of the meeting
suspension paint
sweep
Swiss cheese
switchboard
switcher
symposium
synchronization
synch sound
system
tabbouleh
tableau curtain

table center
table chair
table d'hôte
table microphone
table service
table tent
tabletop display
tabletop presentation
table wine
tabs
taffeta
tag
take down
take stage
talent agent/booking agent
talk
tallow carving
tap
tape blip
tape deck
tape player
tape recorder
tapered edge
tapping
tare weight
target language
TCP/IP (Transmission Control
    Protocol/Internet Protocol)
teach-in
team of interpreters
teardown
teaser
tech check
technical director
technical meeting
technical rehearsal
technical tour
technical visit
technician
Teflon

Telecine
teleconference
telefax/telecopier
teleinterpreting
telephone connection
teleprojector
TelePrompTer
telescopic pipe
Telnet
tempered pressed wood
template
temporary labor
tension structure
tent
tent specialist
terfer
terminal
terrine
theater setup
theatrical case
theatrical gauze and bobbinet
theme break
themed/special interest tour
theme party
think tank
thin wall
three-dimensional (3-D)
through bill of lading
throw
TIAA (Travel Industry
    Association of America)
tie beam/tie rod
tie-off
tiered
timber batten
timecoding
time delay
tiramisu
title role
TL

toastmaster
toe base
toggle switch
tongue and groove
tormentor
tortoni
touch-up paint
tour
tour conductor
tour consultant
tour departure
tour escort
tour guide
tour guide/travel guide
tourist office
tour leader
tour operator
tour option
tour organizer
tour package
tour series
tower
tow motor
track lighting
trade
trade association
trade day
trade mission
Trade Show Exhibitors
    Association (TSEA)
trade show organizer
trade show producer
trade visitor
traditional dress
traffic low
tragedy
trainer
training meeting
tramp steamer
transfer

transit
translation
translation service
translucence
translucency
Transmission Control Protocol/
    Internet Protocol (TCP/IP)
transmission fibers
transparency
transport
transport coordinator/officer
travel agent/agency
traveler/traveler curtain
Travel Industry Association of
    America (TIAA)
travel mission
traverse
treadmill stage
treads
trestle table
trim props
trip director
triple sheet
trip tray
troubleshoot
truck loader
truffle
truss
tryout room
TSEA (Trade Show Exhibitors
    Association)
T-shaped setup
tube lights
tunnel
turnaround
turnbuckle
turndown service
turnkey exhibit
turnover
turntable

turret projector
TV monitor
twenty-footer
twin bed
twin double room
twinkle lights
twin room
twist lock
two-by-two
two-way loudspeaker
typecasting
typeset copy
Tyrex cord
ultraviolet lamp
underliner
underscore
under the auspices of
under-the-glaze decoration
under the patronage of
unidirectional microphone
union
union call
union seating
union steward
uplinking
Upson board
upstage
U-shaped setup
utility box
vacuum forming
valance
valley
van shipment
vapor lights
variety artist
variety entertainment
VCR (videocassette recorder)
Vega
vegetarian
Velcro

velour
velouté
Velox
vendor
ventilation
venue
veronique
vertical cuisine
vertical union
VHS
vibrancy
vichyssoise
videocassette recorder (VCR)
video character generator
videodisc/videodisk
video enhancement
video formats
video magnification
video projector
videotape recorder (VTR)
vinaigrette
vinyl
vinyl top
VIP (very important person)
VIP identification
visitor
visqueen
vitrified
vol-au-vent
voltage
V-shaped setup
VTR (videotape recorder)
WA (with average)
wake-up call
walkie-talkie
walk-in/walk-out music
walk-through
wallboard
wardrobe
wardrobe mistress

warehouse
warm-up
wash light
waste removal
water closet (WC)
water connection
water cooling
water lily fold napkin
water station
water weights
watt
waybill
WC (water closet)
wedding
wedge
welcome cocktail
welcome reception
well brand
wet lease
wet mount
wharfage
wheeler
whispered interpretation/
    interpreting
whistles
W&I

wide-angle lens
windscreen
wing nut
wings
wipe
wire nut
wired system interpreting
wireless infrared interpreting
    system
wireless microphone
wishbone leg
with average (WA)
without reserve
wonton
word processor
working drawing
working foreman
working language
work lights
world meeting
woven design
writing chair
xenon lamp
yoke
zoom lens

Marketing

AAA (Advertising Standards Authority)

AAAA (American Association of Advertising Agencies)

AAF (American Advertising Federation)

above-the-line advertising

advertised air tour

advertised price (in television or radio)

advertising

advertising agency

advertising merchandise

advertising specialties

Advertising Standards Authority (AAA)

aerial advertising

aftermarket

AMA (American Marketing Association)

ambush marketing

amenity

American Association of Advertising Agencies (AAAA)

American Advertising Federation (AAF)

American Marketing Association (AMA)

assortment

barter

below-the-line advertising

best time available

billboard

brand

brand loyalty

brochure

brushed finish

bullet/bullet point

buying team

cause-related marketing

civic celebration

classified advertising

collateral

color wheel

commodity

concentrated marketing

concert rider

concessions

consumer advertising

consumer/trade show

cooperative advertising

core competencies

corporate event

corporate exhibit

corporate identification

corporate show

corporate travel

cross-cultural marketing

destination management system (DMS)

destination marketing organization (DMO)

differentiated marketing

differentiation

direct channel

direct marketing

director of sales (DOS)

direct selling

distributor

DMO (destination marketing organization)

DMS (destination management system)

DOS (director of sales)

event marketing

event sponsorship

exclusivity

exhibition prospectus

exhibitor's kit

exhibitor's manual

exhibit prospectus

flyer

fragmentation

Garcy Strip

geographic segmentation

giveaway (or novelty)

global marketing strategy

header

headline

horizontal show

Hotel Sales and Marketing Association International (HSMAI)

HSMAI (Hotel Sales and Marketing Association International)

impact

import

industrial show

intangibility

interactive marketing

international sales agent

introductory offer

inventory loss

investment spending

limited distribution

local advertising

local media

logo

logotype

market

marketing

marketing flights

marketing mix

marketing public relations

market profile

market research

market response

market segment

market subgroup

markup

mass marketing

merchandise gift

niche market

nonprofit marketing

package insert

partial sponsorship

penetration

people magnet

personal selling

place

positioning

posting

potential audience

premium

press agency

price

price flexibility of demand

price leader
primary audience
primary market
print production
product
production manager
product launch
product life cycle
product show
profit
promotion
promotional fare
prospecting
prospectus
PSA (public service
  announcement)
publication
publicity
public relation
public service advertising
public service announcement
  (PSA)
public show
pull strategy
reach
ready for press
regional show
relationship marketing
repetition
retail event
road show
sales blitz
sales force/sales team

sales meeting
sales portfolio
sales promotion
scientific marketing
scientific meeting
SC&S
segmentation
service
show daily
signature item
SMERF (Social, Military,
  Educational, Religious, and
  Fraternal)
Social, Military, Educational,
  Religious, and Fraternal
  (SMERF)
special events market
special market
sponsor
sporting service
target audience
target market
target price
telemarketing
tourism
tourist service
tractor trailer
trade fair
trade-out
undifferentiated
vertical show
white tie
world's fair

Risk Management

accident report

actionable

act of God

ADA (Americans with
Disabilities Act)

ADAAG (Americans with
Disabilities Act Accessibility
Guidelines)

additional insured

advanced life support (ALS)

affirmative action

affirmative action plan

Age Discrimination in
Employment Act

alcohol risk management

all-risk coverage

ALS (advanced life support)

Americans with Disabilities Act
(ADA)

Americans with Disabilities Act
Accessibility Guidelines
(ADAAG)

antidiscrimination law

antitrust laws

area of rescue assistance

assist animal

association agreement

automobile liability insurance

barratry

barrier-free

basic life support (BLS)

binder

blanket contract

BLS (basic life support)

by-laws

cancellation clause

cancellation insurance

cancellation or interruption
insurance

certificate of insurance

certificate of insurance currency

claim

class action

clean draft

coinsured

collective agreement

collective bargaining

commercial general liability

comprehensive general (public)
liability insurance

contingencies

contingency contract

contractual liability

copyrights

creditor

credit rating

credit report

credit-risk insurance

credits
crime reports
current liabilities
damages
damages, punitive
debtor
declared value
deductible
deductible aggregate
defendant
deferred airfreight
DFWA (Drug-Free Workplace
    Act)
disability
dog guide
double-booking clause
double lock
dram shop laws
Drug-Free Workplace Act
    (DFWA)
electrical codes
emergency exit
errors and omissions insurance
event stewards
excess insurance
exclusion
exposure
express insurance
FDIC (Federal Deposit Insurance
    Corporation)
featherbedding
Federal Deposit Insurance
    Corporation (FDIC)
filed
financial responsibility law
fire exit
fire insurance
fire wall
force majeure clause
forward contract
full coverage

governing statutes
hold harmless
hold harmless clause
Immigration Reform and Control
    Act (IRCA)
inaccessible
incident
incidental entertainment
incident report
indemnification
indemnify
indemnity
infringement
insurance
IRCA (Immigration Reform and
    Control Act)
jurisdiction
jurisdictional dispute
jurisdictional strike
LC (letter of credit)
legal connection
letter of agreement
letter of credit (LC)
liability
liability insurance
liability laws
liable
lifetime customer value
limits of liability
liquidated damages
lockout
lost business
management prerogatives
marine insurance
mediation
mobility impairment
National Occupation and Safety
    Association (NOSA)
negligence
negligence, contributory
negligence, gross

nerve center
no-fault coverage
NOSA (National Occupation and
    Safety Association)
occurrence
100 percent star billing
open insurance policy
OR
paramedic
party
performance bond
phytosanitary inspection
    certificate
policies, claim made
policies, occurrence
poll
power of attorney
public liability
rain insurance
readily achievable accessibility
reinsurance
rider
risk
risk assessment
risk control
risk financing
risk management
risk monies
SARRAL (South African
    Recording Rights Association
    Limited)

security contractor
security guard
security lock
security service
self-insured
service recovery plan
sight act
South African Recording Rights
    Association Limited
    (SARRAL)
star billing
third party
third-party policy
three wire
top of bill
transit and exhibition insurance
transmitter unit
travel insurance
union contract
union jurisdiction
usability
visa
waiver
waiver of indemnity
Waldorf salad
walk-away clause
walk clause
walkout
Walsh-Healy Act